Bible
Speaks
today

T0310995

the message of

ISAIAH

Series editors:
Alec Motyer (OT)
John Stott (NT)
Derek Tidball (Bible Themes)

the message of

ISAIAH

On eagles' wings
Revised edition

Barry Webb

INTER-VARSITY PRESS
Studio 101, The Record Hall, 16–16A Baldwins Gardens, London, EC1N 7RJ, UK
Email: ivp@ivpbooks.com
Website: www.ivpbooks.com

First published 1996
Reprinted 1997, 1998, 2000, 2003, 2006, 2007, 2009, 2011
This edition published 2023

British Library Cataloguing-in-Publication Data
A catalogue record for this book is available from the British Library.

ISBN: 978–1–78974–439–2
eBook ISBN: 978–1–78359–644–7

Set in 9.5/13pt Karmina
Typeset in Great Britain by CRB Associates, Potterhanworth, Lincolnshire
Printed and bound in Great Britain by Ashford Colour Press Ltd, Gosport, Hampshire

Produced on paper from sustainable sources.

*Inter-Varsity Press publishes Christian books that are true to the Bible
and that communicate the gospel, develop discipleship and strengthen the church
for its mission in the world.*

*IVP originated within the Inter-Varsity Fellowship, now the Universities and Colleges
Christian Fellowship, a student movement connecting Christian Unions in universities
and colleges throughout Great Britain, and a member movement of the International
Fellowship of Evangelical Students. Website: www.uccf.org.uk. That historic association
is maintained, and all senior IVP staff and committee members subscribe
to the UCCF Basis of Faith.*

To Miriam, Simcha and Tabitha,
three beautiful gifts from God

Contents

Bible Speaks today

GENERAL PREFACE

The Bible Speaks Today describes three series of expositions, based on the books of the Old and New Testaments, and on Bible themes that run through the whole of Scripture. Each series is characterized by a threefold ideal:

- to expound the biblical text with accuracy
- to relate it to contemporary life, and
- to be readable.

These books are, therefore, not 'commentaries', for the commentary seeks rather to elucidate the text than to apply it, and tends to be a work rather of reference than of literature. Nor, on the other hand, do they contain the kinds of 'sermons' that attempt to be contemporary and readable without taking Scripture seriously enough. The contributors to The Bible Speaks Today series are all united in their convictions that God still speaks through what he has spoken, and that nothing is more necessary for the life, health and growth of Christians than that they should hear what the Spirit is saying to them through his ancient – yet ever modern – Word.

ALEC MOTYER
JOHN STOTT
DEREK TIDBALL
Series editors

Author's preface

Those who hope in the Lord
  will renew their strength.
They will soar on wings like eagles.
(Isa. 40:31)

As a child I longed to fly. A favourite after-school or weekend activity was to ride my bicycle to the perimeter of an airport a few miles from our home and simply watch the planes landing and taking off, taxiing and turning, warming up and shutting down, flashing their lights, revving their engines and testing those mysterious moving parts on the ends of their wings and tailplanes. Everything they did fascinated me. Their smells and noises filled me with a strange pleasure and set me dreaming of faraway places. I could not see enough of them. Of course, in those days they were mainly lumbering old propeller-driven Dakotas and Constellations (the latest thing), but to me they were awesome. They moved with a grace and power that thrilled me, and to see them lift into the air and soar upwards through the clouds left me breathless. How I envied those who flew in them – the pilots especially, of course, but the passengers as well. I had no doubt that they were mortal as I was, but flight invested them with special qualities. The heavens were theirs as well as the earth.

As an adult I have flown many times, at far greater heights and speeds than those I envied in my childhood. But on the whole the experience has not come up to the expectations I had of it. More often than not I have found myself cramped and uncomfortable, craning my neck and disappointed with the view. Of course, the roar of the engines still thrills me. The exhilarating lift and the burst through the clouds are still wonderful. But after much travel I wonder whether these moments of pleasure are worth the hours of tedium that inevitably accompany them. At least, I am left asking whether there may not be some better way to fly. Like an eagle, perhaps.

The flight of the eagle is pure magic. There is no cramping, no noise but the rush of wind on feathers, and nothing to obscure the view. There is nothing contrived about it. It is a gift, and displays in its every lift and turn the greatness and glory of its Giver. The question is: is such flight possible for you and me? And the brilliant answer that Isaiah gives is: yes, it is! The only requirement is that we 'hope in the LORD', believing that his promises are true and that he can and will do for us what we cannot do for ourselves. Those who hope in the Lord 'will soar on wings like eagles'.

Writing this book has been a flight I will never forget. I have soared into the heavens and seen the glory of God, and with new eyes I have seen this world and my own place in it. The view has been breathtaking. I am not less mortal or sinful than I was before. My awareness of these things has been sharpened, not diminished; but I am surer now than ever before that they are no obstacles to my communion with God or to the full realization of what he has purposed for me. I have heard the seraphim cry, 'The whole earth is full of his glory', and so it is. I live in expectation of the day when he will take his power and reign, and know with absolute certainty that because of one who was pierced for my transgressions, the new heavens and new earth will be my home for ever.

Such flight is not for a privileged few. It is the birthright of all God's people. I invite you to fly with me.

In preparing this exposition, I have benefited from the labours of a host of others who have studied Isaiah before me. Some of the most significant ones are acknowledged in footnotes, but my indebtedness in a more indirect way extends far beyond these few. In particular I want to acknowledge the significant debt I owe to E. J. Young and John Oswalt for their fine Isaiah commentaries (the latter at the time of writing on chapters 1–39 only, the former on the whole book). Alec Motyer's commentary (*The Prophecy of Isaiah*, 1993) did not become available until my own work was almost completed. It is an excellent volume, combining thoroughly evangelical scholarship with refreshing new insights. It demonstrates the value of a judicious use of some of the best aspects of the new literary approaches to the Bible. I have thought it best, however, at this late stage, not to try to revise my own work so that it interacts in any substantial way with Motyer's.

Since he is editor of this series, I have, of course, communicated with him personally, and am grateful for the advice and support he has given in that capacity. At a few points I have incorporated exegetical insights from his work into my footnotes and acknowledged their source. Apart from this, however, the two treatments have developed quite independently of each other, and I believe that while they share a common evangelical commitment, each has its own character and special contribution to make. I trust that both will be of benefit to God's people and help to give fresh impetus to the study and exposition of what is arguably the most theologically significant book in the Old Testament.

BARRY WEBB

Chief abbreviations

ANEP	J. B. Pritchard (ed.), *The Ancient Near East in Pictures* (Princeton: Princeton University Press, 2nd edn 1965).
ANET	J. B. Pritchard (ed.), *Ancient Near Eastern Texts Relating to the Old Testament* (Princeton: Princeton University Press, 3rd edn 1969).
AV	The Authorized (King James) Version of the Bible (1611).
BDB	Francis Brown, S. R. Driver and Charles A. Briggs, *A Hebrew and English Lexicon of the Old Testament* (Boston/New York: Houghton Mifflin, 1907).
Herodotus	Herodotus, *The Histories* (Eng. trans. Harmondsworth: Penguin, rev. edn 1972).
IDB	*The Interpreter's Dictionary of the Bible*, ed. G. A. Buttrick, 4 vols. (New York: Abingdon, 1962).
LXX	The Old Testament in Greek according to the Septuagint (3rd to 1st centuries BC).
NBD	*New Bible Dictionary*, 2nd edn, ed. J. D. Douglas et al. (Leicester: IVP, 1982).
NIV	The New International Version of the Bible (1973, 1978, 1984, 2011).
NRSV	The New Revised Standard Version (1995).
RSV	The Revised Standard Version of the Bible (NT, 1946, 2nd edn 1971; OT, 1952).
RV	The Revised Version of the Bible (1948).

Select bibliography

Works referred to in the footnotes are cited there by surname, or surname and date or volume number.

Bright, J., *A History of Israel* (London: SCM, 2nd rev. edn 1981).

Bruce, F. F., 'The Servant Messiah', in *idem*, *This Is That: The New Testament Development of Some Old Testament Themes* (Exeter: Paternoster, 1968).

Childs, B. S., 'Isaiah', in *idem*, *Introduction to the Old Testament as Scripture* (London: SCM, 1979).

Clements, R. E., *Isaiah 1 – 39*, New Century Bible (Grand Rapids: Eerdmans, 1980).

Clifford, R. J., *Fair Spoken and Persuading: An Interpretation of Second Isaiah* (New York: Paulist Press, 1984).

Conrad, E. W., 'The Royal Narratives and the Structure of the Book of Isaiah', *Journal for the Study of the Old Testament* 41 (1988), pp. 67–81.

Delitzsch, F., 'Isaiah', in C. F. Keil and F. Delitzsch, *Commentary on the Old Testament in Ten Volumes* (Eng. trans. Grand Rapids: Eerdmans, n. d.).

Drane, J., *Introducing the Old Testament* (Tring: Lion, 1987).

Dumbrell, W. J., 'Isaiah', in *idem*, *The Faith of Israel: Its Expression in the Books of the Old Testament* (Leicester: Apollos, 1989).

—— 'The Purpose of Isaiah', *Tyndale Bulletin* 36 (1985), pp. 111–128.

—— 'The Role of the Servant in Isaiah 40 – 55', *Reformed Theological Review* 48.3 (1989), pp. 105–113.

Erlandsson, S., *The Burden of Babylon: A Study of Isaiah 13:2 – 14:23*, Coniectanea Biblica Old Testament series (Lund: Gleerup, 1970).

Fleming, D., *Isaiah to Lamentations*, Bridge Bible Commentaries (Brisbane: Bridgeway, 1988).

Hasel, G. F., *The Remnant: The History and Theology of the Remnant Idea from Genesis to Isaiah* (Berrien Springs: Andrews University Press, 2nd edn 1974).

Kidner, D. F., 'Isaiah', in *New Bible Commentary*, 4th edn, ed. D. A. Carson et al. (Leicester: IVP, 1995).

Knight, G. A. F., *Servant Theology: A Commentary on the Book of Isaiah 40 – 55* (Grand Rapids: Eerdmans, 1984).

Leupold, H. C., *Exposition of Isaiah*, 2 vols. (Grand Rapids: Baker, 1968).

Miscall, P. D., *Isaiah*, Readings: A New Biblical Commentary (Sheffield: JSOT Press, 1992).

Motyer, J. A., *The Prophecy of Isaiah* (Leicester: IVP, 1993).

North, C. R., 'The "Former Things" and the "New Things" in Deutero-Isaiah', in H. H. Rowley (ed.), *Studies in Old Testament Prophecy* (Edinburgh: T. and T. Clark, 1950).

—— *The Second Isaiah: Introduction, Translation and Commentary to Chapters XL–LV* (Oxford: Clarendon, 1964).

—— *The Suffering Servant in Deutero-Isaiah* (Oxford: Oxford University Press, 2nd edn 1969).

Oswalt, J. N., *The Book of Isaiah, Chapters 1–39*, New International Commentary on the Old Testament (Grand Rapids: Eerdmans, 1986).

Rice, G., 'A Neglected Interpretation of the Immanuel Prophecy', *Zeitschrift für die alttestamentliche Wissenschaft* 90 (1978), pp. 220–227.

Roberts, J. J. M., 'Isaiah in Old Testament Theology', *Interpretation* 36.2 (April 1982), pp. 130–143.

Ryken, L., *How to Read the Bible as Literature* (Grand Rapids: Zondervan, 1985).

—— and T. Longman III (eds.), *A Complete Literary Guide to the Bible* (Grand Rapids: Zondervan, 1993).

Seitz, C. R. (ed.), *Reading and Preaching the Book of Isaiah* (Philadelphia: Fortress, 1988).

Walton, J. H., 'New Observations on the Date of Isaiah', *Journal of the Evangelical Theological Society* 28 (1985), pp. 129–132.

Watts, J. D. W., *Isaiah*, 2 vols., Word Biblical Commentary (Waco: Word, 1985, 1987).

Watts, R. E., 'Consolation or Confrontation? Isaiah 40 – 55 and the Delay of the New Exodus', *Tyndale Bulletin* 41.1 (1990), pp. 31–59.

Webb, B. G., 'Zion in Transformation: A Literary Approach to Isaiah',
    in D. Clines et al. (eds.), *The Bible in Three Dimensions* (Sheffield:
    JSOT Press, 1990).

Westermann, C., *Isaiah 40 – 66: A Commentary*, Old Testament Library
    (London: SCM, 1969).

Whybray, R. N., *Isaiah 40 – 55*, New Century Bible (Grand Rapids:
    Eerdmans, 1978).

Young, E. J., *The Book of Isaiah: The English Text with Introduction,
    Exposition and Notes*, 3 vols., New International Commentary
    on the Old Testament (Grand Rapids: Eerdmans, 1965, 1969, 1972).

Introduction

As I wrote this introduction, rumours were circulating that the aged Deng Xiaoping was on his deathbed, possibly in a coma, and the whole People's Republic of China was holding its breath. So were thousands of China-watchers worldwide, aware that a critical moment was approaching. Deng had been the effective leader of China since the late 1970s, making him a figure of impeccable revolutionary credentials. He helped organize the first Communist enclave in the 1930s, participated in the Long March, and played a leading role in the resistance to the Japanese occupation during the Second World War. In those early days he was a comrade of Mao Zedong himself. Deng represented stability, based on continuity with the past and the wide respect he was still able to command. On the whole his status had been enhanced rather than diminished in recent years by the way he had implemented economic reforms that progressively opened China to the rest of the world. It had been a dangerous balancing act, producing deep tensions between progressive and conservative elements, north and south, rich and poor, but it had given China what was possibly its only chance to avoid haemorrhaging again in a world where the pressure for change was irresistible. But now Deng was on his deathbed and no-one seemed capable of taking his place. China was on a knife-edge, the future heavy with dire possibilities.

It was in similar circumstances, over two and a half millennia ago, that a young man called Isaiah stood in the Jerusalem temple and heard God calling him to be a prophet. By Isaiah's own reckoning it was the year 740 BC,[1] 'the year that King Uzziah died' (6:1).

---

[1] Total precision is impossible in dating the reigns of the kings of Judah and Israel. This is partly because the Hebrew year does not correspond to the January to December of our civil year, partly because two different dating systems are used in the Old Testament itself (one counting a king's accession year as the

1. Isaiah and his world[2]

Judah was hardly the China of the ancient world; it was tiny in comparison to Egypt to its south and Assyria to its north-east. But together with its sister kingdom Israel it occupied a strategic place astride the land routes linking Africa with Central Asia and the Far East. It lay at the centre of the known world and made the astounding claim that its God, the Lord,[3] was the creator and effective ruler of everything. Uzziah and his predecessors in the Davidic line were the Lord's vice-regents whom he had installed on Zion, his holy hill, which would become the centre of a new world. Judah lived in the conviction that the Lord was the true king, and looked forward to the day when all the earth would know it.

This creed had not been difficult to believe during Uzziah's long reign, which spanned the whole first half of the eighth century (791–740 BC).[4] The once-mighty Egypt, well past its prime and weakened by internal strife, was in no position to interfere. Assyria, which still had ambitions to do so, was too preoccupied for the time being with more pressing matters, including harassment along its northern border and uncertainty about the succession.[5] The most it could do was to maintain enough pressure on Damascus to ensure that it, too, remained weak.[6] This left Israel and Judah ideally situated to capitalize on their key location in the region and to reap rich economic rewards. They also engaged in an impressive programme of military expansion, recovering between them most of the territory that Israel had ruled at the height of its golden age under Solomon. It was a proud time of military success, political stability and great prosperity.[7]

(note 1 *cont.*) first year of his reign and the other ignoring it), and partly because of particular problems such as father–son co-regencies. In general I have taken the higher date in each case from the table in *NBD*, pp. 194–200. For a detailed treatment of the issues see S. J. De Vries, 'Chronology of the Old Testament', *IDB* 1, pp. 580–599.

[2] Only the period that Isaiah himself lived in is treated here. Other periods referred to in the book are dealt with at the appropriate points in the exposition. See especially the comments on 39:5–8 (with reference to the Babylonian exile) and chapter 56 (the period following the return).

[3] I use 'the Lord' to represent the personal name 'Yahweh'. While 'Yahweh' was full of the warmth of personal relationship for the Old Testament people of God, it unfortunately lacks this for most Christians today, and contributes to an unnecessary sense of distance between text and reader.

[4] Co-regent from 791; sole ruler from 767.

[5] Shalmaneser IV (782–773) had died young and childless. The enemy to the north was the Urartian Argistis I.

[6] There had been warfare between Damascus and Israel (the northern kingdom) for much of the previous century.

[7] While Uzziah ruled Judah, Jeroboam II (793–753 BC) ruled Israel. Their achievements are summarized in 2 Kgs 14:23 – 15:7 and 2 Chr. 26:1–15.

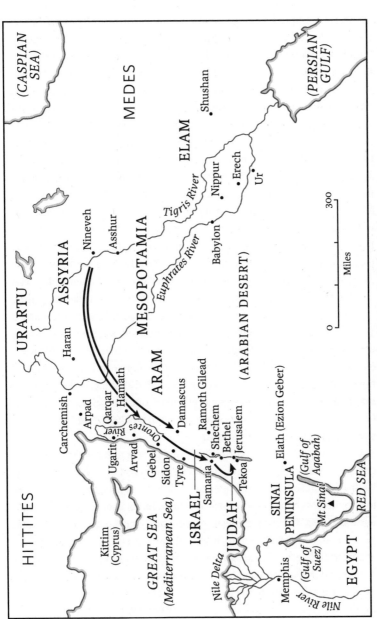

Judah's situation in the eighth century BC

As Uzziah's reign drew to a close, however, it was clear that this state of affairs could not be maintained for much longer. Five years before Uzziah's death, in 745 BC, an ambitious and capable new ruler, Tiglath-Pileser III, had come to power in Assyria. He quickly took control of Babylon, and secured his northern border by a decisive victory over Sardur II of Urartu.[8] By relentless campaigning he put down all rebellion and reorganized the country into a network of provinces controlled by his appointees, and then turned his attention to the west lands. First to feel his wrath was the Syrian city of Arpad, which had been in league with his northern enemies. It was placed under siege for two years and was finally annexed in 740 BC. Seeing the writing on the wall, the rulers of other states in the region soon began to bring tribute, including Rezin of Damascus, Menahem of Israel and Hiram of Tyre. The direction of Assyria's advance was clear, and everything between it and Judah was beginning to crumble. In the year Uzziah died the international scene was full of threat. At home, too, things were far from well. The new-found wealth was not evenly distributed. It was concentrated in the hands of an economic elite who cared little for the have-nots beneath them. Deep fissures were opening up in Judean society as justice was bought and sold, or simply disregarded and replaced by violent exploitation and repression. Religious observance continued, but could no longer conceal the rot that had set in underneath (see 1:10–17, 21–23; 5:8–23). The creed that the Lord was king had become hollow. Its ethical implications were disregarded at home, and it no longer inspired much confidence when one looked out on the changing world beyond Judah's fragile borders. It was going to be a hard creed to live by in the turbulent years that lay ahead.

Under Jotham, Ahaz and Hezekiah, Judah was to lurch from crisis to crisis and Assyrian pressure built relentlessly. In 734 BC Pekah of Israel and Rezin of Damascus formed a defensive alliance and tried to persuade Ahaz to join them. When he refused, they invaded Judah in order to replace him with someone who would. It was a severe test, and Ahaz proved unequal to it. Isaiah counselled him to stand firm and trust the Lord; instead he appealed to Tiglath-Pileser for help and effectively subjected Judah to Assyrian domination (Isa. 7:1–12; 2 Kgs 16:5–9). From then on tribute would be a heavy drain on the national exchequer, and refusal to pay it would constitute rebellion which would attract swift retribution.

---

[8] Modern Armenia.

The northern alliance soon collapsed, beginning with the fall of Damascus in 732 BC. Samaria followed in 722 BC. The northern kingdom of Israel was dismantled and reorganized as a province of an empire whose border now lay only 8 miles north of Jerusalem. In the years that followed, Judah and its southern neighbours struggled on, economically crippled, and restive under the Assyrian yoke. Any sign or rumour of Assyrian weakness sparked fresh talk of rebellion, with hope of Egyptian backing. One such revolt by the Philistine city of Ashdod was savagely crushed in 711 BC (Isa. 20:1). It should have been enough to warn Judah to keep well clear of all such intrigues, but as the century wore on, desperation and opportunity gradually drew her in. The Assyrian yoke was intolerable; it involved acknowledgment of the imperial gods, a price too high to pay. Ahaz had been willing (2 Kgs 16:10–18), but Hezekiah was not. He nailed his colours to the mast by implementing major reforms in the very first year of his reign, and from then on it became a war of nerves as Hezekiah bought time to prepare as thoroughly as possible for the showdown which had to come sooner or later. Abroad, there were signs that events were playing into his hands. Following the death of Sargon II, there were widespread risings against his successor Sennacherib (705–681 BC). In the east, Babylon was already in rebellion and viewed Judah as a potential ally (Isa. 39:1–2). Egypt, too, was experiencing something of a revival and seemed ready to offer support (see on Isa. 18:1–2). A simultaneous uprising in east and west offered the best opportunity to capitalize on Assyria's weakness, and it looked as though it would have to be now or never. This time Hezekiah did not hesitate. He hazarded all by throwing his hat unreservedly into the ring. He withheld tribute, forced the reluctant Philistines to fall into line, and strengthened Jerusalem's defences (2 Kgs 18:7–8).[9]

It was a fateful move; well intentioned perhaps, certainly courageous, but dreadfully mistaken, and it brought Judah to the brink of extinction. Sennacherib moved more quickly, and proved to be far stronger, than anyone had reckoned on. In less than a year he got the reins firmly in his hands at home, brought Babylon to heel and secured his northern border. By 701 BC he was ready to move west, determined to settle matters once and for all. It was a massive campaign in which he systematically ravaged

---

[9] Sennacherib's annals tell how Hezekiah took Padi, king of Ekron, back to Jerusalem as a prisoner (*ANET*, pp. 287–288). It was also at this time that Hezekiah constructed his famous tunnel to bring vital drinking water from an outside spring back under the wall and into the city itself (2 Kgs 20:20; 2 Chr. 32:30; *ANET*, p. 321).

Palestine from Sidon in the north to Lachish in the south and finally placed Jerusalem itself under siege.[10] 'Hezekiah the Judean' had been a key player in the uprising and Sennacherib was determined to make him pay in full.[11] Hezekiah's last hope, humanly speaking, was Egypt, but in the end it proved to be a broken reed whose help was completely ineffective.[12] It looked like the end, and would certainly have been so if the Lord had not intervened (see on 37:36–37). Miraculously, Jerusalem survived, but the whole Judean countryside was a smoking ruin.

Through all this Isaiah clung to the truth that had been etched into his consciousness by his call. In the year that King Uzziah had died he had seen *the* King, high and exalted, and the whole earth full of his glory. So when Sennacherib's men stood at the gates and proclaimed, in the name of 'the great king, the king of Assyria', that Jerusalem was utterly at his mercy, Isaiah knew it was a lie (Isa. 36:13–20; 37:21–29). The truth behind appearances was that the Lord himself was the supreme ruler, and would determine the fate of Assyria and Judah alike. Isaiah lived by the old creed. Ahaz and Hezekiah found it hard to translate into practical politics, the common people gave it only lip service, and Sennacherib mocked it as madness, but Isaiah charted his entire course by it.

The meagre biographical details we have indicate how completely Isaiah's mission dominated and consumed him. Jerusalem, which featured so much in his preaching, was his home city (Isa. 7:1–3; 37:2). His ready access to the king suggests that he was high-born and moved in the most elite circles.[13] Yet there was nothing effete or fawning about him. His presence was a constant reminder that royal power was not absolute, and privilege entailed heavy responsibility. His tense confrontation with Ahaz in chapter 7, for example, speaks volumes for his courage and unswerving commitment to his high calling, qualities that were eventually to cost him his life. His wife is called 'the prophetess' in 8:3, suggesting that she, too, prophesied. Certainly she did so indirectly, for she bore sons to Isaiah whose symbolic names expressed key aspects of his message.[14] Beyond this we know nothing of his family life, what solace he drew from it, or

---

10 *ANET*, pp. 287–288.

11 'Hezekiah the Judean' (*hazaquiau mat yaudaya*) is Sennacherib's own expression (*ANET*, p. 288).

12 See comments on Tirhakah, king of Ethiopia, at 37:9.

13 'According to Jewish tradition, he was of royal blood' (N. H. Ridderbos in *NBD*, p. 521).

14 Shear-Jashub, 'a remnant will return', and Maher-Shalal-Hash-Baz, 'quick to the plunder, swift to the spoil' (7:3; 8:3–4).

what strains it suffered. All we know is that he was not a divided person; his call had an impact on and shaped his home life as it did every sphere he moved in. We catch a glimpse in 8:16–18 of a small band of disciples gathering around him, with a strong suggestion that it included his sons (see on 8:18).[15] That, at least, must have been a tremendous comfort to him and a most fitting reward for his faithfulness (cf. Gen. 7:13).

Most of the material in chapters 1–39 of the book relates in one way or another to his ministry during the crises of 734 and 701 BC respectively. But rarely is he seen directly, and even then the focus is not on himself, but on others: Ahaz, Hezekiah, Sennacherib, and of course the Lord, whose word shapes and directs everything. The servant is hidden behind his Lord, and the messenger behind his message. But he was destined to become more hidden still, for a time came when it was impossible for him to appear in public at all. Within five years of the debacle of 701 BC,[16] Manasseh had completely reversed his father's policies, plunging Judah into one of the darkest periods of its history. Submission to Assyria became the new political orthodoxy, pagan rites of the most detestable kinds were reintroduced, and all dissent was ruthlessly crushed (2 Kgs 21:1–16). Tradition has it that Isaiah was martyred at this time, sawn in two by Manasseh's men.[17] If so, it was a cruel end indeed, but not a defeat, for it is likely that it was in those last silent years, when he was confined by old age and persecution, that he plumbed the depths and scaled the heights of spiritual understanding, and committed to his disciples the inestimable treasures preserved for us in chapters 40–66. They completed and rounded out the insights of his earlier preaching. For something larger occupied his mind now than the particulars thrown up by this or that political crisis. It was the whole shape of God's future plans for his people and for his world. It was what the opening verse of the book calls his 'vision'.

2. The vision of Isaiah (1:1–2a)

These opening lines are like the first stirring chords of the overture to a great oratorio. They summon us to listen and give us the first indication of the character of the work we are about to hear.

---

[15] The 'children' of that verse are probably his literal children, who form the nucleus of his larger band of disciples.

[16] Hezekiah's death, probably in 698 BC, cleared the way for Manasseh's change of policy. On the difficulties surrounding the dating of Hezekiah's reign, see note 2 on page 137.

[17] See the opening comments on 40:1 – 51:11.

a. The vision is objective

We are told at once of both the human agency and the divine origin of the vision. It is the vision of 'Isaiah son of Amoz'; he saw it, lived it and died for it. In this sense it is *his* vision.[18] It comes to us clothed in a human person, alive with human passion and cast in human language. It is the human aspect of the vision that makes it accessible to us. But at the same time it has a quality that transcends this. The very term 'vision', especially in this and similar contexts, stands for divine revelation (cf. Obad. 1; Hab. 2:1–2). It is received by a human person, but originates outside the prophet. At the most fundamental level, it is *God's* vision, and exists only because 'the LORD has spoken'.

b. The vision is big

The vision which is introduced here spans the whole sixty-six chapters of the book. It is big in terms of its sheer bulk; big enough to daunt most readers, let alone preachers and commentators.[19] But, more significantly, it is conceptually big. The vision begins with heaven and earth being summoned to listen (1:2), and it ends with their being so affected by what they hear that they are transformed into new heavens and a new earth (66:22). It is about renewal on a massive scale; the recreation of the universe. Isaiah's vision begins with the historical Jerusalem of his own day, corrupt and under judgment (1:8), and finishes with the end-time city of God, the new Jerusalem, the joy and delight of the whole earth (65:17–19). It deals with God's dealings with his people from the eighth century BC (1:1) right down to our own time and beyond, to the things that will bring history to a close and usher in eternity (66:22–24). Its sweep is huge. In a very real sense the vision is as big as the mind of God himself.

c. The vision is a unity

There is no denying that the book contains a great diversity of material. It moves from verse to prose and back again many times. There are lawsuits, hymns, narratives, terrifying descriptions of judgment and tender passages of comfort. The many changes of character and scene, mood and style, can be quite bewildering. Scholarship has generally responded to this diversity by separating out the various elements and

---

[18] Cf. Paul's use of the expression 'my gospel' (Rom. 2:16; 16:25; 2 Tim. 2:8).

[19] As I can testify from experience!

subjecting each of them to independent, intense scrutiny, a strategy which has not been without its value. But the opening verse points the reader in a fundamentally different direction. It subsumes all this diverse material under the heading '*the vision* of Isaiah'. It tells us that what we are about to read is fundamentally one thing, an integrated whole. It is not just that it is all attached in some way or another to one person (the 'visions' or 'words' of Isaiah would have served well enough to convey that; cf. Ezek. 1:1; Jer. 1:1), but that *the varied content itself* amounts to a single thing, one gigantic vision, and that we will have to apply ourselves to reading it as such if we are to understand it.

d. The vision is historical

In one sense the vision transcends history, reaching above it to the heavens and beyond it to eternity. But at the same time it arises from a particular time and place, and takes the particulars of history with the utmost seriousness. Isaiah saw it, we are told, 'during the reigns of Uzziah, Jotham, Ahaz and Hezekiah, kings of Judah'. As we have seen, these were turbulent times, and the immediate future promised to be even more so. Battles were won and lost, kingdoms rose and fell, the world was an unstable and dangerous place in which people struggled to survive and make sense of their lives. History as they experienced it was characterized by constant change – intense, threatening and confusing. And so it must have remained if God had not spoken into it.

But verse 2, with its announcement that 'the LORD has spoken', breaks on the scene like the 'Let there be light' of Genesis 1:3. It pierces the chaos of history with the brilliance of divine revelation. The vision breaks into history to expose its true shape, character and goal. It is not history-denying but history-affirming. It draws back the curtain and shows us that history, with all its confusing particulars, is the stage on which a great drama is being enacted, a drama scripted and directed at every point by God himself. Assyria is the rod of his anger (10:5); the sufferings which lie ahead, including the Babylonian exile, are a furnace in which God will purge his people (1:25). The outcome will be not just a new people, but a new city and a new universe (65:17–19).[20] History has meaning because God is taking it somewhere, and what the vision does

---

[20] Cf. Paul in Rom. 8:18–19: suffering leads to glory, and the whole creation waits eagerly for the process to be complete and the children of God to be revealed.

is to set the end firmly before us and call us to live every moment in the light of it (2:1–5).

But the end is guaranteed only because of something else. It is the fulcrum on which all history turns, and it lies at the very centre of Isaiah's vision.

e. The vision is sharply focused

I imagine we have all had the experience, at some time or other, of viewing a great work of art. At first we receive only a general impression, of beauty perhaps, or energy or sadness. But then as we look more closely and become aware of the lines of composition, or the distribution of light and shadow, we find our eye being drawn to one particular point. Something is thrown into prominence, something which, if we are only sensitive enough to it, will unlock the whole work to us. This focal point contains the answer to what the work is *about* at the most fundamental level.

The careful reader will find that the vision of Isaiah is the same. Its lines radiate out from one clear focal point and lead back to it. And just in case we are too obtuse to see for ourselves what it is, we are told at once: the vision is 'concerning Judah and Jerusalem'. But I think we can go further even than this. There is a sharper focus still.

Not very long ago I stood with my two daughters one Sunday morning in the huge, circular forecourt of St Peter's Basilica in Rome. There was the usual press of tourists, pilgrims, officials and traders. Would we like a postcard, a cross, a souvenir spoon, or perhaps a rosary or holy picture? No, we found our way past these distractions as quickly as possible; they were so tawdry compared with the magnificence of the place itself. At first it was the basilica that captivated us. The whole forecourt seemed designed to produce precisely this effect; the magnificent curving colonnade, the fountain, the grand staircase, all drew us towards it. But then we noticed the barricades, the seats, the music and the children's choir and realized that a quite deliberate strategy was being put in place to focus our attention elsewhere, at least temporarily. The crowds seemed to be aware of it too, for they were obediently falling into line, so to speak, and expectantly looking across the square towards a far less impressive building situated to the right of the basilica and partly hidden behind a wall. It had long rows of identical windows, so there was no obvious point of interest until about ten minutes to eleven, when a figure appeared briefly at one of the windows and draped a richly coloured banner from it.

The effect was immediate. A murmur of anticipation went through the crowd, the volume of the music lifted as the choir went into its carefully rehearsed routine, and the basilica receded entirely from our consciousness as every eye became riveted on that one small window. We were soon rewarded. At exactly eleven o'clock the Pope appeared at the window and addressed us.

The vision of Isaiah contains many impressive elements. First Assyria looms large, and then Babylon, and many other nations and persons vie for our attention as well. But what the superscription effectively does is to drape a banner from one particular window. It tells us to keep our eye firmly fixed on Judah and Jerusalem, and as we do so, a figure appears before our eyes. He has royal titles which link him in the most intimate way with God himself (9:6). He is a shoot from the stump of Jesse, an ideal king from the line of David (11:1). He is endowed with the Spirit and rules with perfect justice, and under him all that God has purposed for his people and his world is fully realized (11:2–9). The term 'messiah' properly belongs to every king of the house of David, even the unworthy ones; each, by virtue of his office, is 'the LORD's messiah'.[21] But this is *the* Messiah, the final and perfect one, and on reflection we can see how fittingly the window frames him and anticipates his appearance. For 'Judah' and 'Jerusalem' both have the strongest possible links in the Old Testament with the house of David (Gen. 49:10; 2 Sam. 5:6–7).

But then, as we watch, he is strangely altered, or more correctly he appears again in a different guise. It is so different, in fact, that at first we have difficulty recognizing him as the same person. He is a humble and gentle servant (42:1–3), he meets discouragement and opposition (49:4), he is cruelly persecuted and killed (50:6; 53:8–9), but at last he is raised and glorified, and all God's purposes prosper in his hand (53:10). And then at last it becomes clear: the two figures are one. For the Servant, too, is a royal figure. He brings forth justice to the nations (42:1), the distant lands wait for his law (42:4), and through him the blessings promised to David are at last fully realized (55:3–5).

At the heart of Isaiah's vision is the startling revelation that the Messiah must suffer. Its sharpest focus is on the one who came to the window for us all. That is, if you like, the depth of it, the truth that lies at the centre.

---

[21] The Hebrew word *māšîaḥ* (messiah) is translated in most English versions as 'anointed'. 'The LORD's messiah' = 'the LORD's anointed'. See 1 Sam. 2:10; 16:6; 26:11; 2 Sam. 22:51; Pss 2:2; 18:50; Lam. 4:20.

But like a well-cut diamond, the vision has surface as well as depth, and we will be able to appreciate its many facets only as we attend carefully to the way it has been shaped and presented to us as Holy Scripture.

3. The book of Isaiah

a. Structure

Chapters 1–35 and 40–66 are predominantly verse, reflecting the powerful rhythmic style characteristic of prophetic preaching.[22] But at the centre, in chapters 36–39, stands an extended block of material which is predominately prose.[23] It has two parts. The first (chapters 36–37) describes Sennacherib's invasion and its outcome, and finally resolves the Assyrian crisis which has dominated the whole first half of the book. The second (chapters 38–39) deals with Hezekiah's illness and his reception of envoys from Marduk-Baladan. It anticipates the Babylonian crisis, which casts its shadow over the entire second half of the book.[24] So chapters 36–39 are effectively the structural pivot on which the whole book turns. It is preceded by three units (chapters 1–12; 13–27 and 28–35), all of which end with the redeemed singing God's praises in Zion, or on their way to it. It is followed by another three units (40:1 – 51:11; 51:12 – 55:13; and chapters 56–66) which end in the same way.[25]

We observed earlier the overall movement from Jerusalem to new Jerusalem and from fallen creation to new creation. But in fact this movement takes place again and again *within* the book as well as across the whole of it. While the fullest description of life in the new creation is reserved until the last two chapters (65:17–25; 66:10–24), we are given frequent anticipations and pledges of it all the way through, especially at the conclusion of parts 1, 2, 3, 5 and 6.[26] We glimpse the end many times before we finally arrive and rest there.

The basic plan of the book, then, can be set out as in the following table.

---

[22] The main exceptions are 6:1–8 (the first part of Isaiah's call), most of chapter 7 (his encounter with Ahaz), and chapter 20 (Isaiah goes stripped and barefoot). But these represent only a very small proportion of the whole. 19:16–25 is in rhythmic prose, not greatly different from verse.

[23] The two verse sections (37:22b–35 and 38:9–20) are framed by the surrounding prose narrative.

[24] In chapters 56–66 Babylon is no longer directly in view, but the legacy of the exile lives on and contributes significantly to the troubles of the restoration period as it is envisaged here.

[25] Singing as such is not mentioned at the end of the final unit, but is implied by the activity of joyful worship (65:17–19; 66:23).

[26] In fact the book has scarcely begun before the end is in view (2:1–5; 4:2–6).

Jerusalem	Part 1	1 – 12		
	Part 2	13 – 27		Assyria
	Part 3	28 – 35		
	Part 4	36 – 39	- -	
	Part 5	40:1 – 51:11		
	Part 6	51:12 – 55:13		Babylon
New Jerusalem	Part 7	56 – 66		

b. Themes

We have already noted some key aspects of the book's message: the truth that the Lord is creator and universal ruler, the movement to new heavens and a new earth, and the key role of Jerusalem and the Messiah. But now that we have clarified the book's structure we are in a position to go further and ask how the various aspects of its message relate to one another.

Of key significance here are the two passages, in chapters 6 and 40, in which Isaiah finds himself summoned into the presence of God to receive a specific commission. Both the nature of these passages (commissionings) and their strategic location (at or near the beginning of parts 1 and 5) confirm their great importance for an understanding of the book's major themes. The first commits Isaiah to a ministry of judgment, the second to a ministry of comfort; and these become the dominant notes of the first and second halves of the book respectively. It is a book about demolition and reconstruction (cf. Jer. 1:9–10), judgment and salvation. And the order is significant: paradoxically, salvation emerges out of judgment and is possible only because of it. But of course there is much more to it than this. The two themes we have identified are developed on at least three different levels.

The first has to do with the discipline that is brought to bear on the people of Judah and Jerusalem. We meet them in chapter 1 as the Lord's rebellious children. They are so estranged that they hardly know him any more. They are laden with guilt and have given themselves to corruption. They have spurned the Lord, turned their backs on him, and resisted every attempt he has so far made to bring them to a better mind (1:2b–6). But he will not leave them so. He first takes up Assyria as a rod to chastise them in their land (10:5–6). Then he uses Babylon to take them out of it (39:5–7), and finally, when they are broken by suffering, he summons Cyrus of

Persia to set them free and give them the chance to go home and start again (44:24–28). Out of this scourging process there emerges, by the end of the book, a group of people who are truly repentant. They are described as those who 'mourn' (61:2–3), the 'servants' of God (65:13–15), and the 'humble and contrite in spirit' who tremble at the Lord's word (66:2). They are the nucleus from which a new people of God will grow.

At the second level a more profound issue is addressed. This, too, is introduced (though more obliquely) in chapter 1, for there for the first time we meet Isaiah's characteristic description of God as 'the Holy One of Israel' (1:4).[27] It is this Holy One who has been spurned by the people of Judah and Jerusalem, and the unspoken question at this point is: how can he forgive them (or any sinner for that matter) without compromising his holiness? Failure to see it as an issue is simply an indication of how small is our appreciation of the holiness of God and the gravity of human sinfulness. The same issue surfaces much more pointedly in the call passage of chapter 6. When Isaiah is summoned into the presence of this holy God he knows himself to be ruined, for he is unclean and lives among an unclean people (6:5). But no sooner is the confession made than a live coal is taken from the altar and applied to his lips, and he is told that his guilt is taken away and his sin atoned for (6:6–7). The implication is clear. Forgiveness is possible only when atonement is made, and atonement is provided by God himself. It is a gift from his altar. This is the key to understanding the ministry of the Servant of the Lord in the second part of the book. He is the final answer to the mystery of how God can forgive and remain just. He does it through a perfect sacrifice which he himself provides. And at last, in 53:5, the forgiven ones see it: 'The punishment that brought us peace was on him, and by his wounds we are healed.' There is more to judgment than being exiled from the land, and more to salvation than returning to it. There is separation from God or reconciliation with him. At this level the themes of judgment and salvation are focused on the vicarious suffering and exaltation of the Servant.

But this opens up a wider perspective, which brings us to the third and final level at which the two themes are worked out. The people of Judah and Jerusalem have a history which reaches right back to Abraham (41:8; 51:2), and it was always God's intention that they should be the channel

---

[27] This expression occurs twelve times in chapters 1–39, thirteen times in chapters 40–66, and only five times in the rest of the Old Testament.

through which his blessing would flow out to the world at large (Gen. 12:1–3). This is why heaven and earth are summoned to hear what God has to say about these people at the beginning of the book (1:2). Whatever God does among them will have an impact on the entire creation (cf. Rom. 8:19). This is really the seed from which the great missionary vision of the book springs. Already in chapter 2 Isaiah sees the nations streaming to Zion to share in the salvation that has been realized there. But again we have to wait until the second part of the book to find out how this will be brought to pass. Again the key is the work of the Servant. He is a covenant for the people, and a light for the Gentiles (42:6). His sacrifice is sufficient for all and provides the rich food of pardon and forgiveness of which all who are hungry and thirsty may partake, if only they will come (55:1–7).

But now we see that the inward flow of the nations to share in the gospel banquet presupposes and requires another movement which is directed outwards – a great missionary movement of gospel proclamation and invitation. And such a movement does indeed unfold in the closing chapters of the book. It begins with the repeated statement 'You are my witnesses' in 43:10, 12 and 44:8. It is given further impetus by the final appearance of the Servant as a Spirit-anointed preacher (61:1–3), and it climaxes in the sending out of messengers far and wide to proclaim God's glory among the nations (66:19). But as servants of the Servant, their message has the same two-edged nature as his,[28] and divides the world into the saved and the lost. In the end, salvation and judgment become absolutized as eternal life and eternal death (66:22–24), and both alike express the truth of who God really is, the *Holy One* of Israel.

c. Unity and authorship

It will be apparent by now that I am convinced that the book of Isaiah is a unity. But there are various kinds of unity, of which unity of authorship is only one. A book may be from various hands, but have an editorial unity imposed by someone who has worked over the material and given it its final form. It may have tensions within it but have a fundamental theological unity because it is the expression of one theological tradition. I would argue that the Old Testament as a whole (and by extension the whole Bible) has this kind of unity. And on a smaller scale, a book may have

---

[28] See 61:2: 'the year of . . . favour and the day of vengeance . . .'

a unity because it is a product of a 'school' of writers who have drawn their inspiration from one very influential founding figure (e.g. an 'Isaiah school', consisting of Isaiah himself and several generations of his disciples). Most scholars have accepted that the book of Isaiah does have some sort of unity, but exactly what kind of unity it is has proved to be an extremely vexed question.

This is not the place for a detailed review of the history of Isaiah research; that can be readily accessed elsewhere.[29] Suffice it to say that since the late nineteenth century, the vast majority of scholars have opted for some form or other of the 'Isaiah school' approach. In principle this has much in its favour. It enables full recognition to be given to the differences of style and setting in the book without denying its underlying theological unity. And there is prima facie evidence of the existence of such a school in the reference to Isaiah's disciples in 8:16–17. In practice, however, this approach in its various forms has so stressed the distinctives of the different parts of the book that its unity has almost ceased to be a subject of scholarly concern at all. Chapters 40–55 have been assigned to a 'Second Isaiah' of the late exilic period, and chapters 56–66 to a 'Third Isaiah' of the early restoration period. This was the basic analysis made by Duhm in his landmark commentary of 1883. Since then the study of each part of the book has more or less gone along separate ways. Most scholars have continued to regard chapters 40–55 as a unity, but the tendency has been to see chapters 1–39 and chapters 56–66 as complex compositions of material from various periods, with only a relatively small nucleus of material (from chapters 6–8 and 28) being from Isaiah himself. In this process the notion of 'disciples' has become very elastic, and the connection between Isaiah himself and the book which bears his name extremely tenuous. At the opposite extreme E. J. Young continued to attribute everything to Isaiah and nothing at all (except faithful preservation) to his disciples.[30] The truth probably lies somewhere in between.

The most natural way of taking the superscription in 1:1 (which refers to Isaiah in the third person) is that it is from the hand of the final editor, who wishes to affirm that the book as a whole is a faithful expression of

---

[29] See any standard Bible dictionary or encyclopaedia. A more thoroughgoing review and analysis can be found, for example, in Childs.

[30] 'The prophet Isaiah himself was the author of the entire book; he himself committed it all to writing, and he was responsible for collecting his messages and placing them in the present book which bears his name' (Young, 1, p. 8).

the vision (revelation) which was given to Isaiah. From the editor's own point of view the period of the prophet's life is now past. It was 'during the reigns of Uzziah, Jotham, Ahaz and Hezekiah, kings of Judah', that the vision came. A similar backward look occurs in the third-person accounts of events in Isaiah's life in chapters 20 and 36–39. These are quite different in style and viewpoint from the autobiographical material in chapters 6–8. In the present arrangement of the book, Isaiah's account of his call does not occur until chapter 6. It is preceded by material that has apparently been placed before it for thematic reasons, some of it drawn from quite late in his ministry.[31] In short, there is clear evidence of editorial activity in the production of the present book, and it makes good sense to attribute this to Isaiah's disciples. The question, however, is how long this activity went on, and how close the editors stood to the prophet himself.

Of particular interest here, again, is the arrangement of the material in chapters 36–39. Marduk-Baladan, who had been a leader of rebellion against Assyria in the east, was finally ousted from the Babylonian throne in 703 BC, two years before Sennacherib's invasion of Judah.[32] This is one of a number of indications that the events of chapters 38–39 in fact occurred before those of chapters 36–37.[33] Hezekiah's reception of envoys from Marduk-Baladan, king of Babylon (39:1–2), was part of his anti-Assyrian activity which provoked Sennacherib's subsequent invasion of Judah in 701 BC. In other words, it seems that the material in these chapters has been arranged quite deliberately in reverse chronological order to form a bridge between the two halves of the book. The same basic material occurs in 2 Kings 18:13 – 20:19, in the same order, but without any apparent explanation in terms of its context there. It is likely, therefore, that it is primary in Isaiah and secondary in 2 Kings. But there is virtually universal agreement that the books of Kings, as part of the 'Deuteronomic History' (Joshua–2 Kings), are from the period immediately following the fall of Jerusalem in 587 BC.[34] If this is so (and there seems to

---

[31] As explained in the exposition, the description of Jerusalem under siege in 1:7–8 probably relates to Sennacherib's invasion in the reign of Hezekiah (701 BC).

[32] The details of Marduk-Baladan's stormy career, as documented in Assyrian records, are given in C. Boutflower, *The Book of Isaiah I – XXXIX* (London: SPCK, 1930), pp. 134–147. Oswalt (p. 693) provides a brief summary.

[33] For more detail, see note 2 on p. 137 (on the dating of Hezekiah's reign), and the opening comments on 38:1–22.

[34] See Martin Noth's influential work *The Deuteronomistic History* (1943; Eng. trans. JSOT Supplement Series 15; Sheffield: JSOT Press, 1981). Subsequent modifications of his thesis have tended to suggest earlier rather than later dates for the work, including the bulk of 1 and 2 Kings. See R. D. Nelson, *The Double Redaction of the Deuteronomistic History* (JSOT Supplement Series 18; Sheffield: JSOT Press, 1981).

be no good reason to doubt it), it follows that not just chapters 36–39, *but the whole book of Isaiah in substantially its present form,* is pre-exilic. Assuming that Isaiah survived into the reign of Manasseh, this means that the book that bears his name was completed by his disciples within, at the most, the next ninety years.

This explains a number of features of the book which continue to puzzle scholars. Brevard Childs, for example, argues that while a general situation of exile and restoration is in view in chapters 40–66, these chapters are remarkably light on historical specifics compared with chapters 1–39. 'The one notable exception to this generalization is the reference to Cyrus (44:28 – 45:1), but even here the references to the historical events associated with Cyrus are minimal.'[35] Childs is unclear whether this stems from 'an intentional removal of historical data' (for theological reasons) or is the result of 'a peculiar transmission process' which we do not fully understand.[36] But surely the more natural explanation is the one the book itself offers us: that in chapters 40–66 Isaiah is addressing a future situation which is clear to him in outline only. Of course the naming of Cyrus will make this impossible for many to accept, but this detail should be seen for the exception that it is. Only a dogmatic adherence to a particular view of the nature of prophecy would allow it to decide the issue.

This is not to say, of course, that the material concerning Cyrus is of no consequence. In fact, a key aspect of the theology of Isaiah 40–55 hangs on it. The author is insistent that the Lord has proved himself to be the only true God by predicting the rise of Cyrus. He declared it in advance, even naming Cyrus, so that when the fulfilment came there could be no mistake about who controlled history (41:21–29; 45:3–7). The whole force of the argument depends on the existence of a prophecy concerning Cyrus which precedes his rise. This presents a considerable problem, however, for those who hold the 'Second Isaiah' hypothesis, *for no such prophecy is to be found outside Isaiah 40 – 55 itself.* It has usually been assumed that the oracle(s) at issue cannot be identified or has been lost.[37] But this dilemma is resolved at once if the book's own testimony is accepted. Isaiah 40 – 55 is a continuation of the vision of the eighth-century Isaiah. The 'missing' oracles are not 'missing' at all, and the theology of Isaiah 40 – 55

---

[35] Childs, p. 326.

[36] Ibid.

[37] Ibid., p. 329.

does not hang in the air but rests on the solid evidence of the Lord's sovereignty that the Cyrus oracles provide.

Equally difficult for the majority view is the need to maintain that the author of chapters 40–55 should have had his name either completely forgotten or deliberately suppressed by those who transmitted his words to us. It is understandable that a mere editor should remain anonymous, but the author of Isaiah 40 – 55 is much more than this. Chapter 40 opens by presenting us with his credentials. He has stood in the heavenly council, heard the Lord's word and received a divine commission. He is a prophet in his own right, whom many would acknowledge to be the greatest of all the Old Testament prophets, and yet his identity is never disclosed. This is strange indeed. In every other instance of prophetic commissioning in the Old Testament, the prophet is either addressed by name or clearly identified in the framing narrative,[38] and the names of those so called are revered and honoured.[39] Even where there is a close 'master–disciple' relationship between two prophets, as with Elijah and Elisha, each is remembered by name. But in the case of 'Second Isaiah', we are required to believe that a 'disciple' who receives a separate commissioning almost a century and a half after the death of his master, and whose own ministry rivals or even surpasses that of his mentor, has had his identity completely suppressed!

The canonical book of Isaiah presents a very different account of what actually took place. The one called in chapter 40 is not named there because he has already been named in chapter 6. There are many connections between the two passages, including the references to the Lord's glory in 6:3 and 40:5. The glory which Isaiah saw in the heavens is soon to be revealed on earth in the deliverance he will bring to his people. What Isaiah alone saw in chapter 6, 'all people' will one day see. His question here, 'What shall I cry?', echoes his earlier one in chapter 6, 'For how long, Lord?' Like Elijah at Horeb, Isaiah finds himself back at the source of his prophetic ministry and is commissioned afresh for the second phase of his work (1 Kgs 19:1–18).

This exposition has been written in the conviction that the account that the book of Isaiah itself gives of its own origins is far more plausible

---

[38] Cf., e.g., Moses (Exod. 3), Samuel (1 Sam. 3:1–14), Micaiah (1 Kgs 22:19–22), Jeremiah (Jer. 1:4–19), Ezekiel (Ezek. 1 – 3) and Jonah (Jon. 1:1–2). The nearest thing to an 'anonymous call' is the commissioning of the Servant in 42:1–9, but the reason is that he is a future (eschatological) figure whose identity is yet to be revealed.

[39] Especially in intertestamental literature. See the 'praises of famous men' in Ecclesiasticus 44 – 50.

than any alternative that has so far been proposed. It is supported by Jewish tradition from a very early period, as the following passage from Ecclesiasticus shows:

> Hezekiah did what was pleasing to the Lord,
> and kept firmly to the ways of his ancestor David,
> as he was instructed by Isaiah,
> the great prophet whose vision could be trusted.
> In his time the sun went back,
> and he added many years to the king's life.
> With inspired power he saw the future
> and comforted the mourners in Zion.
> He revealed things to come before they happened,
> the secrets of the future to the end of time.[40]

This same tradition is reflected in the New Testament.

d. Importance

In terms of theological significance, the book of Isaiah is the 'Romans' of the Old Testament. It is here that the threads come together and the big picture of God's purposes for his people and for his world is most clearly set forth. Something of its importance can be gauged from the fact that it is quoted no fewer than sixty-six times in the New Testament, being exceeded in this only by the book of Psalms.[41] These quotations are spread through all the major sections of the New Testament, from Matthew to 1 Peter. And if more or less transparent allusions are taken into account, its influence is even more obvious. The New Testament moves to its climax by echoing Isaiah's promise of death conquered, tears wiped away, and new heavens and a new earth (Rev. 21:1–4). In fact, it was Isaiah who, via the LXX, gave us the term 'gospel' by drawing it out of the reserve of common words available to him and charging it with profound new theological significance (see on 40:9–11).

By far the greatest importance of this book, however, lies in the witness it bears to Jesus Christ. In the synagogue, at the very outset of his public

---

[40] Ecclus. 48:22–25 (New English Bible version of the Apocrypha). Ecclesiasticus is a Jewish work from approximately 180 BC.

[41] Psalms is quoted seventy-nine times.

ministry, this book was placed in Jesus' hands and he read from it the passage we now know as 61:1–2 (Luke 4:16–21). It was as though he had received it, not just from human hands, but from the hands of God. By reading from it as he did, he assumed the role of the Servant with all that that would mean for him in terms of willing submission to the Father's will. It was the beginning of his journey to the cross. And in handing the scroll back to the attendant, it was as though he gave it to all of us who would be his followers. If we want to understand fully who he is and what he came to do, we must read this book.

The apostle John understood this well. At the midpoint of his gospel he quotes twice from the book of Isaiah (John 12:37–41), first from chapter 53 ('Lord, who has believed our message . . . ?'), then from chapter 6 ('He has blinded their eyes and hardened their hearts . . .'). Finally he binds them together with his own comment: 'Isaiah said this because he saw Jesus' glory and spoke about him.' It is the point in the gospel where the rejection of Jesus has become obvious, and it is clear that the time has come for him to descend into the darkness of his passion. And this, says the apostle, is the glory of the Messiah that Isaiah saw and spoke about: the glory of his servanthood, the glory of his suffering for those who rejected him. This exposition will show (if demonstration is needed) that he correctly grasped the heart and true significance of Isaiah's total vision as the book which bears his name presents it to us.[42]

Finally, in Acts 8:26–35 we catch a glimpse of how this same understanding of Isaiah's vision was to open into the great outward thrust of the gospel from Jerusalem to the ends of the earth. In the midst of a remarkable ministry in Samaria, Philip is told to go southward to the desert road that leads from Jerusalem to Gaza. There, in one of those amazing moments made by God, he comes upon an Ethiopian eunuch, returning home from Jerusalem and reading the book of the prophet Isaiah. It is not just any passage he is reading, but Isaiah 53, where the Servant is led like a lamb to the slaughter. He is fascinated and puzzled by what he reads and asks Philip for an explanation: 'Tell me, please, who is the prophet talking about, himself or someone else?' Luke gives Philip's response in words of immortal simplicity: 'Then Philip began with that

---

[42]   On the related complex issues surrounding the authority and unity of Scripture, and the use of the Old Testament in the New, see the essays in D. A. Carson and J. D. Woodbridge (eds.), *Scripture and Truth* (Grand Rapids: Baker, 2nd edn 1992).

very passage of Scripture and told him the good news about Jesus.' It was the beginning of the gospel going to Africa.

This exposition of the book of Isaiah is sent forth with the prayer that it may help all who read it to see and speak of the glory of Christ with the same clarity and power.

4. Two final comments

a. The nature of prophecy

It has not been possible to provide here the kind of introduction to Old Testament prophecy as an oral and literary phenomenon which might be expected in a longer, more technical commentary. For those who are interested, the chapter on prophecy by Richard Patterson in *A Complete Literary Guide to the Bible*[43] is excellent. Patterson deals with the characteristic forms of prophecy as an essentially oral genre, but then goes on to offer sound advice on how to read it in the final, literary form in which we now have it in the canon. He notes Ryken's characterization of prophecy as 'visionary literature', which 'transforms the known world or present state of things into a situation that at the time of writing is as yet only imagined'.[44] Patterson himself prefers 'proclamation' as perhaps the most apt designation of the prophetic genre, but recognizes that it moves beyond preaching to inscripturation, and has a visionary dimension which transcends the boundaries of the prophet's own time.

All this is very relevant to this exposition, which seeks to do justice to the structure and unity of Isaiah's vision in its final, literary form, without ignoring the original historical context in which that vision originated.

b. Israel in the book of Isaiah

In the broad sweep of Isaiah's vision the term 'Israel' is used in a variety of ways, depending on the particular situation in view or the theological agenda which is operating.

Most commonly it is used to refer generally to the covenant people of God who could trace their ancestry back to 'Jacob/Israel' (Gen. 32:28) and, before him, to Abraham.[45] The same general sense is implied in the divine

---

[43] R. Patterson, 'Old Testament Prophecy', in Ryken and Longman, pp. 296–310.

[44] Ryken, p. 166.

[45] E.g. 1:3; 8:18; 14:1; 19:24; 40:27; 41:8, 14; 43:1, 22; 44:1, 5, 21, 23; 45:4, 17, 25; 46:3, 13; 48:1, 12; 49:3, 5; 63:7.

title 'the Holy One of Israel', which is so characteristic of Isaiah.[46] Less frequently the term is used specifically of the northern kingdom of Israel, in contrast to Judah, the southern kingdom, reflecting the political situation which existed between the death of Solomon and the fall of the two kingdoms in 722 and 587 BC respectively (e.g. 7:1; 9:8, 12; 11:12; cf. 1:1). To assist the reader I have included an explanatory comment, usually in a footnote, where it may not be clear in what sense the term is being used, either in the text of Isaiah itself or in my exposition of it.

---

[46] E.g. 1:4; 5:19; 12:6; 17:7; 29:19; 30:11; 37:23; 41:14; 43:3; 45:11; 47:4; 48:17; 49:7; 55:5; 60:9, 14.

Isaiah 1 – 12

1. The Lord is king

1. The great vision (1:1)

This opening verse has already been expounded at length in the Introduction (pp. 7–12), so all we need to do here is to remind ourselves of its key significance before moving on.

It stands here as a title for the book as a whole and is packed with information vital for a correct understanding of its message. It describes the contents of the entire book as a single *vision*. It tells us whose vision it is, and the period in which Isaiah exercised his prophetic ministry.

In the days of the four kings named here, especially after the death of Uzziah (see 6:1), when Judah and Jerusalem lay under the ever-increasing threat of destruction by Assyria, Isaiah *saw*, by divine revelation, what God was doing with the nation, why he was doing it, and where everything was heading under his sovereign control.

While the vision concerns a specific city and nation in the eighth century BC, we shall see when we get to the beginning of chapter 2 (in particular 2:1–4) that this is merely the vantage point from which the prophet looks out. The vision is in fact breathtaking in its scope, embracing all nations and reaching to the very end of time. Here is a vision which is bound to deliver us from spiritual myopia and small-mindedness if only we can grasp it, or, better still, allow it to grasp us.

2. From the Jerusalem that is to the Zion that will be (1:2 – 2:5)

a. The sinful nation (1:2–9)[1]

At once it becomes apparent why the vision concerns 'Judah and Jerusalem'. Like us Christians, the people of this city and nation were the Lord's own *children* and *people* (2–3), language which strongly recalls the exodus from Egypt and the forging of the covenant at Sinai.[2] It must have seemed as strange to the more powerful nations round about as it does to the world today that, as the Lord's people, they, like us, had been chosen to play a key role in his purposes for the world (Exod. 19:5–6). But they were in no state to fulfil their high calling. The Lord had been a father to them, but, like headstrong, ungrateful *children*, they had rebelled against him (the details will be given later), and already this rebellion had cost them dearly. The image of verses 5–6 is followed by a stark description of their condition in verses 7–9: burnt cities, devastated countryside, and the capital, Zion (Jerusalem), isolated and under siege. For these people the judgment of God was no mere theological abstraction, or something that existed somewhere else or might be experienced at some future time, as we tend to think of it. It was a very present, painful reality. The situation reflected here is probably the invasion of Judah by Sennacherib the Assyrian in 701 BC.[3]

In bringing his rebellious sons[4] to trial, the Lord was doing no more than the law of Moses required (Deut. 21:18–21), but his was a special grief, for he was judge as well as parent (cf. verse 9 with verse 2). Isaiah, too, longed for the people to repent rather than to go on suffering (see his appeal in verse 5), but everything now depended on the attitude of the remnant whom the Lord had so far graciously spared (9). Would they at last learn from the experience and turn back to the Lord?

The call to heaven and earth to listen in verse 2 serves two purposes. It underlines just how high the stakes are in this confrontation between the Lord and his people. In a very real sense the welfare of the entire universe

---

[1] An indictment of the nation by the Lord in verses 2–3 is amplified by Isaiah himself in verses 4–9 (notice the *us* and *we* in verse 9).

[2] Exod. 6:6–7; 9:1–2; 20:1–2. *Israel . . . my people* (3) clearly has this broad covenantal framework in view. See the comment on 'Israel in the book of Isaiah', above, pp. 22–23.

[3] Cf. verse 7 with 36:1, and verse 8 with Sennacherib's boast in his annals that he shut Hezekiah up in Jerusalem 'like a bird in its cage' (*ANET*, p. 288).

[4] *Children* in verse 2 is literally 'sons', as in the RSV.

depends now, as then, on how God's people respond to his word (cf. Matt. 5:13–16). It also foreshadows the climax towards which the whole vision of Isaiah moves. For, as we have already seen, the word which God speaks to his people here is destined to have its final outworking in a new universe – new heavens and a new earth (65:17; 66:22).

b. Corrupt worship (1:10–17)

The summons to *hear* in verse 10 (cf. verse 2) marks the beginning of a new unit, linked to the previous one by the repetition of *Sodom* and *Gomorrah*, which are now invested with terrible sarcasm. The *rulers* and *people* of Jerusalem were involved together in something every bit as offensive to the Lord as what had gone on in those two notorious cities of old.

The rebellion referred to generally in verse 2 is now specified: worship had been divorced from justice, and *the fatherless* and *the widow* had become the chief victims (17). Such disregard for justice was a fundamental violation of the Sinai covenant for which no amount of cultic observance could compensate. The exodus itself had flowed out of God's concern for the oppressed (Exod. 2:23–25), and from the very beginning he had demanded that his people should have a special concern for the poor and defenceless among them (Exod. 22:21–24). Furthermore, it is a requirement which has been intensified rather than diminished under the new covenant within which we ourselves now stand. If proof is required we need look no further than Jesus' parable of the good Samaritan (Luke 10:25–37), or James's description of 'religion that God our Father accepts as pure and faultless' (Jas 1:27). The cross places us under a far greater obligation to love than the exodus ever could.

Isaiah is at one with the other eighth-century prophets in insisting that ceremonial worship and even *prayer* (15) are worthless if they are not accompanied by active concern for justice (cf. Amos 5:4–7, 21–24; Mic. 6:6–8). But in the long and prosperous reign of Uzziah such concern had dried up. The rich grew richer while the rights and needs of the poor were disregarded, so that when Isaiah was called to his prophetic ministry at the end of Uzziah's reign (6:1), the nation was already ripe for judgment.

c. An ultimatum (1:18–20)

This is deservedly one of the most famous expressions of the grace of God in the Bible.

The theme of rebellion has been progressively developed through verses 2–17. The guilt of the accused has been amply established, and they are reminded of it here in vivid language: their sins are *scarlet, red as crimson*, the colour of blood (cf. 15b). We have reached a point of crisis.

But at the very point when judgment is expected, grace intervenes. The divine judge 'reasons' (see rsv) with the accused, and makes an offer which is truly amazing in its generosity: nothing less than total pardon (18)! What they had wrongly tried to achieve by cultic manipulation is now offered to them freely, on the one condition that they cease their rebellion (19–20a). The alternative is certain destruction: they can *eat* the good from the land (19b) or 'be eaten'[5] by the sword (20a). The choice is theirs. The Lord is gracious, but he is not to be trifled with.

The just basis for the forgiveness freely offered here will be unfolded later in the book. But it did not require the suffering of the exile to make it possible. It was always possible if only the people would repent. But grace is always hard for rebels to understand; their view of God is too small.

d. The purification of Zion (1:21–31)

The lament by the prophet in verses 21–23 clearly implies that there has been no change of heart among the people. The way of forgiveness has been rejected, and judgment is now announced by the Lord in verses 24–26. But there is a surprise here. The judgment is described in terms which imply purification rather than annihilation. Even in judgment, the Lord remembers mercy.

The central image is of crude ore being passed through a furnace and emerging as refined metal (25). The city which was once *faithful* (21) will be faithful again (26), but only after it has passed through the fires of God's judgment. The same basic image underlies verses 27–28: the pure metal which emerges from the furnace is a remnant of those who repent while the rest are destroyed. But now a different way of viewing the whole process is triggered by the rich word 'redeemed': *Zion will be delivered* [or 'redeemed'] *with justice, her penitent ones with righteousness*. The full treatment of the redemption theme will come in chapters 40–66,[6] but

---

[5] niv obscures the pun by its switch to *devoured* in verse 20b. The same verb is repeated in the Hebrew.

[6] See 43:1; 44:22–23; 48:20; 51:10; 52:3, 9; 62:12; 63:9. The significant reference to 'the redeemed' in 35:9 anticipates what is to come.

already we are alerted here to a vital element of it. It will not involve any bypassing of *justice* and *righteousness*. God will redeem (rescue)[7] his people in a way which is in complete accord with his holiness. That is how he always acts, and how he acted supremely in the cross of Christ. Redemption and judgment are inseparable; the one can come only through the other.

A cluster of secondary images in verses 29–31 throws further light on the corrupt state of the once-faithful city. It became polluted with pagan worship, involving *sacred* trees and *gardens* where fertility rites were practised. But those who were guilty of these practices would become like drought-stricken plants themselves, tinder-dry and ready for burning.

There is a particular emphasis in this passage on the culpability of the present leaders (23, 31) and on the promise of good leadership in the purified and restored city of the future (26).

e. The mountain of the Lord (2:1–5)

The heading in 2:1 is an abbreviated version of the book's title in 1:1, and taken together these two headings alert us again to the comprehensive nature of the vision which the book contains. Temporally it moves between the twin poles of the days[8] of Uzziah (1:1) and *the last days* (2:2). Notionally it is centred on *Judah and Jerusalem*. This opening unit of chapter 2 completes a movement which anticipates the movement of the book as a whole, from the Zion that is to the Zion that will be, via purifying judgment.

Mountains played an important part in the religions of Israel's neighbours. They were the points where heaven and earth were thought to meet and were therefore highly favoured as sites for altars and temples. The Canaanites worshipped their gods at the 'high places', and these became a snare to the Israelites. Even when such high places were removed from within Israel's borders in times of religious reform (36:7; cf. 2 Kgs 18:4, 22; 2 Chr. 14:3; 32:12), the surrounding nations continued to worship their gods on their holy mountains.

---

[7] 'Redemption' (root *pādâ*) in the Old Testament is fundamentally 'rescue', frequently through the payment of a price (cf. Exod. 13:13; Lev. 27:27). The corresponding passive participle from the same root is translated 'those . . . rescued' in 35:10, where it is parallel to the complementary term 'the redeemed' (root *gāʾal*) in 35:9. For comment on the technicalities of redemption involving a *gōʾēl* ('kinsman-redeemer') see the note provided there.

[8] 'Reigns' (NIV) is literally 'days'.

Isaiah here foresees the day when one holy mountain will stand supreme, reducing all others to utter insignificance. In this sense Isaiah's vision is exclusive. It is also inclusive, however, because it envisages *all nations* and *many peoples* coming to Zion to share with Israel in the blessings of the Lord's rule. Finally, it is a vision of universal peace, described in terms which have reverberated down through the centuries (4). But Isaiah sees that this peace will become a reality only when the nations are willing to submit to the word that goes forth *from Zion* where the one true God has revealed himself. Peace on any other terms is a cruel delusion, a truth we need to bear in mind constantly as we seek to be faithful to God's word in our own, modern world of religious pluralism.

The mountain of the LORD, then, is a symbol of the coming kingdom of God, in which a purified and restored Zion is destined to play a crucial role.[9] And Isaiah summons his contemporaries to live now in the light of that glorious prospect (5).

Isaiah was not blind to present realities. He spoke out against injustice, faithless politics and hypocritical religion with a passion that few could match today. But it was this vision of the future which inspired him. Religion for him was never an escape from reality, but the source from which he drew the strength he needed to face it squarely. It is how we must live too (1 Pet. 1:13).

3. The day of the Lord (2:6–22)

The scope and content of the book's message have been laid before us in outline in 1:1 – 2:5. Now it is time for the basic themes to be elaborated: first judgment (2:6 – 4:1), and then salvation (4:2–6). The movement from Zion under judgment to Zion restored is the same as in 1:1 – 2:5, but now the judgment aspect of the message is dwelt upon at much greater length.

In verses 6–11 the prophet is in the grip of strong emotions. His appeal of verse 5, like his earlier one in 1:5 and the Lord's own appeal in 1:18, has met with no response. What is the explanation for this unresponsiveness? At first, somewhat recklessly, Isaiah blames God: *You . . . have abandoned your people* (6a). But a more sober perspective soon returns. If the Lord has

---

[9] In this context 'Zion' itself takes on symbolic significance. There may well be a literal new Jerusalem in the new heavens and the new earth, but it will far exceed anything that could fit within our current concept of 'city'. It will be the home of all the redeemed from the beginning to the end of human history (35:10; 51:11; Rev. 21 – 22).

in fact abandoned them it is not without just cause. Zion was once 'full of justice' (1:21), but now it is 'full' of other things: *divination*, unholy alliances and idolatry (6–8). The people trust in their wealth and their military might rather than in the living God (7). Such people do not deserve forgiveness (9b). In his wrestling with God in these verses Isaiah follows in the footsteps of Abraham and Moses (Gen. 18:16–33; Exod. 32:30–32), and anticipates the later struggles of Jeremiah and Habakkuk (e.g. Jer. 8:18 – 9:1; Hab. 1:12–17).[10]

The hub of the problem is *pride* (11), and it is not Judah's problem only; it is a universal disease, and one to which, alas, none of us is immune. It has a thousand subtle and devious ways of manifesting itself, and is ugliest of all when it dons religious garb (Luke 18:9–14; 3 John 9). Such pride can eventually have only one outcome: a confrontation with God in which the proud will be finally undone. The expression Isaiah uses for this ultimate confrontation is *that day*, the day of the Lord (11–12).

Many of Isaiah's contemporaries looked forward to the day of the Lord as the time when he would step in and destroy Israel's enemies, just as he had done long ago in the days of Moses and Joshua (Amos 5:18). But Isaiah and the other eighth-century prophets realized that this confident expectation was grounded in arrogance rather than faith, for Israel and Judah had taken on the ways of the surrounding nations and were therefore just as deserving of judgment. In fact, they were more guilty than others because of the greater privileges they had enjoyed (Amos 3:2). This is a most sobering thought, and one that we ourselves would do well to ponder. Interest in the last things – the second coming of Christ and events associated with it – has always been, quite properly, a strong dimension of our evangelical tradition. But our excitement about such things has not always been accompanied by the concern to amend our lives that it should have been. We are in danger of being 'caught napping' because we have sat far too light to the solemn warnings that our Lord has given us (e.g. Matt. 24:42–44; cf. 2 Pet. 3:11–12).

Isaiah warns that the day of the Lord will be a day of terrible judgment for Judah in particular (6–11), but also for the whole world (12–22). Everything in which people have trusted instead of trusting in the living God will be brought down: trees and *mountains*, fortifications, ships and money (12–17). Even religion will prove worthless on that day if it is

---

[10] As we shall see, the theme of intercession returns strongly in chapters 63–64.

man-made (18–20), for man-made religion (represented here by idols) is the supreme expression of human arrogance. It is an attempt to bend God to our will by remaking him in our own image.

The day of the Lord is pictured as a great earthquake, a mighty shaking (19, 21), which leaves nothing standing and sends people running in terror to *caves* and crevices in a vain attempt to save themselves. It is an image that would have been understood only too well by Isaiah's compatriots, because a massive earthquake which had taken place in the days of Uzziah was still within living memory (see Amos 1:1).[11] But any terror they felt then would be as nothing compared to what they would feel when the Lord intervened in judgment. Similar language is used in the book of Revelation to describe that same fearful day (Rev. 6:12–17).

There is also a positive aspect, however, to the day of the Lord. Proud people will be humbled, but the Lord (and he alone) will be exalted (11, 17) and seen in all his *splendour* (21b). There is therefore a sense in which it is right to long for the day of the Lord, because it will mean the final triumph of God and his purposes. What may be apprehended only by faith now – that the Lord is supreme ruler of the world – will then be plain for all to see (cf. Phil. 2:9–11). This, among other things, is what we pray for in the Lord's Prayer when we ask for God's kingdom to come. But if we are so bold as to pray such a prayer, we must make sure that we are prepared for the answer!

The day of the Lord is the ultimate threat, and poses in its most acute form the question of where our ultimate trust is placed. The profound insight of the passage as a whole is that human wickedness in all its rank variety is a manifestation of one basic evil, namely, trust in ourselves rather than trust in God – pride, in other words. The closing appeal, therefore, to *stop trusting in mere humans* (22), is a fitting climax. It is also an appropriate transition to 3:1 – 4:1, where the folly of trusting in human leaders will be explored specifically.[12]

Isaiah is clear that if the people of Judah and Jerusalem place their ultimate trust where the surrounding nations have placed theirs, then they have forsaken the Lord, and will not escape the judgment that will overwhelm the proud everywhere on the day of the Lord. So then, just as in verses 1–5, a vision of the end issues in an urgent call to action in the present. Verse 22 does not deny the truth, taught elsewhere, that human

---

[11] It was still remembered approximately 200 years later (Zech. 14:5).

[12] Oswalt, p. 129.

beings are made in God's image and therefore have a certain dignity. It does assert, however, that as objects of ultimate trust they are of no account at all.

4. Judgment on Judah and Jerusalem (3:1 – 4:1)

Two short judgment oracles dominate this rather long and complex unit. The first (3:13–15) is against the *elders* and other (male) *leaders*; the second (3:16–17) is against the women of Zion, their female counterparts. The first twelve verses of the chapter provide the background to the first oracle, climaxing in the prophet's cry in verse 12, *My people, your guides lead you astray*. The final ten verses (3:18 – 4:1) are an amplification of the second oracle.

a. What is about to happen (3:1–7)

Verse 1 (*The Lord . . . is about to take . . .*) introduces a note of immediacy in contrast to the 'last days' perspective which has been dominant in chapter 2. But the two perspectives should not be too sharply distinguished, because, for Isaiah, every occasion when the Lord intervenes in judgment is a 'day of the Lord' and an anticipation (and therefore a warning) of the final one.

What is anticipated here is famine caused by siege (1), the removal of the community's leaders by death or deportation (2–3), and, as a consequence, a complete breakdown of social order (4–5). It was the Babylonians who would eventually bring this fully to pass more than a hundred years after Isaiah's death, as described with grim matter-of-factness in 2 Kings 25:1–12. But the prophet could already see in his own lifetime the direction in which things were moving (cf. 39:5–7); Babylon would finish what Assyria had begun.

Paradoxically, the final evidence of the collapse of order will be the desperate way the distraught populace will go about trying to re-establish it. The mere possession of a cloak will do as a qualification for leadership if only its owner can be persuaded to take it on. But no-one will be willing (6–7).

The mention of *the diviner*, the *skilled craftsman*[13] and the *clever enchanter* in verses 2–3 anticipates the denunciation of the leaders that will follow (12). But already it is clear that the rot had begun at the top.

---

[13] The NRSV has 'skilful magician'.

b. Why it is going to happen (3:8–12)

With verse 8 we move from description to explanation.[14] The prophet begins with the wickedness of the people in general (8–9), but then traces it back to bad leadership as its root cause (12). Like a skilful camera operator he first pans the turbulent crowd, and then zooms in on those chiefly responsible. The common people are in a sense victims (feel the pathos in the repeated *my people* of verse 12), but they have passed the point where their behaviour can be excused, for they have become openly defiant and quite brazen in their wickedness (8–9).

There is a paradox in verse 12a. The corrupt leaders are tyrants (they *oppress* the people), but the terms in which they are described (*youths, women*) suggest that their bad behaviour sprang from weakness. They copied the ways of the powerful nations they feared and so ended up being exactly like them. The people, in turn, became like their leaders (5).

But the general populace is not uniformly evil, and the Lord's judgment, when it comes, will not be an outburst of unbridled anger. It will be controlled and discriminating, sifting the righteous from the wicked and giving to each what their *deeds* deserve (10–11). The notion of a righteous remnant which will be preserved to form the nucleus of a new Zion is in fact quite fundamental to Isaiah's message, and will appear under a variety of images as the book proceeds.[15]

c. Indictment of the elders and princes (3:13–15)

In the first twelve verses the Lord has been portrayed as a warrior ('the Lord Almighty', 3:1);[16] now he is portrayed as judge (13). A hush descends as the heavenly court comes to order, for the divine judge has taken his place and the judgment foreshadowed in verses 1–12 is now to be put into effect. Isaiah has singled out the leaders as those chiefly responsible (12); now they are to be formally indicted by the Lord himself.

Leaders (14) is literally 'princes', men closely associated with the court and the royal family. The *elders* were a wider group, representing local communities. The charge brought against them both is oppression of *the poor*. They have used their position to exploit the very ones they should

---

14 NIV conceals the presence of the conjunction *ki* ('because') in verse 8. Contrast NRSV: '. . . Judah has fallen, because their speech and their deeds are against the Lord'.

15 The changes have already begun to be rung on the idea, from the few 'survivors' of 1:9, through Zion's 'penitent ones' in 1:27, to *the righteous* here in 3:10. See comments on 1:21–31.

16 This is literally 'Lord of hosts', as in the NRSV, where 'hosts' means 'armies', both heavenly and earthly.

have protected. The language of the indictment is particularly strong (*ruined . . . crushing . . . grinding*), expressing the intensity of the Lord's revulsion at their actions. For the Lord is on the side of the poor, as the parallel between *my people* and *the poor* in verse 15 makes clear.[17] Moreover, if he is presently acting as judge, this does not mean that he has relinquished his power to put his own righteous anger into effect. He is still *the Lord, the* Lord *Almighty* (15b), and there is surely an ominous ring to the reappearance of this expression at the very end of this unit. The divine judge will certainly avenge those who have been so grievously wronged.

It is sobering to reflect that the same high standards of accountability still apply today. Those who lead God's people are answerable, not just to those they lead (1 Tim. 5:19–20), but to the Lord who has entrusted his precious people to them, and it is to him that they will finally give account for how they behave (Matt. 24:45–51; Acts 20:25–28; 2 Tim. 4:1–2; Jas 3:1). We should pray for them daily.

d. The women of Zion (3:16 – 4:1)

This unit has two parts. The first consists of an indictment of the women of Zion (16) followed by an announcement of judgment on them (17). The second (3:18 – 4:1) is an announcement of judgment from beginning to end, but is closely related to the first part. Verses 18–23 of chapter 3 give more detail about the behaviour of Zion's women, and 3:24 – 4:1 more detail about the judgment the Lord will visit upon them. As indicated earlier,[18] it is likely that an original short oracle, delivered as the very words of the Lord (16–17), has been supplemented with an inspired commentary on it (3:18 – 4:1).

The reference to their *men* in verse 25 suggests that these *women of Zion* were married. Their husbands must have been rich to deck them out so extravagantly (18–23), and we need look no further than 'the plunder from the poor' in the previous oracle to guess how such wealth was acquired. The elders and leaders indicted in verses 14–15 were probably the husbands of these very women.[19] The essential sin of the men was oppression; that of the women was ostentatious vanity.[20] But clearly the

---

[17] See comments on 1:10–17.

[18] In the introduction to 3:1 – 4:1 as a whole, p. 32.

[19] At least some of them could be expected to have doubled up as *warriors* (25).

[20] But there are also hints of other things, e.g. loose morals (*flirting*, 16), and dabbling in occult practices (*charms*, 20; cf. 3:2–3).

common factor is ill-gotten wealth. The women have been partners in their husbands' crimes.

The judgment to be visited on them is closely bound up with what will befall their men (25) and their city (26).[21] As a result of the siege and fall of Zion, these women of Zion will suffer disfiguring disease (17a), sexual abuse (17b),[22] captivity (*a rope*, 24) and bereavement (25). In desperation these proud women will finally be reduced to throwing themselves at any surviving male who will have them (4:1).

5. Beyond judgment – glory! (4:2–6)

The expression 'in that day' has run like a refrain through the whole preceding judgment section, from 2:6 to 4:1 (2:11, [12], 17, 20; 3:7, 18). In the foreshortening so typical of prophetic literature, the day of Zion's fall has merged with the great and final 'day of the LORD', of which it is an anticipation.[23] But now here in 4:2 the expression is used climactically as the prophet's attention is fixed again on the very end of history, the goal towards which everything is moving under God. This vision of Zion's glorious future, beyond judgment, is the climax of 2:6 – 4:6, just as the matching vision at the beginning of chapter 2 is the climax of 1:2 – 2:5.

The great, final day of the Lord, then, has a double aspect. It is both terrible (2:6–22) and glorious (4:2–6). But the way the text refers to glory as the climax reminds us that God's ultimate purpose for his people is not destruction but salvation, a truth confirmed by the apostle Paul with resounding clarity in 1 Thessalonians 5:9: 'God has destined us not for wrath but for obtaining salvation through our Lord Jesus Christ' (NRSV). Peter is no less definite: '[We] are being protected by the power of God', he says, 'through faith for a salvation ready to be revealed in the last time' (1 Pet. 1:5, NRSV). That salvation, which will be fully realized when Christ returns to draw history to its triumphant conclusion, is represented here under four images.

a. The Branch of the Lord (4:2a)

In some later Old Testament books 'the Branch of the LORD' or simply 'the Branch' is used as a technical term for the Messiah (Jer. 23:5; 33:15; Zech.

---

21 The women are literally 'daughters of Zion' (16, NRSV). The city has itself been referred to as 'the Daughter Zion' in 1:8.

22 The Hebrew of v. 17b is obscure, but the NRSV is probably correct with 'the LORD will lay bare their secret parts', i.e. subject them to sexual humiliation. Cf. Motyer, p. 63.

23 See comments on 3:1–7.

3:8; 6:12), and the motif of a 'shoot', 'branch' or 'root' springing up (the terminology varies) will later be used in some fairly specific ways within the book of Isaiah itself (e.g. 11:1; 53:2). Here, however, it seems best to take the full-grown plant, in conjunction with what follows, as a general image of the Lord's saving purposes come to fruition and on display for all to see on the last day.

Every gardener knows how a healthy plant in full bloom reflects credit on the one who planted and cultivated it. That is why visitors are discreetly guided towards such prize specimens on their tours of the garden. In a similar way the salvation that the Lord will achieve for his people will reflect great credit on him on that final day. *The Branch of the LORD will be beautiful and glorious.* The next three images reveal just what that salvation will involve.

b. A fruitful land (4:2b)

The fruitful *land* of Canaan had been God's gift to the Israelites in the days of Joshua in fulfilment of the promises made to their ancestors (Deut. 6:10–12; 8:7–10; Josh. 21:43–45). The land therefore had religious significance for them. It was a visible sign or sacrament of the grace that the Lord had shown in choosing them to be his people.

In Isaiah's day that relationship was strained almost to breaking-point, and the land lay desolate and ravaged by Israel's enemies, right up to the gates of Jerusalem itself (1:2, 7–8). But Isaiah was confident that the ancient promises would not fail.[24] God would not utterly destroy the nation; nor would he divorce her permanently from the land. A remnant would survive and enjoy in full measure what had been promised to their ancestors long ago. *The fruit of the land* would be their *pride and glory.* It is an image of abundant provision and deep contentment. Farmers would particularly appreciate this image, as gardeners would the previous one. The third is more attuned to city-dwellers like Isaiah himself.

c. A holy city (4:3–4)

Now the focus narrows from the land to *Zion* or *Jerusalem*, the city which had acquired a special significance for Israel in the time of David. In those days it had been holy in a double sense. It had been holy in that God, the Holy One of Israel, had chosen it as the place where David (his chosen king)

---

[24] According to Gen. 17:7–8, the promises were to have everlasting validity.

and his descendants would rule over his people for ever (2 Sam. 7; Ps. 2:6), and where God's people would assemble to meet with him in his temple (Pss 76:1–2; 87; 122). But it was also holy in the sense that it had exhibited in its corporate life the very character of the one who had chosen it (cf. Lev. 19:2; 22:31–33). It had been 'faithful' and 'full of justice' (1:21).

The Zion of Isaiah's day had become a corrupt, harlot city, but Isaiah never doubted that it was still chosen to play a key role in the Lord's purposes. In these two verses he sees the Zion of the future inhabited by an elect remnant,[25] living in a city which has been purged of its moral corruption by divine judgment.[26] Zion will then once more be holy in both senses: elect and faithful. The holy city represents perfect community.[27]

d. A canopy of glory (4:5–6)

The final image is of journey's end, of the pilgrim people of God at last secure in God's presence for ever. There are many allusions here to the period of the exodus. At that time Israel was protected and guided on its journey through the wilderness by a pillar of cloud by day and a pillar of fire by night, the manifested presence of the Lord (Exod. 13:20–22; 14:19–20). That journey was punctuated by encampments, and at such times, according to the ancient record, the fiery cloud covered the tabernacle like a protective shield (Num. 9:15–18). But the ideal which they hoped for, rest in the land, had never been perfectly achieved, even in the time of David. Now, in Isaiah's time, it seemed further off than ever. So, metaphorically at least, their pilgrimage continued.

Isaiah believed that the final encampment of God's people would be in the new Zion. There, at last, their journey would end. But notice the democratization of the ancient ideal which takes place here. In the final encampment the *glory* of the Lord's presence fills the whole camp, and the protecting *cloud*, like a vast *canopy* or pavilion (cf. Exod. 40:34), covers the entire site and all who are assembled there (5). There will no longer be any need for the tabernacle or temple, for the glory of the Lord will be directly

---

[25] *Recorded among the living* (3) is probably an allusion to Exod. 32:32; cf. Ps. 87:5–6.

[26] RSV correctly renders the tense of the verb 'wash' as future perfect, 'shall have washed away'. *The filth of the women of Zion* (4) is singled out for special mention, perhaps as the most revolting instance of Zion's corruption, but also as a link with the preceding context (3:16–17); those who were a focal point of corruption there are here a focal point of cleansing. *Spirit* (small 's') in verse 4 is probably an instance of the idiomatic use of the word to introduce abstract terms, as in 'spirit of dizziness' (19:14) and 'spirit of justice' (28:6). Oswalt renders the phrase as a whole, 'through a process of burning and judgment', p. 148.

[27] Interestingly, there is no Davidic ruler envisaged here. The messianic strand of Zion theology will be developed later, e.g. 11:1.

accessible to all. And those with whom God is present in this way will be perfectly secure for ever (6). This is no out-of-date dream, but one which Jesus prayed to be realized (John 17:24), and which the apostle John sets before us again at the climax of the Bible as the vision of our own future in God which should still inspire us and draw us on (Rev. 21:22–27). We, too, are pilgrims.

6. A worthless vineyard (5:1–30)

a. The song of the vineyard (5:1–7)

Isaiah lives always with the tension between what will be and what is; between the glorious destiny which beckons Israel and the awful reality of its present condition. It is a tension which ultimately only the Lord can resolve. Here, once again, as in 2:6, we plunge from the heights to the depths as the prophet returns to the thankless task of exposing the sins of his fellows and warning of judgment to come.

But it will not be easy for him to gain a hearing for such an unpleasant message, and so he presents himself as a minstrel and beguiles his unsuspecting audience with a song. It is a striking example of just how creative and skilful the prophets could be in communicating their message (gospel preachers take note!)

The opening words of the song must have puzzled his original hearers as much as they puzzle us. Who is the prophet's 'beloved',[28] and if it is a *song* he sings, why is it about his beloved's *vineyard* instead of about the beloved himself (1)? In fact, the 'love song' turns out to be a parable, and before long the entranced listeners find themselves face to face with its hard-hitting message. The prophet's beloved is the Lord, and Israel (here represented by Judah) is the Lord's vineyard.[29] In spite of all the patient care he has lavished upon it, it has produced only worthless 'wild grapes' (2, NRSV). Would he not be fully justified, then, in removing its protective wall and abandoning it?

The end of the grape harvest, a traditional time for entertainment and festivities, may have provided the setting for the original performance of the song. Its occurrence at this particular point in the book has been anticipated by the use of 'vineyard' as a metaphor for Judah in 3:14. The

---

[28] RSV; *the one I love* (NIV).

[29] See the comment on 'Israel in the book of Isaiah,' above, pp. 22–23.

bad fruit which the vineyard has produced is explained in the six 'woes' which follow it (5:8–25).

The song itself is in four parts. Verses 1–2 are an introduction which catches the attention of the audience and sets the scene; in verses 3–4 the Lord himself speaks and asks the audience for a verdict; in verses 5–6 the Lord, as owner of the vineyard, announces his own decision; and finally, in verse 7, the prophet again speaks in his own voice and makes a specific application to Israel.[30]

Two matters are worthy of particular comment. First, Isaiah's double reference to the Lord as *the one I love* and *my loved one* in verse 1 is bold,[31] but not for that reason insincere or a mere literary conceit. Love for God is an important dimension of Old Testament piety, as both the law of Moses and the Psalms testify (Deut. 6:5; Pss 42:1; 116:1). Isaiah loved the Lord passionately, and it was because of this that he could identify so closely with both the outrage and the grief that the Lord felt at the wilful sinfulness of the nation. (We should note this carefully if our religion has become passionless. Our capacity to share God's anger can be an indicator of how much we really love him.) Finally, verse 7, which concludes the song, gives us further insight into Isaiah's powerful use of language:

> *He looked for justice* [mišpāṭ], *but saw bloodshed* [miśpāḥ];
> *for righteousness* [ṣĕdāqâ], *but heard cries of distress* [ṣĕʿāqâ].[32]

The demand for social justice as a basic covenant obligation could scarcely be more succinctly and forcefully presented.

b. Bad fruit (5:8–25)

The six woes of this passage specify the 'bad fruit' of verses 2 and 4. The list is damning; greedy land-grabbing (8), drunken debauchery (11–12), arrogant defiance of God (18–19), self-justifying sophistry (20), conceit (21) and perversion of justice (22–23). Taken together, these woes probably reflect the conditions that developed in Judah during the reign of Uzziah (= Azariah, 791–740 BC: 2 Kgs 15:1–7; 2 Chr. 26:1–23). As we have already

---

30 Cf. Oswalt, p. 152.

31 Cf. the use of similar language by the lovers in the Song of Songs.

32 '*Justice* is the righting of wrongs, while *bloodshed* is the inflicting of wrongs. *Righteousness* is right living and right relationships while to cry (ṣĕʿāqâ, 'scream') indicates wrong relationships and the anguish of the oppressed' (Motyer, p. 69).

seen,[33] this was in many ways a golden age of impressive achievements, but it also had a darker side. A new, wealthy elite emerged, who grew more and more corrupt and oppressive as they became intoxicated (in more ways than one!) with materialism and the pursuit of pleasure.[34] In the year that Uzziah died, as we see in the next chapter, Isaiah saw the Lord taking his place in the heavenly court to pass judgment on the nation. As well as documenting the charge of the preceding song, then, these woes provide the backdrop to Isaiah's call which follows.

The passage as a whole is structured by the words *Woe* and *Therefore*. *Woe* introduces denunciations of particular sins; *Therefore* introduces the judgments which either have been or will be visited on the offenders. There is a growing intensity as the unit progresses: first one woe (8), then another (11), and then four strung together in quick succession (18, 20, 21, 22). Similarly, there is first a single announcement of judgment introduced by *The Lord Almighty has declared* in verse 9, then a double *Therefore* in verses 13 and 14, and finally another in verses 24 and 25, where the judgment takes on cosmic, world-shattering proportions (especially in 25). This is a passage of powerful denunciation, but also of deep pathos, for the cry of 'Woe' is capable of expressing both, and almost certainly does so here. Isaiah is no self-righteous, detached observer. The final woe he pronounces is on himself (6:5).

Here, then, is a classic passage on the corrupting power of riches (or at least of the desire to acquire them; cf. 1 Tim. 6:9–10). The land-grabbing of verse 8 was contrary to the basic principle of the law of Moses that the Lord owned the land, and that all his 'tenants' were to have a fair share of it (Lev. 25:23–28). The wealth was gained by oppression and could be held on to only by further oppression (23). When confronted with their sin, the offenders either became brazen (18–19) or resorted to specious arguments to justify their actions (20). But nothing could conceal the fact that they had *rejected the law of the Lord Almighty* (24). Pretending to be wise (21), they actually became fools (cf. Rom. 1:22). In their drunken debauchery they could no longer understand God's ways or see what he was doing (12; cf. 1:3).

In contrast to all this stands the God of *justice* and *righteous acts* (16), whose word they have despised. God's holiness consists essentially in his

---

[33] See Introduction, pp. 2–7.

[34] It seems, from the preaching of Amos and Hosea, that similar things happened in the northern kingdom, Israel, during the equally long and prosperous reign of Jeroboam II (793–753). See, e.g., Amos 2:6–7; Hos. 4:1–3.

moral character, and this means that he cannot be indifferent to evil. But the judgments foreshadowed here – desolation of *houses* and land (9–10), *exile*, famine and death (13–14) – will affect rich and poor, noble and commoner alike (13b, 14b). By their actions the ruling elite have brought about the ruin of the nation. How this will happen is explained in verses 26–30, which follow.

c. The vineyard ravaged (5:26–30)

The destroyer of the Lord's vineyard is to be a foreign invader, and he is to come at the Lord's express command (26). The phrase *lifts up a banner* is unexceptional in this military context, but the word *whistles* is more telling (cf. 7:18). It expresses the Lord's contempt for the arrogant pretensions of the great military powers who were struggling for control of Palestine. Their armies on the move, swift, disciplined, equipped and ruthless, inspired terror (27–30). But it was the message of Isaiah and the other eighth-century prophets that it was the Lord, not these nations, who called the tune. Nor is this a quaint view of history which can or should be relegated to a museum of intellectual antiquities. It is a biblical revelation about how history has always worked and still does today. The first Christians, in their time of testing, cried out to God in full confidence that the worldly powers ranged against them, both Jewish and Gentile, could do nothing but what God, by his power and will, 'had decided beforehand should happen' (Acts 4:28). Even Herod and Pontius Pilate, in conspiring to bring about the death of Jesus, had merely played roles that God had scripted for them (Acts 4:27–28). 'The authorities that exist', Paul tells us, 'have been established by God' (Rom. 13:1), and the closing book of the New Testament points us with complete confidence to the day when God's lordship over the nations will be manifested in final judgment (Rev. 11:15).

Isaiah was absolutely certain of the Lord's sovereignty over history; he was using the nations to accomplish his purposes and would continue to do so. It is a theme that will be developed more fully as the book proceeds.

The invader is not named here, but is almost certainly Assyria. The last two lines of verse 25 will be heard again and again in chapters 9 and 10 (9:12, 17, 21; 10:4), where Assyria is explicitly in view. Judah had already begun to experience the Lord's hand *upraised* in judgment when the song of the vineyard was sung,[35] but worse was to come.

---

[35] The date is uncertain.

7. 'I saw the Lord' (6:1–13)

Chapter 6 towers like a majestic peak over the surrounding terrain and is clearly of central importance for the message of the book. It was in this encounter with the Lord that Isaiah's understanding of both God and his own mission was crystalized. It stands centrally within chapters 1–12 and is intimately related to both what precedes and what follows.

We have already noted how the woes of chapter 5 prepare the way for Isaiah's call in the year of Uzziah's death.[36] But chapters 1–5 as a whole have posed a bigger problem than the corruption that affluence bred and the judgment that this must entail. It is the question of how spiritual renewal can take place so that Israel may become the centre of world blessing that it is destined to be (2:1–5). Judgment may purge away the dross, but how can inner transformation be brought about?

The present chapter moves from a vision of God (1–4), to confession of sin (5), to cleansing (6–7) and finally to commissioning (8–13). That is the path by which Isaiah enters into his servanthood, and it is the path Israel must take also. The prophet's experience in this chapter shows them the way. His identification with the sinful nation is made explicit by his confession in verse 5.

The connections with what follows are more obvious. Chapters 1–5 were very general in character, laying out the broad themes of judgment and salvation without relating them to specific historical events. But chapters 7–12 show how the judgment passed on Israel by the Lord in chapter 6 began to be worked out in the specifics of the historical circumstances of Judah and Jerusalem. In particular the hardening foreshadowed in 6:10 is at once reflected in Ahaz's response to Isaiah in chapter 7. In chapters 7–11 the faithless nation is cut down, but a stump remains (11:1), and from that stump life springs anew, as anticipated somewhat enigmatically in 6:13.

a. Vision of God (6:1–4)

In the implied contrast between *King Uzziah* (1) and '*the* King, the Lord Almighty' (5),[37] we are taken at once to the central theme of the chapter

---

[36] See on 5:8–25.

[37] Kidner (p. 595) comments that 'Uzziah died after, not before, Isaiah's call, as 1:1 makes clear. If his death has significance apart from its date, it is that he died a leper, for flouting God's holiness . . . (2 Chr. 26:16).'

(divine kingship) and the root problem underlying Israel's failure (trust in mere humans rather than trust in the Lord; cf. 2:22). As is so often the case, increased wealth had brought a diminished view of God, so that people felt secure in their sins as long as they performed the appropriate rituals (1:12–17). But here Isaiah sees the Lord as he is, *high and exalted*, beyond manipulation, *seated* on his judgment *throne* (cf. 1 Kgs 22:19–23). The time of reckoning has come.

Heaven and earth merge[38] in this blinding vision of the one who is above all *holy* (3), a term which, in view of 5:16, includes both transcendence and righteousness.[39] The accent here is on transcendence (he is *exalted* and his rule is universal); in the latter part of the chapter it will shift to his righteousness. The *seraphim*,[40] by their words and actions, show that the appropriate response is reverence, service and praise.

b. Confession (6:5)

The vision of God produces not rapture but sheer terror in the prophet. He knows himself to be utterly *ruined*,[41] for two reasons: he is unclean, and he has seen God.

The belief that no-one could see God and live appears to have had its roots in the encounter with God at Sinai, when he hid himself in a thick cloud and the people were warned to keep away on pain of death (Exod. 19:21; cf. Exod. 33:20). A privileged few, both then and at other times, had been permitted to see him, though how clearly and in what form is uncertain (Exod. 24:11; Gen. 28:12–13; Judg. 6:22; 13:22–23). Moses was regarded as uniquely privileged in being permitted to 'know' the Lord face to face (Deut. 34:10).

Isaiah is not proud at being admitted to the inner circle. He is aware only of being *unclean*, like his fellows. 'Unclean' is a general term in the Old Testament for all that is, for whatever reason, unfit to be in God's presence. Here the uncleanness is clearly moral, for it is associated with the *lips* and therefore, by implication, with the heart (cf. Mark 7:20–23). Isaiah

---

[38] The Jerusalem temple expands into its heavenly counterpart (cf. 1 Kgs 8:27; Isa. 66:1).

[39] 'God's holiness' is best summarized, in Old Testament terms, as his distinctiveness, his 'complete moral majesty . . . Holiness is God's hidden glory; glory is God's all-present holiness' (Motyer, p. 77).

[40] The Hebrew term is *śĕrāpîm* from *śārap*, 'to burn' (BDB, pp. 976–977). In Num. 21:6 it is used with reference to the 'fiery serpents' (RSV; 'venomous snakes', NIV) sent to punish Israel in the wilderness. Here the seraphim are clearly heavenly beings, with the accent more on their 'fiery' appearance (4) than their 'serpent' quality.

[41] 'Lost' (NRSV) is too weak to capture the force of the verb. Cf. Oswalt, p. 171.

cannot praise and serve God as the seraphim do because, in the depths of his being, he is unclean, just as his compatriots are. It is remarkable to see the prophet identify himself so completely with those whose sins he has been denouncing in the previous chapters. But in the presence of God degrees of sin become irrelevant. It is the holiness of God which reveals to us our true condition, not comparison with others.

c. Cleansing (6:6–7)

Paradoxically, Isaiah's confession of being unclean like his fellows has set him apart from them, for he, unlike them, has been willing to acknowledge his condition.

The *altar* from which the burning *coal* is taken by the seraph is not named. It may have been the incense altar before the veil (Exod. 30:1–6) or the bronze altar which stood in the inner court (Exod. 27:1–8). But it matters not. The altar, whatever its identity, symbolizes the entire provision which God had made in the temple and its services for the sins of his people.[42] Isaiah is cleansed, not by his own efforts, but purely by the grace of God. The same grace was available to Israel as a whole (1:18), but by their arrogance they had cut themselves off from it.

d. Commissioning (6:8–13)

It now becomes apparent why the 'lips' and 'mouth' have been so prominent in verses 5–7. The Lord seeks a messenger, and Isaiah, now cleansed, is ready and willing to be his mouthpiece.[43]

Verses 9–13 reveal that his message is to be essentially one of judgment, but it is described more in terms of its effects than its content: it will harden hearts (9–10) and lead to devastation of both land and people (11–12). Sentence has been passed on the nation in heaven; Isaiah's preaching will put it into effect on earth. Verses 9–10 indicate that the very unresponsiveness of the people will be an aspect of God's judgment on

---

[42] It is probably impossible to pinpoint where Isaiah finds himself standing within the temple of his vision. Is he in the inner court near the bronze altar, in the Holy Place before the incense altar and the veil, or within the Holy of Holies itself? The fact that he sees the Lord enthroned suggests he has been transported into the inmost sanctuary. Cf. Ps. 80:1, where the Lord is thought of as 'enthroned between the cherubim' above the ark of the covenant. There is little point, therefore, in trying to identify the *altar* of verse 6 by speculating about which altar may have been visible to him or which of the two symbolizes God's provision for sin. While the bronze altar with its bloody sacrifices may represent this provision more obviously, according to Hebrews 9 the entire temple complex, including 'the golden altar of incense' (verse 4), represents Christ's priestly work of sacrifice and intercession for us.

[43] There may be a secondary allusion, in the 'unclean lips' of verse 5, to Uzziah who, as a leper, would have had to cover his lips and cry, 'Unclean!' (2 Chr. 26:21; Lev. 13:45).

them. They have chosen arrogance and indifference; they shall have them in full measure and experience their bitter fruits: devastation and exile (12). Judgment is now inevitable.

There is a slender thread of hope, however. Verse 13 likens the land and its people to a tree whose *stump* remains in the earth after it is felled, and speaks of a righteous remnant (*holy seed*) within the nation. In the final line the *holy seed* and the *stump* are equated. The verse as a whole is ambiguous, but the term 'seed' suggests regrowth, and (especially in view of what follows in chapters 7–12) it is better to take these closing words of the chapter as a promise (NIV) rather than a threat (NRSV). The righteous remnant will not be destroyed, but survive and grow into a new people of God. As we shall see in chapters 7 and 8, Isaiah himself is the nucleus around which this righteous remnant begins to gather.

As well as giving us an awesome view of God, this chapter provides us with a succinct portrait of his servant Isaiah. He was a man with a big vision of God (1), a deep awareness of his own sinfulness (5), a profound experience of the grace of God (7), and a willingness to spend and be spent in his service, whatever the cost (8). May God help us to be more like him.

8. Ahaz at the crossroads (7:1–25)

a. The threat of invasion (7:1–12)

The setting for this encounter between Isaiah and Ahaz is briefly sketched in verses 1–2. A resurgent Assyria under Tiglath-Pileser III has begun to push west and south into Palestine. The kings of Israel[44] and Aram have formed an anti-Assyrian pact and are determined to force Judah to join them by deposing Ahaz and installing a puppet king in his place (6). It is the year 734 BC.

Ahaz is torn between two fears. He is panic-stricken in the face of the invasion by Aram and Israel (2), but he is even more fearful of joining them against Assyria. When Isaiah confronts him he appears to have already decided to try to hold out[45] in the hope of finding security through

---

[44] Israel, the northern kingdom, is called *Ephraim* in verses 2, 5 and 9, probably because Jeroboam I, its first king, was an Ephraimite (1 Kgs 11:26) and Ephraim continued to be one of its leading tribes. See the comment on 'Israel in the book of Isaiah' above, pp. 22–23.

[45] He is inspecting Jerusalem's water supply in preparation for a siege (3).

submission to Assyria (see 2 Kgs 16:7–9). Isaiah offers him a radical alternative: forswear all alliances and trust wholly in the Lord (7–9). In view of Ahaz's refusal to do this (10–11), Isaiah announces that Judah will soon be overrun and devastated by that very Assyria that Ahaz has foolishly decided to turn to for help (17–20).

b. The Immanuel sign (7:13–25)

Verses 13–16 are clearly the theological key to the chapter. The encounter with Ahaz in verses 1–12 leads up to them, and verses 17–25 which follow are an extended commentary on them. It is certain that verse 14 finds its ultimate fulfilment in Christ (Matt. 1:23), but what of its meaning here in its immediate context?

In verses 9–10 of chapter 6 Isaiah was told to make the ears of the rebellious people dull and close their eyes,

> lest they see with their eyes,[46]
>> hear with their ears,
>> understand with their hearts,
> and turn and be healed.

In chapter 7 we see him doing this to Ahaz. Ahaz has rejected the clear word of the prophet (7–9) and the offer of a clear sign to confirm it (10–12). Therefore he is given a sign which is veiled and enigmatic, a sign which he cannot understand (13–16).

But the sign is not meaningless. It *can* be understood, but only from the perspective of faith, and again chapter 6 provides the key. The final verse of that chapter spoke of a righteous remnant, a 'holy seed', that would survive the coming judgment. At the beginning of chapter 7 Isaiah is pointedly told to take his son Shear-Jashub with him as he goes to meet Ahaz (3). 'Shear-Jashub' means 'a remnant shall return' or 'a remnant shall repent'. Both are possible,[47] but since the immediate context here is one of faith versus unbelief rather than exile and return, the latter meaning is almost certainly the primary one.[48] Isaiah comes to challenge Ahaz to repent and join the remnant who believe, but he refuses. The

---

[46] RSV.

[47] The word used is *šûb*, commonly used in both senses in the Old Testament.

[48] Exile is implied later in the chapter (20–22), but no return is envisaged.

Immanuel saying of verse 14 is therefore given to Ahaz as a veiled message of judgment.

Zion has already been pictured as a woman (literally, 'daughter Zion') in 1:8. Now, in the crisis of invasion and imminent siege, she is depicted as a sexually mature woman (literally, 'young woman', ʿalmâ) who has already conceived and is even now in the pains of childbirth. The central statement of verse 14 is literally: 'The young woman has conceived and is giving birth to a son . . .' If the 'young woman' is Zion, then her *son* is the faithful remnant who will emerge from her sufferings.[49] That is why he is given the name *Immanuel*, 'God with *us*'. God will be with the faithful remnant who gather round Isaiah (cf. 8:16), not with the unbelieving Ahaz and the rebellious nation as a whole. This is the implication of the ominous shift from 'your God' in verse 11 to *my God* in verse 13.

The rest of the chapter unfolds in explicit terms the threat implied in the Immanuel saying. The image of the *son* or 'child', however, continues only to the end of verse 16.[50] By the time this child has reached an age of accountability (within a few years at the most), the land will have been so devastated and depopulated by Assyria that cultivation will be impossible; the survivors will have to exist on the products of the few animals they have and any wild food they can gather (15a, 17–25). But even *before* this (16a), the land of the two kings presently invading Judah will be deserted. In fact, Aram fell to the Assyrians in 732 BC (2 Kgs 15:29), followed by Israel in 722 BC.[51] Finally, Judah herself was all but devastated in 701 BC (2 Kgs 18:13 – 19:31; Isa. 36 – 37).[52]

But the Immanuel sign contained a promise as well as a threat. For Isaiah and his followers it meant the promise of God's protecting presence and the eventual fulfilment of God's good purposes for his people. The preservation of the remnant in Isaiah's day was part of a process which led finally to the coming of Jesus, the perfectly faithful and righteous one (Luke 1:35), in whom all God's promises come to fulfilment (2 Cor. 1:20; Gal. 3:16). So Matthew was right to see the ultimate fulfilment of the

---

[49] Cf. 66:7–8, where the same imagery recurs in a much less ambiguous fashion.

[50] So the survivors left in the land in verse 22 are not necessarily identical with the righteous remnant of verse 15, although the occurrence of *curds and honey* in both places suggests that Isaiah expected the faithful to be among the survivors.

[51] 2 Kgs 17:1–6. Esarhaddon and Ashurbanipal subsequently made final deportations of Israelites in 670/669 BC, approximately sixty-five years after the crisis of the present chapter (see Isa. 7:8b).

[52] See Introduction, pp. 2–7.

Immanuel saying in Jesus Christ.[53] What was death to Ahaz is life to us who believe.

Two important themes from previous chapters are strongly developed here in chapter 7. The first is the Lord's supreme, universal sovereignty, which was so forcibly set before us in 6:1–13. There he sat upon 'a throne', 'high and exalted' (1), and his glory filled the entire earth (3). He was *the* King (5), before whom all others paled into insignificance. Here in chapter 7 we see him exercising that sovereignty as he summons the nations to do his bidding. To him Egypt and Assyria, the two superpowers of the day, are but insects which swarm at his *whistle* (18–19; cf. 5:26). Assyria in particular is but a *razor* which he takes up temporarily (*hired*) to clear Palestine of its inhabitants, as a man shaves unwanted hair from his body (20).

The second theme is closely related to the first, namely, the absolute necessity of wholehearted reliance upon the Lord. In chapter 2 the alternative to such trust was reliance upon 'mere humans' (22); here that general notion is developed in terms of trusting in the nations (especially Assyria) for protection instead of the Lord. The choice is put squarely to Ahaz in verse 9b: 'If you do not stand firm in your faith, you will not stand at all.' Whatever we rely on instead of trusting in God will eventually turn and devour us.[54]

9. From darkness to light (8:1 – 9:7)

This unit deals with the same events as chapter 7, and the fact that the name *Immanuel* occurs in 8:8 and is alluded to again in 8:10 suggests that, in general, what we have here is the further outworking of the word spoken to Ahaz in 7:14. That word was doubled-edged, involving both judgment and salvation. Its outworking is now depicted in terms of darkness and light. In the short term it means gathering darkness (judgment), but in the long term brilliant light (the coming of the Messiah and the dawning of a new age).

The passage as a whole consists of four oracles, in which Isaiah delivers messages given to him directly by the Lord, and two brief reflections on

---

[53] In applying this verse to Christ, Matthew quotes from the LXX, which uses the more specific term *parthenos*, 'virgin' (Matt. 1:23).

[54] Cf. Oswalt, p. 214.

their significance by the prophet himself. Its structure is as shown in the table below.

Darkness	1st oracle: a name and its meaning	8:1–4	Judgment
	2nd oracle: the rising river	8:5–10	
	3rd oracle: the stumbling stone	8:11–15	
	1st reflection: the gathering darkness	8:16–22	
Light	2nd reflection: the coming of the dawn	9:1	Salvation
	4th oracle (climax): a great light shines	9:2–7	

a. A name and its meaning (8:1–4)

These verses are strikingly reminiscent of 7:14–17, but the birth and naming of Maher-Shalal-Hash-Baz ('quick to the plunder, swift to the spoil')[55] is clearly different in character from the Immanuel sign given to Ahaz. That was cryptic, given to Ahaz alone; this is a much clearer sign, written in common characters and openly placarded so that all the people can read it (1). The summoning of leading men as *witnesses* (2) strongly suggests that both the name and its meaning (given to Isaiah in verse 4) were openly published from the start, so that there could be no doubt when it was fulfilled that this was an authentic word from the Lord. The people are to be left in no doubt that the Lord is in control of the events unfolding to the north, and that Isaiah is his true spokesman.

Like Ahaz in chapter 7, the people as a whole are being given a last chance to abandon their faithless scheming (see verse 12) and rely entirely on the Lord as their deliverer, for the sign does not speak of judgment on Judah, but rather of the destruction of her two northern enemies (4). It does have a cryptic element, however. It certainly invites faith, but does not compel it. To those determined to be faithless it could be taken as confirmation of Ahaz's wisdom in seeking help from Assyria, signifying nothing more than the destruction of Judah's enemies (4). The people, like Ahaz, were at the crossroads. They had to choose whether to respond in faith or in unbelief. As the next unit shows, they made the same disastrous response as their king.

---

[55] See NIV footnote. The *prophetess* (3) is presumably Isaiah's wife.

b. The rising river (8:5–10)

King and people alike have rejected the Lord's help (compared to *the gently flowing waters of* the *Shiloah* spring in Jerusalem) and preferred the help of Assyria (likened to the water of the mighty Euphrates).[56] But if they thought that the river, once in flood, would stop at their own borders,[57] they were mistaken. It will sweep on into Judah, all but engulfing it (*reaching up to the neck*, 8). For all that, however, the clever schemes of the nations (whether they be Israel, Aram or Assyria) are, in the final analysis, of no consequence. It is what the Lord has purposed, not what they have planned, that will ultimately be achieved (9–10).

Two sub-units are clearly recognizable. The first (5–8) ends with the name *Immanuel*; the second (9–10) with the matching statement *God is with us*.[58] This provides an important link between chapter 7 and 8:1 – 9:7, as we have already noted. But the name Immanuel here points forwards as well as back. It reminds us that in the midst of this land and people which are now descending into darkness, there is emerging a community of faithful believers. The land is their inheritance (8) and God is with them (10). So despite the worsening situation, there is hope.

c. The stumbling stone (8:11–15)

Unlike the previous two oracles, this one is not for the nation as a whole. But neither is it for Isaiah alone. The verbs are plural, indicating that the *you* in view are the prophet and his disciples (16), the inner circle of believers.

It does, however, have a logical connection with what has gone before. The schemes of the nations will come to nothing (10), because they stem from the *fear* of mere humans (12). Isaiah and his followers are to have nothing to do with such schemes. Instead, they are to fear the Lord alone (13). To those who do this the Lord *will be a holy place* (or 'sanctuary'; he will protect them),[59] but to those who do not he will be like a great *stone*

---

[56] Cf. Fleming, p. 24.

[57] NRSV's 'melt in fear before' in verse 6 is conjectural. NIV's *rejoices over* is more faithful to the Hebrew. The people had rejoiced over Assyria's victories in the north, seeing only the immediate benefit to themselves.

[58] In the NRSV the first is in prose and the second in verse.

[59] *Miqdāš*, 'sanctuary' or 'holy place', is applied elsewhere to the tabernacle (Exod. 25:8) and the temple (1 Chr. 22:19). It was supremely the place where God, the Holy One, dwelt among his people. But it was also a place where those in danger of their lives, for whatever reason, could come to seek divine protection (Exod. 21:12–14; Ps. 27:5). For a striking example, see 1 Kgs 1:49–53. Here, Isaiah applies the term directly to the Lord, and the context suggests that protection is the primary idea. The Lord himself is the true place of refuge for the faithful (cf. Ezek. 11:16).

in their path, over which they will *stumble* and *fall* (14–15). The bottom line is that the Lord cannot be ignored. Whether he is experienced as saviour or as judge depends on how we respond to him.

The reference to the *strong hand* of the Lord resting on Isaiah in verse 11 suggests the great importance of this oracle for the believing remnant. They have chosen rightly, but they must never cease to be vigilant. The alternative will always be there as a temptation.

d. The gathering darkness (8:16–22)

As an actor sometimes deliberates with him- or herself out loud so that the audience can share his or her thoughts, so Isaiah does here (17). At times he appears to be addressing an unspecified individual (16) or his disciples collectively (19),[60] but the mixed speech forms are in reality an indication of his inner turmoil as he reflects on the preceding oracles and their implications.

Those who have rejected the clear message he has brought from God will turn in their lostness to the occult, and in so doing plunge themselves into ever deeper *darkness* and ruin (19, 21–22). Isaiah therefore sees the urgency of committing his teaching to his disciples. They will need it to turn to as the darkness closes about them (20), and they will preserve it for a future generation who may be more willing to hear (16). But if Isaiah has hope in this dark moment (and he does), it is not grounded finally in the disciples but in the Lord (17). Even the disciples may fail to live up to the expectations Isaiah has of them, but the Lord himself will never let him down.

Before passing on, we must pause and reflect here, because something profoundly important has been happening in the second half of this chapter. There has been a marked sharpening of the demarcation between the faithful and unfaithful within the visible community of God's people, between those who respond to the word of God with obedient faith and those who do not, between the true and the false. This will happen more and more as the book runs its course until it becomes a major strand of its message in the final two sections (51:12 – 55:13 and chapters 56–66).[61] This should not surprise us, for the Bible never confuses formality with

---

[60] Because of the context, it is tempting to take the *children* of verse 18 as also referring to the disciples, but the expression *signs and symbols* suggests that it is the literal children of 7:3 and 8:3 who are in view here.

[61] See my treatment of the remnant theme in the book of Isaiah in my essay 'Zion in Transformation', in D. Clines et al. (eds.), *The Bible in Three Dimensions* (Sheffield: JSOT Press, 1990).

actuality, mere participation in the externals with the heart response which alone can make those externals meaningful. Even the original company that came out of Egypt with Moses included a 'mixed multitude' (Exod. 12:38, AV) whose true heart condition was soon exposed by the rigours of the wilderness (Num. 11:4). Jesus, too, warned us about those who 'have no root' and 'last only a short time' (Mark 4:17). Often the difference between the true and the false is very hard to discern; wheat and tares, sheep and goats, can look very much alike to the untrained eye. But the divine judge sees the difference clearly, and the testings of life increasingly distinguish them from one another. On the last day, of course, the separation will be absolute and permanent (Matt. 13:24–30; 25:31–46). We can ill afford to take such truth lightly. The line that was being drawn in Isaiah's day is still being drawn today, with the same ultimate issues at stake. Scripture urges us to examine ourselves to see whether we are in the faith (2 Cor. 13:5). We cannot afford not to do so.

e. The coming of the dawn (9:1)

This brief unit introduces a sharp contrast (*Nevertheless . . .*) which prepares the way for what follows in verses 2–7. The change of mood from 'fearful gloom' (8:22) to *no more gloom* (9:1) is possible only because of Isaiah's confidence in the Lord (8:17).

With his gaze once more fixed on *the future*, the time of fulfilment (cf. 2:2; 4:2), the imminent devastation of the northern kingdom by Assyria (cf. 8:1–4)[62] is relegated to *the past*. By faith he sees a glorious reversal that will one day be effected by God's grace. Devastation will give way to glory. The dawn will break in the very region that was the first to experience God's judgment. No wonder Matthew draws our attention to the fact that it was in these northern parts, with their mixed population, that Jesus first proclaimed the gospel (Matt. 4:12–17).

f. A great light shines (9:2–7)

This oracle of salvation is clearly the climax of the whole movement from *darkness* to *light* in 8:1 – 9:7. At the same time it represents the final reversal of the situation in chapter 7 where the Davidic house, represented by Ahaz, was rejected.

---

[62] The geographical terms *land of Zebulon* etc. refer to the northern and eastern parts of the northern kingdom, which were the first to be overrun.

The logical structure is signalled by the threefold 'for' of verses 4, 5 and 6 (NRSV). The rejoicing of verse 3 is occasioned by release from oppression (4), cessation of war (5) and the birth of an ideal ruler (6). The alternation of past and future tenses expresses the bold confidence with which the oracle is delivered. That which is plainly future is spoken of as already accomplished, for *the zeal of the LORD Almighty will accomplish this* (7c).

In retrospect, *the people walking in darkness* (2a) must include both northerners and southerners (9:1; 8:19–21), but in verse 3 they are simply *the nation*. Thus the oracle subtly anticipates the reunification of Israel and Judah under a single, ideal, Davidic ruler of the future (7).

But who is he? Some have suggested that it is the crown prince, Hezekiah, who is in view, and that the titles of verse 6b are simply grandiose throne-names expressing the high expectations that people like Isaiah had of him. But this can hardly be so. At the very most, Davidic kings were regarded as the adopted 'sons' of God (2 Sam. 7:14; Ps. 2:7). Furthermore, Hezekiah was born in 737 BC, three years before the events of chapter 7 (see 2 Kgs 18:1–2),[63] whereas the birth of the ideal ruler in this chapter is regarded as a future event. In fact, the anticipation of a time when there will be 'no more gloom' (1) strongly suggests that this announcement of salvation refers to the same future situation as the visions of 2:2–4 and 4:2–6. In the final analysis the language of verse 6 can apply only to one who is God incarnate.[64] There can be little doubt, then, that this oracle points directly to the coming of the Messiah, the great Son of David and the true light (Luke 1:32–33; John 1:9).

Finally, it is fascinating to reflect on the fact that the outworking of God's purposes in history through the whole of chapters 7–9 is associated (either figuratively or literally) with the birth of children (7:3; 7:14–15; 8:1–4; 9:6). Truly his strength is made perfect in weakness!

10. 'His anger is not turned away' (9:8 – 10:4)

We are at another of those points in the book where the focus returns suddenly to present realities (cf. 2:6; 5:1), in this case the sad condition of the northern kingdom and its imminent demise. We are also at the

---

[63] He came to the throne in 716 BC.

[64] And hence 'God with us' acquires a whole new dimension of meaning.

beginning of another movement which will climax in the appearance of an ideal ruler (11:1–9).

In both form and content these verses have a lot in common with 5:8–25. The refrain which divides the present passage into four strophes (9:8–12, 13–17, 18–21 and 10:1–4) was first met at the very end of the previous one (5:25c), and the *Woe* which introduces the final strophe here (10:1) recalls the catalogue of woes there (5:8, 11, 18, 20–22). Moreover, the evils denounced in the two passages are essentially the same: arrogance, bad leadership, civil strife and oppression.[65] But while the first passage dealt with Judah and Jerusalem, this one deals with Israel (*Ephraim*) and *Samaria* (9:9).

It is remarkable to see a southerner like Isaiah so even-handed in his assessment of the two kingdoms. But he understands that 'Israel' in a theological sense is one people ruled by the Lord,[66] so what happens in the north is just as significant for him as what happens in the south. But there is probably another reason for his attention to the northern kingdom here. Its demise took place almost 140 years before that of the south. But Judah was already infected with the same evils. Isaiah elaborates on the sign of Maher-Shalal-Hash-Baz as it applied to Israel and Samaria (8:3–4) because its fulfilment would serve as a timely warning to the equally corrupt Judah and Jerusalem.

Four matters call for particular comment. First, a progression is discernible in the passage as a whole from moral decay (9:9, 17) through social disintegration (9:20 – 10:2) to national collapse (10:3–4). There is also a progression from harassment by neighbouring states (9:12) to outright conquest by Assyria (10:3–4).[67]

Second, the tenses of the verbs throughout the four strophes are mixed, but we are probably not intended to distinguish between events which happened before, during or after the time at which the words were spoken. The strophes are tightly bound together by a single refrain, and so it is best to take the opening couplet (9:8) as setting the time reference for the whole:

> *The Lord has sent* [past] *a message against Jacob;*
> *it will fall* [future] *on Israel.*

---

[65] Drunkenness does not feature here as it does in chapter 5.

[66] See on 9:2–3, and also the comment on 'Israel in the book of Isaiah', above, pp. 22–23.

[67] The foe *from afar* (10:3) is subsequently named in 10:5.

The descriptions of the nation and its fate are spoken in the interval between the issuing of the decree in heaven and its implementation on earth.

Third, the power and effectiveness of the Lord's word are of course ideas which are of fundamental importance for all the Old Testament prophets. But they are of particular significance for Isaiah, as we shall see later (see especially 40:8; 55:10–11). It is noteworthy therefore that the opening two lines of this present passage, cited above, already give striking expression to this concept. Here the *message* (literally, 'word') which the Lord[68] *has sent* almost seems to have a life of its own; *it will fall on Israel* with devastating results. Any notion of magic is excluded, however, by two considerations. In the first place, Isaiah resolutely opposed superstition and magic in all its forms (see 8:19; 47:12), and in the second, the verb 'sent' here is the same as that used for the commissioning of Isaiah himself in 6:8. The 'word' is powerful and effective precisely because it is the Lord's word; it is no more independent of him than the messenger who is commissioned to bear it. Moreover, the book of Jonah provides a memorable example of the Lord's continuing sovereignty over his word.[69] He who sends it can also recall it (Jon. 3:1–5, 10), but there is no suggestion that he will do so in the present case. The words *will fall* point to the suddenness with which the Lord will put into effect what he has said he will do.

Finally, the refrain of 9:12, 17, 21 and 10:4 not only links the four strophes together, but points forward[70] to the further outworking of the Lord's righteous judgment, in this case against Assyria.

11. The Lord's anger redirected (10:5–34)

In one sense the unity of this passage is very clear; it deals from beginning to end with the future downfall of Assyria. Its message also is clear: neither fear nor rely on Assyria; she is merely a tool in the Lord's hand and her time, too, will come. Its structural unity is less obvious, but emerges readily enough on closer examination. The main sections are arranged as follows:

---

[68] Here referred to as *the Lord* ('*adōnāy*), as in 6:1.

[69] Cf. Oswalt, p. 252 (citing the German commentator H. Wildberger).

[70] As it does also in 5:25.

A. (5–19) Proud, 'invincible' Assyria will be judged.

    B. (20–27) Don't rely on Assyria. Identify with the remnant who rely on the Lord.

A'. (28–34) Proud, 'invincible' Assyria will be judged.

Each of the three parts has two subsections: A (5–11, 12–19), B (20–23, 24–27) and A' (28–32, 33–34). The unit as a whole is connected to the previous one by the link word 'anger' in verses 4 and 5.

a. Assyria (10:5–19)

Verse 12 stands out because of its central position (at the junction of 5–11 and 12–19) and because it alone in verses 5–19 is in prose. It is in fact a thematic statement which sums up the whole of 5–19. It alerts us to the fact that, while the northern kingdom has not been lost to view entirely (10–11), the focus has shifted back to the south, and to Jerusalem/Zion in particular. This progression is exactly the same as we observed in 8:1–8, and reflects what actually happened. The Assyrian 'flood' which overwhelmed the north eventually swept on into Judah as well. It was at Jerusalem that the Lord *finished all his work*[71] of judging the two kingdoms.

Nor should it surprise us that the Lord should then, as verse 12 also tells us, redirect his anger towards arrogant Assyria. For chapter 2 has already put on record God's abhorrence of arrogance and his intention to judge it, not only among his own people (6–11) but also in the world at large (12–22). Of course the judgment on Assyria here, like that on Israel and Judah, is envisaged as taking place within history rather than on the final day, but it is nevertheless entirely in keeping with the character of God as revealed in the earlier chapters.

What *is* surprising is that the Lord should have chosen to use such a proud, pagan nation at all, especially against his own people.[72] But two things are strongly affirmed. First, the Lord did in fact do so (5–6), and second, this did not absolve Assyria of moral accountability (7–11, 15). It is not that Assyria resisted her calling (she was not even aware of it), but that she sinned in the manner in which she fulfilled it (arrogantly, 15). The

---

[71] This must be taken as referring to the Assyrian crisis. The Babylonian crisis is not yet in view.

[72] His similar choice of Cyrus, this time as deliverer, will later cause consternation among the exiles in Babylon (44:24 – 55:6).

twin truths of divine sovereignty and human responsibility are held together in a fine tension here, as they are in Scripture as a whole (see especially Acts 2:23).

b. The remnant (10:20–27)

This is the central pivot on which verses 5–34 as a whole turn. The units which precede and follow predict Assyria's demise; this central unit draws out the implications of this for Isaiah's contemporaries. The link word, in verse 20, is *remnant*. When Assyria is at last reduced to a remnant (19), the remnant of Israel will no longer lean on her, but will lean upon the Lord (20). If this first paragraph (20–23) is simply a prediction of what will happen, it is followed in verses 24–27 by an exhortation about how to act now in the light of it: *My people . . . do not be afraid of the Assyrians* (24).

The focus moved back to Jerusalem/Zion in verse 12, as we saw, and it remains there in this central pivot. *Israel* in verse 20 is not the northern kingdom, but the whole twelve tribes, as the repetition of the name *Jacob* (the common ancestor) in verses 20 and 21 confirms. And verses 22b and 23 reaffirm the Lord's intention fully to execute his threatened judgments. *The whole land*,[73] both north and south, will be devastated, and only then will Assyria herself be dealt with (25–27).

The target group is in fact quite specifically the people of Jerusalem (24), and the issue before them is exactly the one which was put to their representative, Ahaz, in chapter 7. Will they act out of fear or out of faith? Will they look to Assyria to save them or return to a wholehearted reliance on the Lord (20–21)? Verses 24–27 assure them that if they do so *return* (21) they need have no fear of the Assyrians. The Lord will deliver them as he rescued their ancestors from the Egyptians and the Midianites (26).

This key passage harks back to the name Shear-Jashub (7:3), just as 9:8 – 10:4 harked back to Maher-Shalal-Hash-Baz (8:1). And there is both confidence and wistful resignation in the prophet's words. A *remnant will* finally[74] turn back to the Lord, but only a remnant (22). Ahaz refused to return. When the same challenge was put to Hezekiah at a later stage in the Assyrian crisis, it met with a more positive response (chapter 37).

Essentially, the choice that Isaiah and his compatriots faced was whether to respond to the circumstances that threatened them with calm

---

[73] NRSV's 'earth' in verse 23 is misleading.

[74] *In that day* (20); the day when Assyria is judged.

reliance on God or with a frenzy of self-help, using whatever means the wisdom of the age deemed most likely to succeed. And since the world is always with us, and has the same basic character from age to age, it is an issue which always faces the people of God in a multitude of ways small and great. In the book of Isaiah the issues of faith and unbelief are constantly related to the very pressing and practical business of political, national and personal survival, and this has a most important lesson to teach us. Faith is more than a means of justification; it is also a practical approach to the challenges of daily life, just as much for us as it was for those who faced the Assyrian threat. We are not only saved by faith; we live by it (2 Cor 5:7).

c. Assyria again (10:28–34)

The last line of verse 27 is somewhat obscure. The NRSV emends it and reads it with what follows. The NIV adheres more closely to the Hebrew and treats it as the concluding line of the previous unit. With or without this line, however, the structure and general import of verses 28–34 are clear.

The first paragraph (28–32) depicts the Assyrian army closing in on Jerusalem with terrifying speed and efficiency, and captures the horror felt by those in its path. The outlying towns mentioned are all to the north of the city, whereas when Sennacherib actually approached Jerusalem in the time of Hezekiah he did so from the direction of Lachish to the south (36:1–2). That is proof enough, if proof is needed, that this is not a literal description of that event written after it happened. Rather, it is a vivid poetic portrayal of the apparent invincibility of the Assyrians. They sweep all before them and shake their fists at the very place which symbolizes the Lord's rule on earth (32).[75]

In the second paragraph, however, this proud and powerful Assyrian army is pictured as a forest of towering trees (like the famous forests of Lebanon) which the Lord will suddenly fell *with great power* (33–34).[76] We have already met this imagery in verses 15–19, but now it is reworked with savage irony. The nation which was an axe in the Lord's hand (15) will finally be axed down by him (34). While God may use evil people to accomplish his purposes, this does not in any way diminish their accountability.

---

[75] This is particularly suggested by the reference to *mount . . . Zion*. Cf. Pss 2; 46; 48.
[76] For the fulfilment see 37:36.

We are in touch here with something we will not fully understand this side of heaven; it is part of the mysterious interplay between divine sovereignty and human freedom. We should, however, grasp it firmly and be profoundly grateful for it, for it will preserve us from either denying the reality of evil or fearing that it will ultimately triumph. Wicked men served God's purpose by nailing Jesus to the cross, but the resurrection lays on them, and on all of us, the urgent need for repentance (Acts 2:23, 36–38; 17:31).

In both its concepts and its imagery this unit corresponds to verses 5–19, giving a balanced A B A' structure to the passage as a whole, as we noted above.

12. Messiah's kingdom (11:1–16)

Clearly the two major sections of this chapter (1–9, 10–16) belong together. They both concern the rule of the *shoot* or *Root* of Jesse (1, 10). But what is first presented in general and symbolic terms in verses 1–9 is then reduced to concrete particulars in verses 10–16.

a. The ideal king (11:1–9)

The movement from the overthrow of the human kingdom (represented by Assyria) to the setting up of the kingdom of God (represented by the Messiah) is a natural one theologically, even though it involves a radical foreshortening of the historical processes involved (cf. Dan. 2:44; Rev. 11:15). Appropriate also, in another sense, is the movement from the felling of a forest at the end of the previous chapter to the emergence of *a shoot* from a *stump* at the beginning of this one. But this is only a surface continuity. The deeper reality involves a sharp contrast. Assyria is felled never to grow again; Judah is felled only to have new life emerge from its stump.

This is not the first time in the book that the transition from judgment to salvation has been depicted as the springing up of a plant, but clearly there is a more particular application of that imagery here. In 4:2 the full-grown Branch was a general image of the Lord's saving work for his people at last come to fruition. Here the shoot/Branch[77] is a metaphor for

---

[77] 'Branch' in both 4:2 and 11:1 of the NRSV translates two different but synonymous terms. The same basic image is reworked.

the Messiah, through whose advent and rule this will be accomplished. In 6:13 the stump was symbolic of the faithful remnant of the nation, the 'holy seed' from which a new people of God would grow. Here in chapter 11 the stump is the felled Davidic house, from which will come at last their leader and standard-bearer.

In a sense every king of Judah, from Saul onwards, had been the messiah.[78] Moreover, in view of the promises made to David it was natural that the Davidic house should have held a central place in the hopes of those who looked for God's will to be done in their midst. But it is also natural that, as the Davidic dynasty proved to be more and more of a disappointment, their expectations should have moved away from the current kings in Jerusalem towards a future ideal ruler, *the* Messiah, whom God would send to lead them.[79] This process is clearly at work in chapters 8–11 of Isaiah, against the background of the faithlessness of Ahaz in chapter 7. We first met this ideal figure in 9:6–7; now we are given a fuller account of his character and reign. The passage moves from his fitness to rule (1–3a) to the character of his rule (3b–5) to the ideal state of affairs that will result from his rule (6–9).

The expression *the stump of Jesse* (1; cf. 10) indicates his humble origins, bypassing all the ostentation of the Davidic house as it subsequently developed. His fitness to rule will consist essentially in his endowment with *the Spirit*, giving him true *wisdom*, grounded in *the fear of the LORD* (2–3; cf. Prov. 1:7; Job 28:28). This too, by implication, is a reflection on the current kings, whose false wisdom arose from fear of an altogether different kind (7:2). The fundamental characteristic[80] of his rule will be righteousness, which in practical terms will mean justice for the *poor* and meek (4–6), something which the current kings had conspicuously failed to bring about (cf. 3:12–15). And he will be in a position to execute perfect *justice* because he will be possessed of perfect knowledge (3b). There is a strong suggestion here, and in the extraordinary power of his spoken word (4b), that he will be more than an ordinary mortal (see on 9:6–7).

The effect of his rule will be universal peace (6–9), an ideal described here in symbolic language which recalls the paradise of Eden. It is a picture of the whole creation put back into joint. The entire earth, not just

---

[78] The Hebrew *māšîaḥ* (messiah) simply means 'anointed'. Both priests and kings were anointed, but 'the LORD's anointed' was shorthand for 'the king' (1 Sam. 24:10; Lam. 4:20).

[79] Cf. Drane, p. 340.

[80] Implied by *belt* (5; 'girdle' in RSV), probably an undergarment. Cf. Oswalt, pp. 282–283.

Jerusalem/Zion, will be the Lord's *holy mountain* (9; cf. 2:2; 4:5). In other words, he will be known, and his rule will be experienced, everywhere.

In this passage, then, as in 9:6–7, Isaiah looks beyond the disappointments of his own age to the coming of one who, in the last analysis, can only be God in the flesh, the Lord Jesus Christ. But the two passages are complementary. The first focuses on his birth, the second on the actualization of his reign over the earth. In New Testament terms, 9:6–7 was fulfilled in his incarnation, and 11:1–9 will be fulfilled in his second advent.

b. The ensign (11:10–16)

The opening words of verse 10 make it clear that this unit has the same end-time focus as verses 1–9, and in view of this the many particular *nations* mentioned must be understood in a figurative rather than literal sense.[81] Collectively they represent the enemies, great and small, of God's people.

The repetition of *In that day* in verses 10 and 11 subdivides the larger unit into two parts. What the whole envisages is a vast, end-time assembly. In the outer ring (10) will be the Gentile nations, who will at last come to recognize the Lord's rule. In the inner circle (11–16) will be the people of God, at last finally delivered from all their enemies. But this inner group will not be passive. They will participate in the Lord's rule over the outer group (14). The *banner* which the Lord will raise to convene this vast assembly will be *the Root of Jesse* (10, 12).[82] In other words, all that was envisaged in 2:2–4 and 4:2–5 will be realized when the Messiah at last reigns.

Three things should be noted. First, the *remnant* in view in verses 11–16 comprises, in one sense, simply the survivors, people of Israel and Judah who will still be alive, although scattered, when the Messiah comes (12). But since they are also the inheritors of final salvation, they are also the remnant in another sense, namely, the final generation of the elect, faithful people of God. These two senses of 'remnant' finally converge in the Old Testament, as they do in the New (see Mal. 4:1–2; 1 Thess. 4:17).

Second, because of the end-time focus of the unit as a whole, the gathering of the scattered people of God here cannot be seen as fulfilled

---

[81] Some, such as the Philistines, had already ceased to have any distinct national identity in Isaiah's own time.

[82] Verse 12, in effect, is the reversal of 5:26.

in the later return of the exiles from Babylon, even though both are depicted as a second or new exodus (cf. 11:15–16 with 43:16–17; 50:2). The return from Babylon was a particular deliverance that took place within history; this is a comprehensive one that will take place at its end (11).

Third, as Christians it is important to recognize that the nationalistic categories of a prophecy like this are transcended in the New Testament's vision of the end. In New Testament terms the scattered people of God are all those, Jew and Gentile alike, who gladly acknowledge Jesus as the Christ (i.e. the Messiah; 1 Pet. 1:1–2; Rev. 5:9–10; Phil. 2:9–10).[83] These are the ones who will finally be gathered from every nation to share in Christ's rule over those who will only reluctantly bow the knee on the final day. As we shall see, however, this expansion of the remnant concept to include Gentiles as well as believing Jews is already anticipated within the book of Isaiah itself (e.g. 56:6–7).

13. The Lord praised in Zion (12:1–6)

In one sense this paean of *praise* is simply the conclusion of the account of the Messiah's reign which began in 11:1. The repeated 'In that day' of 11:10–11 finds its sequel here in the phrase *In that day you will say* in verses 1 and 4. The praise foreshadowed in this chapter is to be in response to the blessings anticipated in chapter 11. The final salvation of God's people is described at the end of chapter 11 as a second or new exodus (15–16). The singing in this chapter then follows in the same way that the song of Exodus 15 followed the original exodus. Verse 2b is in fact an almost exact quotation of Exodus 15:2a, and verse 5a echoes Exodus 15:21.

But chapter 12 has a much more wide-ranging function within the book than this. The text to this point has consisted of units which are closely related to one another in a more or less obvious fashion. But the oracle against Babylon in chapter 13 introduces a block of material which is so distinct from what precedes as to indicate that a major new departure in the internal development of the book begins at that point. Chapter 12, then, stands at the end of the first major part of the book, and its content indicates that it is not merely the end but the climax. Consider, for example, the closing verse:

---

[83] The Greek term *christos* (Christ) is the equivalent of the Hebrew term *māšîaḥ* (messiah).

> *Shout aloud and sing for joy, people of Zion,*
> *for great is the Holy One of Israel among you.*

Chapters 1–12 have stressed again and again the holiness of God[84] and the fact that the culmination of his saving work would be reached in Zion (2:2–4; 4:2–6; and, by implication, 9:6–7). Here that culmination is described in terms of the final realization of the ancient covenant ideal: *the Holy One* dwelling in the midst of his people (cf. Exod. 25:8). What greater good could be imagined (cf. Rev. 21:1–5)? That is climax indeed and therefore a just cause for celebration!

This double function of chapter 12 confirms that the Messiah of chapter 11 is none other than God himself in the flesh. Chapter 12 celebrates both the rule of the Messiah and God dwelling among his people; they are one and the same thing. This is the goal towards which both the Zion prophecies of chapters 2 and 4 and the messianic prophecies of chapters 9 and 11 point.

The chapter has a simple structure. It contains two brief songs of praise (1–2, 4–6), each introduced by the words *In that day you will say*. Located centrally between the two songs, in verse 3, is a prophetic word of promise: *With joy you will draw water from the wells of salvation*. This promise in effect provides the rationale for the whole chapter. The theme is salvation, and the occasion is salvation experienced in full measure, like water drawn at will from inexhaustible wells. The result is joy, and it is this joy to which the songs give expression.

a. The first song (12:1–2)

The introductory *you will say* is in the singular, and as far as its form is concerned, the song itself is one of personal thanksgiving. It begins with a declaration of intention (*I will praise you*), followed by a reason (*your anger has turned away and you have comforted me*), and it concludes with a confession of faith (*God is my salvation*; cf. Pss 9; 18; 30; 34). But it is clear from what immediately precedes (and from what follows) that it is not a solitary individual who is in view here, but a collection of such individuals: 'the remnant of [the Lord's] people' (11:16). So the opening statement must be understood in a distributive sense: 'Each of you will say in that day . . .' Although it obviously had consequences for the nation as a whole, the

---

84 Especially 6:3, but also 1:4; 5:16, 19, 24; 8:13; 10:17, 20.

decision to trust or to rebel, to rely on the Lord or to put confidence in other things, had to be taken by each individual. Ahaz had to face it as a personal issue (7:9b); so did every other Israelite (28:16), and so must we today. This first song looks forward to the time when final judgment has taken place, and every survivor will have learned at last that salvation is to be found in no-one and nothing else but the Lord, and will thankfully and gladly confess that fact.

Verse 2 celebrates a glorious paradox: the angry God is finally the only source of comfort. This verse marks the final cancelling out of the dreadful refrain of 5:25; 9:12, 17, 21; and 10:4. In the end, 'comfort' (= salvation) can be found only by fleeing into the arms of the righteous God whose wrath we have incurred.

b. The second song (12:4–6)

This second song is a communal hymn in which the worshippers exhort one another to *give praise to the* Lord (4a), to declare his deeds to *the nations* (4b), and to praise him joyfully and loudly (5–6; cf. Pss 105 – 107; 113; 117; 135; 136). The switch to the plural was made in verse 3: 'With joy you [plural] will draw water', and continued in the introductory statement of verse 4: *In that day you* [plural] *will say . . .*[85]

Two reasons are given for the responses that are called for: the Lord's glorious deeds (5a), and his presence in Zion (6b). The second of these is a consequence of the first. It is the Lord's glorious deeds in judgment and salvation that have established his presence in Zion as the *great* and *Holy One*, terms which point unequivocally to his kingship.[86] But as 2:1–4 has made clear, the final establishment of the Lord's rule in Zion will have implications for *the nations*, and this is why the second song in particular places such stress on worldwide proclamation (4b, 5b). The two songs of this chapter celebrate good news which, in the end, cannot be contained. It must be proclaimed far and wide, for only as the nations hear of the Lord's glorious deeds will they be able to recognize at last that he alone is God, and come to Zion to learn of his ways (2:3). Thankfulness and praise overflow, as they always must, into evangelism.

---

[85] The NRSV's 'O inhabitant [singular] of Zion' in verse 6 (fn.) represents an idiomatic Hebrew expression referring to the entire population of the city (cf. Jer. 51:35).

[86] Especially the latter (6:3; 5:16; etc.), but see also Ps. 48, a psalm of Zion.

Isaiah 13 – 27

2. Lord of the nations

As a relatively small nation threatened by great powers, Judah was constantly tempted to look to political and military alliances to save her. Chapters 1–12 began by focusing on Judah and ended with proclamation to the nations. This second major section begins by focusing on the nations and ends with Judah (13:1; 26:1; 27:13). But the net message is the same. Salvation is to be found in the Lord alone. While Assyria falls into the background here, it is not forgotten entirely (see 14:24–27). The nations in view in chapters 13–23 were all threatened by Assyria at one time or other, and were all actual or potential partners with Judah in anti-Assyrian alliances.[1]

1. Concerning Babylon (13:1 – 14:23)

There are two prophecies concerning Babylon here: an 'oracle' (13:1–22) and a *taunt* (14:3–23). Wedged between them is a contrasting announcement of salvation for Jacob/Israel (14:1–2). In one sense this short passage simply introduces the taunt against Babylon by sketching the circumstances in which it will be sung (see 14:3–4). But it also alerts us to the fact that the words spoken against the nations are actually for Israel's ears[2] (the nations themselves almost certainly never heard them). They are spoken to remind Israel that no matter what the nations do to her, her final destiny is secure, because it is the Lord, not they, who shapes the course

---

[1] See Erlandsson, pp. 102–105.
[2] See the comment on 'Israel in the book of Isaiah', above, pp. 22–23.

of history. He is Lord of the nations, and his judgment on them has as its ultimate goal the salvation of his people.

a. The oracle (13:1–22)

Many scholars have proposed that this oracle should be dated to about 550 BC, long after Isaiah's death, when *Babylon* had replaced Assyria as the dominant military power in the region and its own fall to the Medes and Persians was imminent. But the heading in verse 1 flatly contradicts this, and forces us to grapple with the question why Isaiah himself might have spoken so strongly against Babylon in his own day.

The answer is not hard to find. It is clear from chapter 39 that Judah was well aware of Babylon's existence in Isaiah's day and, according to verses 5–8 of that chapter, Isaiah could see that, in the long term, Babylon posed an even bigger threat to Judah's security than Assyria did.

But there is a second reason for Isaiah's beginning here with Babylon. For Babylon was no newcomer to the world stage. It had a history reaching right back to the tower of Babel (Gen. 10:9–10; 11:1–9), and was therefore a fitting symbol of that arrogant pomp and power of the world that were characteristic of the nations as a whole in their rebellion against God. Babylon had already had one great period of glory in Isaiah's day, and it was soon to have another[3] before its end came. But come it would; Isaiah was certain of that. The story of Babylon was, for him, the story of all nations that defy God.

This symbolic significance of Babylon becomes more and more apparent as the oracle unfolds. The historical Babylon was not in fact overthrown by the Medes in a violent bloodbath and its site left abandoned, as verses 17–22 would indicate if taken literally. It surrendered without a fight to Cyrus the Persian, who had already achieved ascendancy over the Medes. But in Isaiah's day the Medes were the barbarians of the Ancient Near East, living beyond the eastern fringe of the civilized world and always threatening to overwhelm it. The Lord's announcement that he *will stir up . . . the Medes* (17) is a declaration that he has already settled upon the destruction of Babylon and all that it represents. Isaiah is not so much describing Babylon's eventual fall as pointing to what that will represent. The fall of Babylon merges, in this oracle, with the final, great *day of the*

---

[3] The period associated with Hammurabi (eighteenth century BC) and the so-called neo-Babylonian period associated with Nebuchadnezzar (sixth century BC).

LORD (6; cf. 9), when *all* human arrogance will be judged, and *all* human pomp and power will be exposed for the hollow things that they are (cf. 2:12–22). The historical event is described in cosmic, larger-than-life terms because of the greater reality that it anticipates and points to: the eventual fall of the whole world system which stands in opposition to God.[4]

b. The promise (14:1–2)

We have already noted how these two verses function in their context.[5] Now we must examine their content.

The terms *Jacob* and *Israel* here, as in 10:20–21, hark back to the ancient ideal of a single nation, descended from a common ancestor, and constituted as the people of God by the covenant forged at Sinai. God's original choice of Abraham, Isaac and Jacob had been confirmed in his deliverance of their descendants from bondage in Egypt. He had, so to speak, chosen Israel again. This act of deliverance had flowed out of his compassion and his faithfulness to his promises (Exod. 2:23–25). Now it was the conviction of Isaiah and the other Old Testament prophets that the Lord would go on choosing Israel in this way until the purpose he had in view in choosing her in the first place was fully realized. He would, of course, make other, lesser choices along the way. He would choose to discipline Israel when that was required, and he would even choose to use pagan nations such as Assyria and Babylon to bring this discipline to bear (e.g. 10:5–6). At times it might even seem that the Lord had rejected Israel, but ultimately he would confirm his original choice by choosing her again as he had at the exodus. It is this theology of election which undergirds the short but comprehensive promise of salvation in these verses.

Salvation as return from exile would have made perfect sense in Isaiah's own time, of course, since the whole of the northern kingdom and much of the south had already been ravaged and depopulated by Assyria (see 1:7–9). But the present passage, like the bracketing oracles against Babylon, is more a statement about what will finally be the case than a prediction of something in immediate prospect of fulfilment. A partial fulfilment came when Cyrus of Persia and his successors not only allowed Judean

---

4 Cf. Rev. 18, and Oswalt's treatment of this passage, pp. 300ff.

5 See the introductory comments, above, on 13:1 – 14:23 as a whole.

exiles to return, but gave them material assistance and forced others to serve them in the same way (Ezra 1:2–4; 7:21–24). But the complete fulfilment awaits the day anticipated in the New Testament when the meek will inherit the earth and share in Jesus' rule over the nations (Matt. 5:5; Rev. 5:9–10).

c. The taunt (14:3–23)

The word *taunt* (4) is perhaps too precise and strong for the Hebrew *māšāl*,[6] but it does capture accurately the tone of the song which follows. It has the form of a funeral lament (cf. 2 Sam. 1:19–27), but instead of expressing sorrow it communicates profound satisfaction, even delight. It celebrates, in this ironic fashion, the downfall of arrogance and oppression, represented here by *the king of Babylon*. It moves from the earth (4b–8) to Sheol[7] beneath (9–11), to heaven above (12–14), momentarily down to Sheol again (15), and finally back to *the earth* (16–21). Verses 22–23 confirm, in the form of a straightforward judgment oracle, that what is anticipated in the song will indeed take place.

The cosmic sweep of the poem led some early interpreters, and many since them, to see here a symbolic description of the fall of Satan. But if this reads too much into the text (and I think it does), it is equally misguided to reduce it to a description of the fall of a particular earthly monarch. The king of Babylon here, like Babylon itself in chapter 13, is a representative figure, the embodiment of that worldly arrogance that defies God and tramples on others in its lust for power. It is this which lies at the heart of every evil for which particular nations will be indicted in the following chapters. It also lies at the heart of all the horrendous acts of inhumanity which human beings and nations still commit against one another today. That is why the tone of this song should not cause us any embarrassment. This is no cheap gloating over the downfall of an enemy, but the satisfaction and delight which God's people rightly feel at his final victory over evil. The same note of celebration is heard at the very end of the Bible where, again, Babylon is a cipher for all that opposes God and his purposes (Rev. 18).

---

[6] See, for comparison, the use of the same term in Num. 23:7; Deut. 28:37; Prov. 1:1; Hab. 2:6.

[7] The meaning of 'Sheol' ranges from the grave, to the underworld, to the state of death. Belief in an underworld of some form was almost universal in the Ancient Near East. While the Old Testament shares this belief to some extent, it does not endorse pagan ideas about it (e.g. that it is ruled by a god or gods of the underworld). If such a realm exists, it too is ruled by the Lord. See the article on 'Sheol' in *NBD*.

The *junipers and the cedars of Lebanon* (8) represent the peoples of northern Israel and Aram who were particularly exposed to aggressors from beyond the Euphrates and had suffered much at their hands. In verse 9 the shadowy remains of former rulers are pictured as greeting the fallen oppressor with astonishment in Sheol. For all his might he has proved to be no more enduring than themselves! The *morning star, son of the dawn* (12) is probably the planet Venus, which seems to rival the sun in its early brightness but is soon eclipsed. *Mount Zaphon* is where the Canaanite gods were reputed to meet, like the Greek gods on Mount Olympus. Isaiah boldly uses imagery from this pagan background to point to the essence of human pride: self-deification (cf. Gen. 3:4; 2 Thess. 2:3–4). The ultimate disgrace of the oppressor, in verses 16–21, is to be deprived of honourable burial, and to have no descendants to perpetuate his name.

2. Concerning Assyria (14:24–27)

This short oracle provides the transition from the general treatment of worldly pomp and power, symbolized by Babylon, in 13:1 – 14:23, to the concrete and particular expressions of it in Isaiah's own day which now follow. First in line, naturally enough, is Assyria. In its size, its arrogance and its oppressive imperialism it was the manifestation par excellence of the spirit of Babel in the eighth century BC.

In one sense there is nothing new here, since the downfall of Assyria has already been treated at length in 10:5–34. But one feature of the present oracle is particularly noteworthy, namely, the tremendous emphasis that is laid here on the Lord's sovereign purpose which nothing can annul or frustrate. This is highlighted by the solemn oath which introduces the oracle, the rhetorical questions which end it, and the almost monotonous repetition of the words *plan* and *purposed* throughout it. This plan of the Lord has as its first objective the deliverance of his own people (25), but it also concerns *the whole world* and *all nations* (26). The destruction of Assyria will simply be one manifestation of it, as will the judgments on other nations announced in the following chapters.

Great care is needed, of course, in moving from a passage like this to the particulars of our own day. The way the rise and fall of specific nations fit into God's sovereign purposes is not revealed to us with the clarity that it was to Isaiah. But the 'spirit of Babylon' is certainly still with us, and, if we take Revelation 18 as our cue, will be until the very consummation of history. The manifestations of it in our world are legion. Furthermore, God's purposes for his people and for the world are still advancing, and, as the reflex to that, his wrath is constantly 'being revealed . . . against all the godlessness and wickedness of people'.[8] Jesus himself spoke of apparently 'natural' events such as war, famine and earthquake as signs of the end (Matt. 24:4–8). So while we lack the kind of detailed knowledge that Isaiah had, we do have warrant for seeing his oracles against the nations as illustrating a general truth about history. Every collapse of a proud, immoral regime in our world too is an interim day of the Lord, en route to the final day.

This theme of the Lord's plan will be developed strongly as the book proceeds, especially in chapters 40–55.

3. Concerning Philistia (14:28–32)

In contrast to the wise and invincible plan of the Lord are the foolhardy plans concocted by people who refuse to acknowledge the Lord. The attempt to implement one such plan clearly provided the setting for this oracle, which is precisely dated to *the year King Ahaz died*, 715 BC (28). Assyria was still suffering internal instability following the death of Shalmaneser III in 721 BC, and rebellion was in the air in southern Palestine. Philistia was already party to an anti-Assyrian conspiracy headed by Egypt (chapter 20), and in 715 BC there was apparently an attempt to involve the new king of Judah, Hezekiah. Hence the reference in verse 32a to *the envoys of that nation* (Philistia, or possibly Egypt), whose visit demanded a response. Isaiah was totally opposed to any participation by Judah, as his words in verse 32b make abundantly clear. The only sure refuge for the people of Zion was in the Lord, its founder (cf. 28:16). This was his consistent message in crisis after crisis. If God's people looked to the nations for their salvation instead of to him they could only come to ruin. Plans which did not spring from faith were recipes for disaster.

Hezekiah appears to have heeded the prophet's warning on this occasion, and just as well! It was not long before the Assyrian army moved in strength against Philistia (as predicted in verse 31), which suffered

---

[8] Rom 1:18. Paul has specifically in view here the kind of present disclosure of the divine anger to which the rest of Romans 1 is devoted, but I take it that a more general principle is implied. See J. Stott, *The Message of Romans: God's Good News for the World* (London: IVP, 2020), pp. 53ff.

the bitter consequences of its action, as did Egypt.[9] Judah, as a non-participant in the rebellion, was spared.

The very colourful image in verse 29, of a *rod* which is *broken* only to put forth a shoot which turns into a *viper*,[10] perhaps refers specifically to the death of Shalmaneser III and the rise, in his place, of Sargon II. Whether this is so or not, the general import of the verse is clear. The weakness of Assyria around 715 BC was not the prelude to its demise, as the conspirators had fondly hoped. In fact, it was just about to come to its full strength in Sargon, Sennacherib and Esarhaddon.[11] The *poor* and *needy* of verse 30a are the hard-pressed people of Judah (see 32b). They will be kept safe if they look to the Lord. But for Philistia there is no hope at all (30b).

4. Concerning Moab (15:1 – 16:14)

From Philistia to the west of Judah we now pass to *Moab* in the east, beyond the Dead Sea. The general background is the same, although this time no specific date is given. According to Assyrian records,[12] Moab was another nation which was invited to join the revolt in 715 BC. The implication of this oracle is that it did, and suffered the same fate as Philistia. It appears from the last two verses (16:13–14) that Isaiah reused an earlier oracle, sensing that the present circumstances had given it a new relevance.[13] The *three years* of verse 14 probably refers to the length of the revolt, from its inception until it was finally crushed by Sargon (see 20:1–4). There are three main sections: chapter 15 is a lament, 16:1–5 is an appeal by refugees seeking sanctuary in Judah, and 16:6–11 is a reflection on the pitiful condition to which the once-proud Moab has come. A summary statement (12) then concludes the oracle, before the appendix (13–14) which points to its imminent fulfilment.

a. The lament (15:1–9)

There is a crescendo of horror in this lament, from wailing (1–4) to flight (5–8) to death (9). The final verse is clearly climactic. Here the place name

---

[9] See *ANET*, pp. 286–287, for the Assyrian account of this campaign by Sargon II.

[10] Cf. Aaron's rod in Num. 17, and Moses' rod in Exod. 4:1–3.

[11] Drane, p. 133.

[12] Sargon's annals. See Bright, p. 279.

[13] Cf. Jer. 48, apparently another reuse of the same material.

Dibon, which first occurs in verse 2, is changed to *Dimon* to echo *dam*, the Hebrew word for 'blood'.

> *The waters of Dimon are full of dam,*
> *but I will bring still more upon Dimon . . .*

This is the ultimate horror, to which the wailing and the flight are despairing, futile responses: bloody slaughter from which there is no escape. Some details in the second half of verse 9 are obscure, but its general sense is clear. Those who manage to evade the sword will be devoured by wild beasts.[14] Running away will prove, in the end, to be as futile as remaining.[15]

The plethora of place names is rather bewildering, but it does help to shed light on both the *weeping* and the flight of the refugees. The weeping takes place in the far north (*Heshbon and Elealeh*, 4), in the extreme south (*Luhith* and *Horonaim*, 5), in the *streets* and on the housetops (3). There does not appear to be any progression. References to the wailing move erratically from north to south to centre to north and to south again. It is as though a great cry goes up everywhere, filling the land from end to end. But in more than one place we are told that people *go up* to *high places to weep* (2a, 5b), partly perhaps because these places offered more protection, at least temporarily, from their enemies, but also because it was here that the Moabites, like the Canaanites, worshipped their gods. But their gods, like their defences, are worthless. The *wailing* is the despairing cry of those who are without hope because they have trusted in what is powerless to save them. Here, surely, is a warning for Judah. It finds an echo in Paul's description of how we all were before God's grace rescued us: 'without hope and without God in the world' (Eph. 2:12).

The direction of the flight is southwards, suggesting an attack from the north. *Zoar*, in verse 5, is at the southern end of the Dead Sea, in Edom, and the *Ravine of the Poplars* in verse 7 is probably the Zered River which marked the Moab–Edom border. At least some, however, sought refuge in Judah, as we shall see in 16:1–5. The condition of the refugees is truly pathetic. *The waters of Nimrim* (6), probably an oasis, are either *dried up* or polluted, and so they struggle on, carrying what remains of their possessions (7), and weeping as they go.

---

[14] Taking *lion* here as representative. Cf. 13:21–22 and Amos 5:18–19.
[15] Cf. Oswalt, p. 339.

The tone of this lament is markedly different from that of 14:3–23, an important reminder that it is possible to rejoice at God's victory over evil without taking pleasure in the death of any individual or nation. Moab was a nation with close ancestral ties with Israel, but whose relationship with her was often strained and sometimes hostile (Gen. 19:36–38; Judg. 3:12–30; 2 Sam. 8:2; Zeph. 2:9–10). There is no gloating here, however. The speaker is so moved by Moab's plight that his *heart cries out* for her (5a). And that speaker, paradoxically, is the Lord himself, who has brought this upon her (9). In this lament, delivered by the prophet as the Lord's mouthpiece, we see God executing judgment with tears in his eyes. It should remind us sharply that there is no conflict between loving people and warning them of judgment to come; the one is a necessary consequence of the other.

b. The appeal (16:1–5)

The appeal itself is in verses 3–5; the preceding two verses give the background to it. The gifts of verse 1 are intended to encourage a favourable response, and are presumably sent by the fugitives of 15:9 or their representatives. The helpless *women* of verse 2 epitomize the defenceless, panic-stricken state of the refugees as a whole.

The long-range background is hinted at by the reference to the *house of David* in verse 5, at the very climax of the appeal. In the time of David Moab had been part of an empire centred in Zion and presided over by David himself, in recognition of which the Moabites had brought tribute gifts to him in Jerusalem (2 Sam. 8:2). But they had cherished their independence and broken away as soon as they were able to do so.[16] Now, by seeking shelter in the house of David (a metaphor for Davidic rule), these Moabite refugees acknowledge that their only hope is in Israel's God, whose chosen king rules in Zion.

That hope has both an immediate and a long-term aspect. What they hope for immediately is shelter from *the oppressor* who is presently ravaging their homeland (3–4a).[17] What they hope for in the long term (presumably for their descendants) is a share in the ideal situation to

---

[16] Probably after the schism that followed Solomon's death. It temporarily came under Israelite control again in the ninth century BC, during the reigns of the northern kings Omri and Ahab, as witnessed by the so-called Moabite Stone (*ANET*, pp. 320–321).

[17] 'Counsel' (NRSV; *'ēṣâ*) in 3a is parallel to 'justice' and has connotations of effective action, a plan put into effect, rather than mere advice (NIV: *Make up your mind . . . Render a decision*). Cf. 14:26.

emerge in the future when an ideal king reigns in Judah (4b–5). This appeal, then, has a messianic ring to it, and what the Moabites do here anticipates what people of all nations will finally do, as foreseen in 2:2–4.

Sela (which means 'rock') in verse 1 may be the place by that name in Edom (2 Kgs 14:7). But more likely, in view of verse 2,[18] it is simply a wilderness fortress somewhere in Moab from which the refugees send their appeal to the greater fortress of Zion.[19]

c. The reflection (16:6–11)

There are two parts here. In verses 6–7 the prophet speaks on behalf of all his countrymen and women (*We have heard*); in verses 8–11 he speaks for himself alone (*I weep*, 9a). Verses 6–7 are a reflection on the pride of Moab; verses 8–11 are a lament over her because of the ruin to which she has now come. But clearly the two parts belong together.[20] The personal lament of verses 8–11 is a response to the general call of verse 7 (clearer in the NRSV, 'let everyone wail for Moab'). Verses 6 and 7 cannot therefore (as is sometimes done) be separated from what follows and read as a callous rebuff of the appeal from the refugees. We simply do not know whether they were given sanctuary or not. Verses 6–11 as a whole are not a direct response to their appeal but a reflection on the complete reversal of Moab's condition that it represents. Its tone, like that of chapter 15, is sympathetic rather than derisive.[21]

Just how Moab's famed pride and arrogance were expressed we do not know. She certainly was not in a position to dominate other nations as some could. Perhaps her pride was tied up with her agricultural wealth, as verses 8–11 suggest. In any case verse 6 is a reminder that the spirit of Babel is not confined to the giants of this world. Moab was just as infected with it as Assyria and Babylon, and it is this for which she is judged. In the lament of verses 8–11 she is pictured as a luxuriant grapevine, laden with fruit, and spreading out to right and left – a picture of great abundance and prosperity. But then, in the midst of harvest celebrations, the songs of the revellers are silenced by the shout of battle (9b), and when the battle is done, all that remains is the pitiful sound of weeping (9a, 11). All is suddenly in ruins. In a moment Moab has plunged from the heights of

---

[18] The Arnon is in northern Moab, far from Edom.

[19] Cf. Oswalt, p. 341.

[20] Note the connecting word *kî* ('for') in 8a (NRSV).

[21] Cf. Oswalt, p. 345.

proud boasting to the depths of utter destitution. It is a lesson from history, a foretaste of that terrible day of the Lord which will finally come upon all the proud (2:12–21).

d. Summary and appendix (16:12–14)

These verses, by implication, draw the conclusions for Judah. Verse 12 recalls the resort to the high places in 15:2, 5. And now the lesson to be drawn from that is underlined: Moab's gods are no gods. There is no salvation in them. Verses 13 and 14 highlight the second major implication of the larger unit: Moab's time is short. How foolish Judah would be, then, to seek security in an alliance with Moab! Indeed, the very reverse is God's purpose. Other nations, including Moab, will find security only as they align themselves, at last, with the God who rules in Zion. The same principle, of course, still holds true today. The saints will reign with Christ (Rev. 5:10)! How foolish then for us, as his people, to seek security in the things the world worships as its gods.

5. Concerning Damascus (17:1–14)

From Philistia to the west of Judah, and Moab to her east, we now pass to *Damascus*, the capital of Aram, to her north. In the following two chapters we will move on to Egypt in the south, thus completing the four points of the compass. The arrangement is not chronological but schematic in a geographical sense. Wherever Judah looks, to the west, east, north or south, she sees only nations whose glory is fleeting and whose fate is sealed. There is nowhere she can look for her own security but to the Lord, who is the Lord and judge of them all.

The unit as a whole begins with Damascus (1) but soon includes *Ephraim* (= Israel, the northern kingdom) in close association with it (3), and concludes with what we shall see is a passage dealing with Assyria (12–14). We therefore have all the ingredients here of the same situation which we met in chapter 7, namely, an anti-Assyrian pact between Aram and Israel which they attempted to force Judah to join. This was an earlier conspiracy than the one involving Philistia and Moab that lies behind 14:28 – 16:14. The clock has been turned back twenty years to about 735 BC, during the reign of Ahaz.

The structure of the chapter can perhaps best be represented as shown in the table overleaf.

		a.	Judgment (1–6)
A.	Aram and Israel	b.	Repentance (7–8)
		c.	Judgment (9–11)
B.	Assyria		Judgment (12–14)

Of course, further refinements are possible. The first part of section A (verses 1–6) is divided into two sub-units by the concluding formula *declares the* LORD, in verses 3 and 6 respectively. And all three parts of section A are linked by the expression *In that day* in verses 4, 7 and 9. Section B is introduced by the exclamation *Woe* in verse 12 (cf. 10:1, 5). But even without these refinements, the broad structure highlights the fact that the judgment on Aram and Israel (section A) is redemptive, issuing in repentance, while that on Assyria (section B) is purely punitive, an end in itself.

a. Aram and Israel (17:1–11)

Assyria was, of course, the destroyer of both Aram and Israel. Damascus fell after a ruinous siege in 732 BC, and Samaria (the capital of Israel) a decade later in 722 BC (2 Kgs 17:1–6). And if the prediction of verses 1–2 was not literally fulfilled (Damascus did not in fact *become a heap of ruins*), it was certainly fulfilled in the sense that the *royal power* departed *from Damascus* (3b). It was transformed from the capital of a sovereign state into the administrative centre of an Assyrian province. The old Damascus, in this sense, simply ceased to exist. It was no more. Its ally Ephraim (Israel) suffered the same fate (3a),[22] and it is on Israel in particular that the focus falls from this point onwards.

In verses 4–6 three images depict Israel's condition after her collapse. She will be like an emaciated man whose *fat* has disappeared, leaving him lean and skeletal (4), like a reaped field in which only a few stalks remain for the poor to glean (5; cf. Lev. 19:9),[23] and like a grove of olive trees that have been so thoroughly *beaten* that only a few pieces of fruit remain on the highest *boughs* (6; cf. Deut. 24:20). The same condition is described in more prosaic terms in verse 9: *all will be desolation.*[24]

---

[22] The disappearance of her *fortified city* ('fortress', NRSV) presumably refers to the collapse of her defences.

[23] *The Valley of Rephaim* was south-west of Jerusalem (Josh. 15:8; cf. 2 Sam. 5:18, 22).

[24] Israel's fate will be like that of the Hivites and Amorites she once dispossessed on entering the land (see RSV).

In one sense, of course, Israel's fall was simply the result of her foolish collusion with Aram. But it had deeper roots. The prophet probes these directly in verses 10–11,[25] and indirectly in the pivotal passage on repentance in verses 7–8. At heart her undoing was her long history of idolatry, which had eroded her single-minded commitment to the Lord, and opened her to a politics of convenience and worldly wisdom instead of trust.

The worship of the Canaanites consisted largely of the performance of rites which were thought to induce fertility in flock and field by a kind of sympathetic magic. One such rite appears to underlie verses 10–11 with their mention of *finest plants* and *imported vines* ('slips of an alien god', NRSV). Slips were induced to grow and blossom at an artificially rapid rate, probably at a shrine.[26] But of course the evidence which they appeared to give of the potency of the god was false, and participation in such rites by Israelites showed that they had turned their backs on the Lord, the only one who could have given them security (10a).[27] As the plants soon withered, so would the hopes of the worshippers (11b).

In verses 7–8, at the centre of the passage, idolatry is described in more familiar terms. A contrast is drawn between gods that are made by human beings, *Asherah poles*[28] and *incense altars* (8), and the one true God who is the *Maker* of all things (7). And a day is spoken of when people will finally recognize the folly of idolatry and acknowledge the supremacy of Israel's God. The repetition of *In that day* in verses 4 and 7 links verses 7–8 closely to what precedes (especially to verses 4–6), and suggests that the repentance spoken of here is something that will happen within Israel as a direct consequence of the disaster which is about to overtake her. But the general term *people* in 7a suggests that the immediate here merges into something more long-term and universal. Isaiah foresees a day when people everywhere will finally forsake their man-made gods (cf. 2:2–4, 20–21). The Lord's immediate purpose, however, is to induce Israel to do so, and judgment is the means he will use to bring it about. The repentance of Israel is central to his wider purposes, as the pivotal position of verses 7–8 in the unit suggests. He has declared war on idolatry.

---

[25] Note the connecting 'For' in verse 10a (NRSV).

[26] Cf. the 'gardens' of 1:29.

[27] Cf. Deut. 8:11–20 where to 'forget' is to turn away in apostasy.

[28] The sacred trees or poles around Canaanite altars, associated with Asherah, the consort of the Canaanite high god, El.

b. Assyria (17:12–14)

While no nation is named here, the close conjunction with the preceding material dealing with the fall of Aram and Israel makes it all but certain that Assyria is the destroyer which is principally in view (cf. 9:8 – 10:4 followed by 10:5–34). In this short unit the imagery of 8:7 is powerfully developed and reworked. There Assyria was a river in flood; here she is the *raging sea*. But her power is illusory. At the Lord's rebuke (13)[29] her mighty waters become *chaff* blown away by *the wind*. She is never really her own master. It is the Lord who calls her and the Lord who chases her away. Verse 14 anticipates the fate which actually befell her, as described in 37:36.

But again, something bigger is hinted at by the words *many nations* and *peoples* in verses 12 and 13. Assyria is representative of all who make war on God's people. They will all suffer the same fate (14b; cf. Pss 46; 48).

6. Messengers from Ethiopia (18:1–7)

In many ways this is a transitional unit. It does not have the introductory formula 'A prophecy against . . .', which is a major structural marker in chapters 13–23 (see 13:1; 15:1; 17:1; 19:1; 21:1; 22:1; 23:1). Instead, the opening exclamation, *Woe*, following the same Hebrew word in 17:12, links it to what has gone before, and especially to 17:12–14. But its content relates it more closely to what follows. The biblical *Cush* was the large region south of the fourth cataract of the Nile, embracing modern Ethiopia, Sudan and Somaliland. In the time of Hezekiah, late in the eighth century BC, it merged with Egypt under the rulers of the twenty-fifth dynasty, who were Ethiopians,[30] and this is clearly the situation reflected in this part of Isaiah (see 20:3–4). So this rather enigmatic passage concerning Cush provides the transition to the following oracle which is explicitly 'against Egypt' (19:1). In fact, chapter 18 introduces a block of material spanning chapters 18, 19 and 20, all of which are concerned with Egypt in one way or another.

But the backward connection to the passage against Assyria in 17:12–14 is equally important for understanding the present chapter, for the general background is the rivalry between Assyria and Egypt for control of

---

[29] An allusion to the Lord's mastery of the primeval waters at creation. Cf. Gen. 1:2; Ps. 104:7.

[30] Approximately 716–663 BC. Bright, p. 471.

Palestine in the second half of the eighth century BC. Humanly speaking, the small states of Palestine could not hope to offer successful resistance to Assyria without the backing of an ally more powerful than themselves. In these circumstances Egypt seemed the obvious place to look, and of course Egypt was quick to exploit this opportunity to extend its influence in the region. Consequently Egypt was a key player in all the anti-Assyrian activity in Palestine in the period. The specific background is clearly very similar to that which underlies 14:28–32. Feverish diplomatic activity is in progress[31] in an attempt to patch together an effective anti-Assyrian coalition in southern Palestine, and Judah is being invited to participate. This time the diplomacy is explicitly with Egypt (cf. 14:32). The passage in chapter 14 relates to the rebellion of 713–711 BC, when Hezekiah did not participate. A second rebellion took place in 705–701 BC, when he did.[32] Egypt was prominent in both, and the present passage may relate to either, since it is undated (cf. 14:28)[33] and gives us only Isaiah's response, not Hezekiah's.

Isaiah's response is more for the ears of Hezekiah and his fellow Judeans than for the messengers, since ambassadors could hardly be expected to take such an enigmatic message as this to their masters. But its general import must have been clear enough to Hezekiah and his courtiers, who were presumably already acquainted with Isaiah and his preaching. For what he says here is a restatement, albeit in a somewhat dazzling rhetorical fashion, of his consistent position regarding international conspiracies. Judah is to have no part in them.

The speech begins, in true diplomatic fashion, with a compliment to the Ethiopians who have sent the *messengers* (2b). It ends in the same way (7), so that as far as its rhetorical form is concerned, it is a carefully rounded whole. But the implication of what lies in between is that the Lord will not support the revolt. *When a banner is raised on the mountains . . . and . . . a trumpet sounds* (both of them calls to arms) he will remain detached, quietly looking on from heaven but taking no part (3–4). But then (and here the speech assumes a more threatening tone), just *before the harvest*, when it looks as though all that the conspirators have worked for is about to come to fruition, he will suddenly put in the knife (5), and

---

[31] The messengers are *swift* (18:2).

[32] Cf. Oswalt, p. 163.

[33] *Whirring wings* (18:1) refers either to insects or, more likely, to the swift-moving 'winged' (i.e. sailing) boats of Ethiopia. See Oswalt, pp. 359–360.

the result will be utter carnage – a grand feast for the vultures (6). And the eventual outcome?[34] Messengers will come to Zion again, this time on a very different errand. They will come to acknowledge the sovereignty of the Lord by bringing *gifts* to *Zion*, *the place* of his *Name*, that is, the place where he has revealed himself (7).

It now becomes even clearer why this unit and the previous one both begin with *Woe*. Neither Assyria nor Egypt will be the victor in the conflict between them. The Lord will. And in the near future both of them will feel the sharp edge of his wrath.

Paradoxically, what these ambassadors hear (at least from Isaiah) is not a diplomatic message but an oracle (4a), and it concerns not Egypt alone but the whole *world* (3a). For Egypt is not the only nation that is destined to come, finally, on humble pilgrimage to Zion (2:2–4). Judah, then, should not join the conspiracy, first because it is destined to fail, and second because to do so would be to betray a lack of trust in the Lord to bring about, through his own people, his declared purpose concerning the nations. That is the import of this brilliant piece of rhetoric by the prophet.

7. Concerning Egypt (19:1–25)

Chapter 18 has established the general context within which this chapter is to be read and understood; it is still Egypt as a potential ally against Assyria which is in view. The message, too, is the same. Judah will find no security in looking to Egypt. On the contrary, Egypt's only hope is in Judah's God, whom she is destined finally to acknowledge as her God also. There are two parts, the first in verse (1–15) and the second in prose (16–25). The first shows the Lord coming to Egypt to visit devastating judgment upon her; the second points to her ultimate repentance and incorporation into the kingdom of God. So this chapter resonates with the two great themes of prophetic preaching: judgment and salvation.

a. Judgment (19:1–15)

It is difficult, and probably wrong-headed, to tie these verses to any particular conquest of Egypt. By Isaiah's time Egypt's era of imperialistic glory, the New Kingdom period, was long since past, and the land was

---

[34] *At that time* (7a) is a typical piece of prophetic foreshortening which passes over the interval between the present and the end time and sets the one in the light of the other. Cf. 17:7 and comment.

ruled by Ethiopians. In the succeeding centuries she was to be a prize sought after and seized by one ambitious tyrant after another, including Esarhaddon and Ashurbanipal (671 and 667), Nebuchadnezzar (568), Cambyses (525) and Alexander the Great (332).[35] The *fierce king* of verse 4 could be any one of them or, more likely, representative of them all. Again and again Egypt proved to be an ineffective and unreliable ally of the small states of Palestine in their struggles against Assyria and Babylon.

In three stanzas the prophet identifies Egypt's three crucial weaknesses: her religion (1–4), her total dependence on *the Nile* (5–10), and her false wisdom (11–15). Egypt's religion was idolatrous and polytheistic, and had its natural reflex in social fragmentation (2). It could not unite the nation, and a nation without unity cannot long endure. Humanly speaking, the Nile was Egypt's lifeline. Should the Nile fail, so would all the nation's life-sustaining activity (5–9). The encroaching desert would soon swallow it up and turn it into a wasteland. And finally, its *wise men* were *fools* (11–12).[36] Because they lacked any understanding of the Lord's plans, they were powerless to counteract them (12, 15). With such *counsellors* Pharaoh, and all Egypt with him, would *stagger* blindly to disgrace and ruin (14). Behind this whole passage lies the memory of the exodus, when the Lord exposed the powerlessness of Egypt's gods, the emptiness of her wisdom, and the vulnerability of her lifeline, the Nile (Exod. 7:14–24; 8:19; 10:16–19). The description of him riding *on a swift cloud* (1) indicates his total mastery of the natural world (cf. Deut. 33:26; Pss 18:10; 68:33; 104:3).[37] Egypt can do nothing to avert his determined action.

b. Salvation (19:16–25)

This second part of the chapter is divided into five brief segments by the recurring formula *In that day* in verses 16, 18, 19, 23 and 24. Here, as so often in Isaiah, this expression points beyond the immediate horizon of unfolding historical events to what will finally be the case when the Lord's purposes are fully realized. This is confirmed by the fact that the thought of this passage has a close relationship, as we shall see, to that of 2:2–4 – Isaiah's vision of what will come to pass 'in the last days'.

---

[35] Bright, pp. 471–473.

[36] *Zoan* (= Tanis) and *Memphis* (13) were major cities in lower Egypt.

[37] This bold imagery appears to be drawn from Canaanite literature in which Baal, the storm god, is similarly described.

The opening segment (16–17) moves against the background of verses 1–15 (the initial *In that day* of 16a points backwards as well as forwards) and indicates that the first step towards Egypt's incorporation into the kingdom of God will be *fear*, fear that arises from judgment already experienced and from the prospect of even worse to come. It will be inspired by *the land of Judah* (17) as the place from which the judgment emanates. It is not fear of Judah per se, but of the manifest power of her God. Such fear is a healthy thing. It leads here, as in the case of Rahab of old (Josh. 2:8–11), to the swearing of a new *allegiance* (18). In this short second segment Isaiah envisages an eventual turning to the Lord so complete that some cities, including one which had been a centre for the worship of the sun god Re,[38] will even go so far as to adopt Hebrew, *the language of Canaan* (18).

The third segment (19–22) is much longer than the other four and is centrally located in the unit as a whole. It shows the new allegiance of the Egyptians being expressed in action and experience. Like Abraham they will build *an altar*, and like Jacob they will erect a *monument* (19; Gen. 12:8; 28:22). Standing at the *border*, the pillar will testify to the fact that the Egyptians serve the same God as their Israelite neighbours, as the altar at the Jordan witnessed to the uniting of the tribes in Joshua's day (19–20; Josh. 22:26–28). Like the Israelites of the judges period, they will *cry out to the* LORD . . . *and he will rescue them* (20b; Judg. 3:7–11), and like Israelites in general they will offer *sacrifices* and *make vows*, and be subject to the Lord's firm but loving discipline (21–22). It is pointless to try to link the building of the altar and pillar in this passage with concrete historical events.[39] The prophet has employed a series of images drawn from the past to point to the central truth of Egypt's incorporation into the people of God in the future. They will *acknowledge* [NRSV 'know'] *the* LORD (21) even as Israel knows him.

The final two segments, in verses 23 and 24–25 respectively, show us a world in which open borders and common worship witness to the fact that ancient hostilities are at last resolved (23), and in which Israel finally fulfils the destiny marked out for her in the promises made to Abraham

---

[38] *City of the Sun* (18); cf. Heliopolis (sun-city), Jer. 43:13 (NIV footnote). The Masoretic text has 'City of Destruction', but 'City of the Sun' has the support of numerous witnesses including the Isaiah A scroll from Qumran. See Oswalt, pp. 177–178, whom I have followed closely here.

[39] The *altar*, for example, is sometimes identified with the Jewish temple at Elephantine (fifth century BC) or with the later one at Leontopolis (second century BC).

so long ago: *a blessing on the earth* (24b; cf. Gen. 12:3). The details are startling, particularly the mention of Egypt and Assyria, the two arch-rivals whose power plays made Isaiah's world so unstable and war-torn in the late eighth century BC. They function here, it seems, as test cases. The day that Egypt and Assyria are at peace with one another and with Israel will be the day the whole world is at peace. And it will be a peace brought about not by human might or wisdom, but by *the LORD Almighty*, whose benediction closes the chapter, arching over the whole scene like a brilliant rainbow (25). Peace of this order can come only from him, and will be bestowed only when he is acknowledged for who he is, the sovereign Lord and creator of all. The vision of 2:1–5 has come back to inspire us again. It is the *worship* of the one true God, the God of Israel, that will finally draw all things together in perfect harmony (23).

There are many questions left unanswered here, but if we are to be guided by the broad sweep of Isaiah's vision as the rest of the book unfolds it to us, we will not look for the fulfilment of this dream in some political or religious realignment of nations in the Middle East, now or in the future. We will seek it rather in the eventual triumph of God's kingdom through the suffering, death and exaltation of Israel's Messiah, and ours (11:1–9; 42:1–4; 52:13 – 53:12; cf. John 12:30–37). True worship is based on reconciliation, and there is no way to true reconciliation that bypasses the cross (Col. 1:19–20).

8. Isaiah goes naked (20:1–6)

In this chapter, which concludes the block of material concerning Egypt (chapters 18–20), we are returned yet again to the concrete historical realities of Isaiah's own day. The general background is the same as for 14:28–31, namely, the Egyptian-backed Philistine revolt against Assyria in 713–711 BC. The oracle of chapter 14 predicted the crushing of the revolt by Assyria. The present passage is set against the precise fulfilment of that prediction in *Sargon's* destruction of *Ashdod* in 711. With Ashdod in ruins the revolt was effectively at an end. Yamani, king of Ashdod, fled to Egypt, but the Egyptians were cowed by Sargon's military might and cravenly handed Yamani over to him (see on 14:28–32).

The chronology of verses 2–4 is difficult to unravel, but the most likely sequence of events is as follows. For the *three years* of the revolt (713–711) Isaiah had gone about *stripped and barefoot*, like a disgraced captive (3).

He may have been completely naked or, more likely, barefooted and stripped of his outer clothing.[40] His feet were certainly bare, and so, probably, were his *buttocks* (4; cf. 2 Sam. 10:1–5). His action was *a sign and portent*, that is, it was invested with special, divine significance.[41] It is highly improbable that he remained stripped round the clock, so to speak. More likely he appeared this way in public at least once each day over the three-year period (cf. Ezek. 4:4–8).

On the day that Ashdod fell he was told to perform his action for the last time (2) and to add an interpretation to it (3). Up to that point the onlookers were no doubt aware of the general import of the sign (the revolt would fail), but had probably thought that it applied particularly to the fate of Ashdod. Now, at the precise moment calculated to give it maximum psychological impact, its true significance is revealed. It points beyond Ashdod's demise to the fate of the Egyptians, on whom the Philistines had relied for support.

That was the crucial significance of the sign for Isaiah's contemporaries in Judah. Egypt did not suffer outright conquest until 671, forty years later, when she was conquered by Esarhaddon,[42] and during the whole of that time Judah was tempted to do what Ashdod had done. But Isaiah, by this sign and its interpretation, had already powerfully pointed out to them the foolishness of such a course of action.[43] Egypt had already suffered tremendous loss of face in 711 (see above), and in the end would fare no better against Assyria than Ashdod had done. To rely on Egypt was the sheerest folly.

This chapter, then, is a fitting climax to the complete block of material concerning Egypt in chapters 18–20. It underlines the basic message of the entire section in a most vivid manner; and it is a message the church needs to hear afresh today. The crises we face will not be solved by looking to the world for solutions. 'The world and its desires pass away, but whoever does the will of God lives for ever' (1 John 2:17).

---

[40] *Sackcloth* here (2) is probably just the customary clothing of a prophet; cf. 2 Kgs 1:8; Zech. 13:4. The Hebrew *'ārôm* (naked) does not necessarily indicate total nudity (see 58:7) and certainly does not do so here (otherwise, why add *and barefoot*?).

[41] Cf. Oswalt, p. 101. There is no clear distinction between the usage of the two words in the Old Testament. Neither a *sign* nor a *portent* is necessarily miraculous, although it may be. See 8:18 and cf. 38:7–8 and Joel 2:30.

[42] *ANET*, p. 293.

[43] *The people who live on this coast* (6) is vague, probably by design. It refers primarily to the Philistines, but also, by implication, to all the small states of southern Palestine, including Judah.

9. Concerning the Desert by the Sea (21:1–10)

The title of this oracle is very enigmatic and really sets the tone for the oracle as a whole. It concerns *a dire vision* of *an invader* who would come *like whirlwinds* (1–2). This vision was so dreadful in its aspect that Isaiah was physically affected by it (3–4). It is not until almost at the end, in verse 9, that we discover, as Isaiah himself apparently did at that point, that it concerns the fall of *Babylon*. The oblique title[44] introduces an atmosphere of mystery and dread which is maintained until the climax is reached. It is the prophet's experience as well as his message which is being communicated to us here. The next chapter begins with a similarly enigmatic title (22:1), and in fact the whole of 21:1 – 22:14 has the same visionary quality.[45]

But why another oracle against Babylon at this point? The answer lies in the fact that, as the eighth century drew to a close, Judah's attention began to swing away from Egypt and towards Babylon as a prospective ally against Assyria (witness the warm reception given to the ambassadors by Hezekiah in 39:1–4). But Isaiah sees in this vision that Babylon, like Egypt, is doomed, and so, by implication, are those who align themselves with her. Hence the warning note on which the oracle ends (10).[46] There is no comfort for Judah in this oracle; only a premonition of her own eventual demise. The tone of this passage (foreboding) is very different from that of 14:3–23 (taunt). 'Babylon' was a symbol in chapters 13 and 14; here it is a concrete nation. It was the only nation which seemed capable of offering effective resistance to Assyria at the end of the eighth century BC, and by looking to Babylon, Judah, potentially at least, made Babylon's fate her own. The difference in tone is best explained in terms of a much closer link to the specific circumstances reflected in 39:1–4 than was the case in chapters 13 and 14.[47]

Babylon was in more or less continuous rebellion against Assyria from 721 to 689 BC, when it was decisively crushed by Sennacherib. He treated the city and its people with great ferocity, destroyed the temple of Marduk

---

[44] Babylon was situated on a vast plain which bordered on the sea. In the word *desert* or 'wilderness' (NRSV) we have, possibly, the first intimation of coming judgment. Cf. Jer. 23:10.

[45] Note the recurrence of the 'vision' motif in 21:2; 22:1 and 22:5.

[46] *Crushed on the threshing-floor* is a metaphor for 'sorely afflicted' (cf. 28:27–28).

[47] Those chapters may well have been written soon after 689 BC (see next paragraph), when an alliance with Babylon was no longer contemplated.

(the national god) and carried his image away to Assyria.[48] But Isaiah's *dire vision* reaches beyond this. For Babylon was to rise again, and its fate would not be sealed finally until its fall to a coalition of Medes and Persians under Cyrus the Great in 539 BC. It is this more distant, final fall of Babylon which appears to be alluded to in verse 2b with its reference to *Elam* (= Persia) and *Media* as Babylon's destroyers,[49] and in verse 5a where the princes of Babylon *eat* and *drink*, unaware that the enemy is at the gate (cf. Dan. 5). However that may be, the general import of the vision is clear: Babylon is doomed. Judah would be foolish in the extreme to link her own fortunes to those of Babylon, no matter how attractive this course of action may appear in the short term.

The *lookout* of verses 6–9 appears to be a visionary figure rather than the prophet himself, since it is Isaiah who appoints him at the Lord's command (6). He is part of the total visionary experience Isaiah has and which he communicates, in turn, to his contemporaries in Judah (10).

10. Concerning Dumah and Arabia (21:11–17)

There are two short oracles here, the first *against Dumah* in verses 11–12, and the second *against Arabia* in verses 13–17. They are very closely related to each other, as we shall see.

Between Judah and Babylon lay the north Arabian desert with its Bedouin tribes, its oases and its overland trade routes. *Dumah*, Dedan and *Tema* (11, 13, 14) all lay in this region. The Babylonian envoys of 39:1 probably passed this way en route to Judah in order to avoid going through the Assyrian heartland to the north,[50] and as they did so they no doubt tried to enlist the support of these desert tribes for their cause. If they succeeded, as they appear to have done, then the subsequent action taken by the Assyrians against Babylon would have had serious repercussions for these people, and that appears to be the situation reflected here. The people of Dumah anxiously await news of what is happening (11–12), while, further south, fleeing refugees seek food and water in Tema (13–14). *Kedar* in verses 16–17 is a collective term for the desert tribes in general, so that these final two verses really act as a conclusion to both oracles.

---

[48] Bright, pp. 280, 284, 287.

[49] Elam was not an enemy but an ally of Babylon in the more immediate context of the eighth century BC. Bright, p. 280.

[50] Cf. Oswalt, p. 398.

They predict a sudden end (*Within one year*) to the prosperity of these proud desert-dwellers, and the decimation of their fighting men. Their involvement with Babylon was soon to cost them dearly.[51] Judah herself felt Sennacherib's wrath at about this time (as we know from chapter 37), and escaped complete destruction only because of the Lord's miraculous intervention (37:36).

The close connection with the preceding oracles against Babylon is confirmed by the *watchman* imagery of verses 11–12 (cf. 6–9), but now it is Isaiah himself who is the watchman.[52] The one who *calls to* him *from Seir* (= Edom), a visionary figure,[53] is probably a fugitive who has fled westward from Dumah (Edom is directly south of Judah). He receives an enigmatic response (12), but its implication is clear: no news yet; Dumah's fate hangs in the balance. It is apparent, however, from verses 16–17, which way the balance finally tipped, not by accident, but by the sovereign determination of *the LORD, the God of Israel.*

11. Concerning the Valley of Vision (22:1–25)

As explained above, the enigmatic title of this oracle and its visionary quality suggest close links with what has gone before.

The 'dire vision' of 21:1–10, with its revelation that Babylon was doomed, filled Isaiah with dread. If Babylon could not stand, how could Judah? But the same news apparently produced quite a different reaction among the people of Jerusalem in general, as summarized in verse 13b: *Let us eat and drink . . . for tomorrow we die!*

The response of some, including the king, was more measured and purposeful: they looked to the city's armaments, walls and water supply in anticipation of an attack (8–11a). But what no-one did was to *look to* the Lord in repentance and faith (11b), and it is this that calls forth the severe announcement of judgment to come in this oracle (14). There are two parts. The first (1–14) pronounces judgment on the general population; the second (15–25) focuses on one leading citizen, Shebna.

---

[51] Cf. Esarhaddon's account of the campaign of his father, Sennacherib, against the Arabs in *ANET*, p. 291.

[52] The Hebrew words for *lookout* and *watchman* are different, but the underlying image is the same. (RSV has 'watchman' for both.)

[53] Cf. the 'man of Macedonia' in Acts 16:9.

a. The people in general (22:1–14)

As suggested by the opening words of verse 5, *The Lord, the LORD Almighty, has a day*, it is best to see the descriptions of Jerusalem beset with armies in verses 2b–3 and 5–8a as the content of a revelation which Isaiah has received rather than the description of a past event. In the midst of a city given over to senseless *revelry* (1–2a) Isaiah sees a very different scene, which causes him to *weep bitterly* (4a). He is inconsolable, for what is portended by the revelation is nothing less than *the destruction of* his *people* (4).

The mention of *Elam* in verse 6 is a further link with the 'dire vision' of the previous chapter, and suggests that, like that vision, this one too reaches beyond the immediate threat to the city (in this case Jerusalem) to its ultimate fall. Warriors from Elam probably formed part of the forces of Nebuchadnezzar which destroyed Jerusalem in 587.[54] Isaiah saw that, whatever her fortunes in the short term might be, Jerusalem's faithlessness would eventually be her downfall (8a, 14).

The first verb in verse 8b is singular (*you looked . . . to the weapons*), while all the following verbs are plural. The *reservoir between the two walls* in verse 11 is almost certainly Hezekiah's famous water tunnel, still to be seen in Jerusalem today.[55] So Hezekiah, as king, is alluded to but not named, partly perhaps out of deference to him, but mainly because he is not being singled out for individual blame (he later evinced a faith not evident here, as we will see in chapter 37). The indictment is general rather than particular at this point, and remains so to the end of verse 14. But there is a sharp shift of focus in what then follows.

b. Shebna (and Eliakim) (22:15–25)

This passage is hinged to the previous one by the repetition of *the LORD Almighty* in 14b and 15a. But there is a much deeper connection than this. Both men named here were court officials under Hezekiah (36:3; 2 Kgs 18:18; 19:2). In *Shebna* in particular the passage gives a concrete example of the faithlessness for which the people as a whole are condemned in verses 1–14. Verses 15–19 predict his fall, and verses 20–25 his replacement by Eliakim.

---

[54] Cf. Clements, p. 185. Elam and Babylon were allies from the late eighth to early sixth centuries. It was only in the second half of the eighth century, under Cyrus, that Elam (Persia) turned against Babylon. The identity of *Kir* ('city') is unknown, but see 2 Kgs 16:9; Amos 1:5; 9:7.

[55] See *ANET*, p. 321.

Shebna	Eliakim
Self-regarding (his tomb, his *chariots*) (16, 18)	*Servant* of the Lord (20) *Father* to the people (21)
Like a ball (unstable) (18)	*Like a peg* (stable, dependable) (23)
Disgrace (18)	*Honour* (23)
Deposed by the Lord (19)	Fixed *into a firm place* by the Lord (23)

The contrast between the two men could not be more sharply drawn. *Eliakim* is the very antithesis of Shebna, an ideal leader called and established by the Lord. Verses 24 and 25, therefore, come as something of a surprise. Eliakim's family are apparently not made of the same stuff as he is. They take advantage of his high position to better themselves and in so doing bring about his ruin. The peg gives way under the strain. Eliakim is destroyed from below.

In the end, then, it is not just the Shebnas of Jerusalem who will bring it down, but the common people as well. What is presented in general terms in verses 1–14 is particularized in verses 15–25, but the message is the same. The failure of the people of Jerusalem to rely upon the Lord will bring both them and their leaders to ruin.

By the time of Sennacherib's invasion of Judah in 701 Eliakim had already become chief minister[56] and Shebna had been demoted to the position of secretary (2 Kgs 18:18). This is a far cry, to be sure, from the disgrace and exile predicted in verses 17–18, but these may have followed later. Nothing is known, apart from what we have here, about the circumstances of Shebna's death.

In retrospect, the enigmatic titles in 21:1 and 22:1 are both ironical. The rich alluvial plain of Babylonia is actually a desert – a place with no prospects. And Jerusalem, Mount Zion, is in reality a valley where no real vision exists. The people of Jerusalem are blind to the Lord's purposes. Isaiah sees them clearly, and weeps.

12. Concerning Tyre (23:1–18)

This prophecy of the fall (1–14) and subsequent rise (15–18) of *Tyre* is a minor landmark within this part of the book.[57] It is the last of the series

---

[56] *The palace administrator* (15), i.e. over the royal court.

[57] See the table on p. 13 above.

of oracles concerning particular nations which began in chapter 13, and is followed by what scholars commonly call the 'Isaiah Apocalypse' (chapters 24–27) in which cosmic acts of judgment and salvation bring history to a close. It stands at the end of a distinct block of material within the larger unit, chapters 13–27.

Tyre probably closes the series of oracles against the nations for the same reason that Babylon opens it; it was so famous for one particular aspect of worldly achievement that it had a symbolic value that could be used to good effect by Isaiah and others who followed him.[58] As Babylon was proverbial for its military might and cultural achievements, Tyre was proverbial for its commercial wealth. Standing in the first and last positions as they do, then, Babylon and Tyre sum up all that is impressive and alluring in the world (cf. 1 John 2:16).

A connection of a different kind is made between Tyre and Babylon in verse 13, which points clearly to the historical setting of the present oracle. This may refer to Sargon's attack on Babylon in 710, or, more likely, Sennacherib's much more devastating attack in 689. At any rate, it is clear that the fate already suffered by Babylon provides the background to the present prediction that Tyre, too, will fall. Again indirectly, but none too subtly, the prophet hammers home his message. Then, as now, the security that seems to be available through unholy alliances with the world is a cruel illusion.

The first part of the prophecy is neatly framed by the repetition of *Wail, you ships of Tarshish* in verses 1 and 14. Tyre and Sidon were the two leading cities of Phoenicia, and Tarshish, in what is now Spain, was one of the many far-flung colonies the Phoenicians had established around the Mediterranean world (see 7b). They served as bases for Phoenicia's lucrative sea-borne trade, of which the ships of Tarshish were the outstanding symbol. These trading ships brought great wealth into her coffers and gave her much influence in the world.[59] Israel had had close diplomatic and trading links with Phoenicia, and with Tyre in particular, since the days of David and Solomon (2 Sam. 5:11; 1 Kgs 5:1; 7:13; 9:11–12, 26–28).

Verses 1–7 picture the stunning news of Tyre's fall reverberating around the Mediterranean world. Home-bound sailors first hear of it in

---

[58] E.g. Ezek. 27:1 – 28:19, and also Rev. 18:11–24, which appears to draw on both Isaiah's and Ezekiel's descriptions of Tyre even though the comprehensive symbol there is Babylon. Cf. Oswalt, p. 427.

[59] One might compare, for instance, the commercial might of modern Japan.

Cyprus (1b); a deathly hush falls over *Sidon* at the news (2–4); *Egypt* weeps because of the impact on her wheat exports (5; cf. 3); and finally refugees carry the news right back to Tarshish (6). There is more involved here than the personal suffering of the inhabitants of the city. A lot of people had a great deal to lose in the collapse of Tyre. When it came it would hit the Mediterranean world like a Wall Street crash of devastating proportions.

Isaiah does not leave it at that, however. In verses 8–12 he presses beyond the event itself to its cause, and in characteristic prophetic fashion bypasses all secondary causes to trace Tyre's fall to the determined purpose of *the* LORD *Almighty* (9). Sentence had already been passed on the city in heaven, not (take note) because of its wealth, but because of its *pride* – another characteristic theme of Isaiah's preaching (9; cf. 2:11–17). There is no intrinsic connection, of course, between wealth and pride, but sadly they do all too often go hand in hand. The wealth of Tyre had made its merchants *princes* (8), but, like the rich fool in Jesus' parable, they had failed to recognize their accountability to him from whom their wealth had come.[60] Wealth had bred in them an illusion of self-sufficiency which had made God – or at least the true and living God – seem irrelevant. It would take his swift and severe judgment to jolt them back to reality.

But God's judgments on nations within history are seldom final, and that is certainly the case here, for in verses 15–18 Isaiah sketches in the longer-term prospects for Tyre in God's purposes. There is hope in the *seventy years* of verses 15 and 17, a conventional number for a long but limited time.[61] Tyre will not rise quickly, but rise she will, and in the continuation of the *prostitute* image through to verse 17 there is more than a hint that she will return to her old ways.[62] But – and this is where history gives way to eschatology[63] – the wealth she has hoarded up will be taken from her. It will flow into Zion as the rightful inheritance of the people of God (18).

In the succeeding centuries[64] Tyre was to suffer at the hands of Esarhaddon (679–671), Nebuchadnezzar (585–573), Artaxerxes III (343)

---

[60] Cf. *stored up* and *hoarded* in verse 18 with Luke 12:18–19.

[61] *The span of a king's life* (15); cf. Ps. 90:10.

[62] Not trade as such, but unprincipled trade – commerce without morals. Verse 16 probably reflects the soliciting techniques of harlots in Mediterranean ports.

[63] Teaching about the last things.

[64] I.e. following 689. See comment on 23:13.

and Alexander the Great (332), before being rehabilitated by Ptolemy II in 274 BC. But in the end it matters little what fulfilments of the prophecy may be discerned in these troughs and peaks of Tyre's fortunes, for Isaiah's words reach beyond them all to set all that Tyre represents in the light of eternity. Wealth is the gift of God and it will eventually return to the giver (18a). The nations may prostitute themselves in the pursuit of it, but the people of God must not. They are to seek God and his righteousness, and in so doing they will eventually inherit all things (Matt. 5:5; 6:32–33; 1 Cor. 3:21–23).

13. The Isaiah Apocalypse (24:1 – 27:13)

These four chapters together constitute the climax of the whole second part of the book (chapters 13–27). Here particular nations are lost to view as the focus broadens to encompass the whole earth (24:1). Devastating judgment (chapter 24) is followed by song (25:1–5),[65] feasting (25:6–8), song (25:9–12), more song (chapter 26) and still more song (27:1–11). The final two verses (27:12–13) act as a summary conclusion to the whole. The theme is the triumph of God, which is good news (hence the singing) because it means that the reign of sin and death is at an end; the kingdom of God has at last come in its fullness. This 'apocalypse' or 'unveiling' of the end (for that is what the word means) in many ways anticipates that better-known apocalypse, the book of Revelation, which serves as the grand finale of the Bible as a whole.[66]

a. The earth laid waste (24:1–23)

The judgment of God is both terrible and glorious, especially when, as here, it is the final judgment which is in view. Much of chapter 24 is taken up with the *terror* of it, but the *glory* breaks through briefly in the middle (14–16) and again, more brilliantly, at the very end (23).

There are both certainty and expectancy in the opening words of verse 1. The New Revised Standard Version captures the sense well: 'Now the LORD *is about to* lay waste the earth.'[67] For Isaiah the final judgment was

---

[65] The praise here and in 25:9 is the positive counterpart of *the song of the ruthless* (which has been stilled) in 25:5.

[66] Admittedly there are great differences of style, but the basic vision is the same, as well as many of the images: the two cities, the eschatological banquet, the song of the redeemed, etc.

[67] The anticipatory use of the Hebrew participle.

not only certain; it could happen at any moment. He lived every day in the light of it, just as we ourselves must do today as those who await their Lord's return (Luke 12:35–36). That is one reason why the judgment of God is glorious; it is a manifestation of his total sovereignty. As one commentator has put it, 'Only a God whose control of history is so complete that he could bring it to a close at any moment is worth worshipping.'[68] And in exercising that judgment, as verses 1–3 make clear, he will be no respecter of persons. In language reminiscent of the account of the great flood in Genesis 7, Isaiah shows us the earth laid *waste*, and *people* and *priest*, *master* and *servant*, *creditor* and *debtor*, all alike swept away.[69] Social position, wealth, and even religious titles will mean nothing.

Flood gives way to drought in verses 4–6, making it clear that we are dealing not with literal description but with a series of powerful images. There is more connection with what has gone before, however, than first meets the eye. *The earth is defiled*, we are told, because its inhabitants have *broken the everlasting covenant* (5). This is almost certainly a reference to the covenant between God as creator and humankind as creature implicit in the very act of creation itself, and reaffirmed to Noah after the flood (Gen. 9:8–17). It is in this context that we must understand *the laws* and *statutes* referred to in verse 5. These are the basic standards of right behaviour given to the man and woman at creation – especially their responsibility to care for their environment as stewards accountable to God (Gen. 1:26–31; 2:15). The present passage shows us a world so abused by those to whom it was entrusted that it can no longer sustain life: it has been *defiled by its people* (5a). God has given us fair warning of where our abuse of his world is leading us! The solution is not to deify the earth, as some do today (allowing paganism to re-enter by the back door), but to turn back to its creator in repentance before it is too late.

Image is now piled on image. The judged earth is like a vineyard without grapes where, instead of harvest celebrations, there is a hush broken only by groans (7–9), like a joyless *ruined city* (10–12), and like a stripped *olive* grove or vineyard where only bits and pieces are *left* (13).

But then, suddenly, this idea of 'leftovers' is turned on its head. For just as at the time of the great flood there were a faithful few who were spared to inherit a new earth, so, it appears from verses 14–16, will there be a

68 Oswalt, p. 444.
69 Cf. also 18b with Gen. 7:11b.

remnant on the final day. Scattered among the nations will be those who acknowledge the Lord and welcome his judgment as the triumph of right over wrong.[70] Over the scene of desolation, a song of praise goes up from *east* and *west* and from the earth's farthest limits (14–16). This is the 'new song' of Revelation 5:9–10, the song of the redeemed. God will not destroy the righteous with the wicked. He will spare those who have turned to him and waited for his salvation (see 25:9). But Isaiah is too burdened to join that song yet. Verse 16b is the transition back to the judgment material which follows. In verses 17–22 the darkness closes in again.

The basic idea of verses 17–22 is the impossibility of escape for those destined for judgment, whether *people* in general or *kings* or heavenly beings (17, 21). They will be like animals vainly fleeing from a hunter who has anticipated their every move (17–18a). There will finally be nowhere to go because the very ground they tread on will break up under their feet (18b–20). Like captive rebels they will be thrown into *prison*, never to be released (22).[71] This message needs to be sounded clearly today when the church has grown squeamish about the truth of divine retribution. There will be no escape for rebels who refuse to lay down their arms. The *day* on which he will *punish* them has already been entered in God's diary (21a; cf. Acts 17:30–31).

The final goal of judgment, however, is the glory of God, the visible display of his character. And so, in verse 23, the chapter ends fittingly with a burst of light so brilliant that it shames *the sun*. This thumbnail sketch of God's glorious reign over a renewed earth reads like a precis of 2:1–5. But there is surely a touch of special grace in the fact that the redeemed people of God are represented here by 'his [the Lord's] elders', since they were the special objects of his wrath in 3:14 and 9:15 (cf. 1:23).[72] The Lord's triumph will not be for himself alone, but for his people as well. His glory consists not only of his righteousness (15–16), but also of his grace (23). How thankful we should be for that tremendous fact!

---

[70] Note their praise of the Lord as *the Righteous One* (16a).

[71] I take the last line of v. 22 with its disjunctive syntax (in Hebrew) to be a summary statement. *They will be . . . punished* refers back to *the Lord will punish* at the beginning of verse 21, and *after many days* has the same moment in view as *In that day*, also in verse 21. The idea is not so much imprisonment with a view to subsequent punishment (as implied by the NIV translation) as imprisonment which is itself the punishment. After many days they will be shut up, and suffer imprisonment as their eternal lot. Cf. Motyer, pp. 205–206.

[72] So Oswalt, p. 456.

b. The great banquet (25:1–12)

It is fitting that the triumph of God should be celebrated with feasting and song, and this is in fact what we have in this chapter. The banquet in verses 6–8 is certainly the centrepiece, and it is framed by songs of praise: a personal song in verses 1–5, and a communal song in verses 9–12. The theme of both songs is the character of God which has been plainly revealed in his acts of judgment and salvation. And this God is no stranger to the singers; they know him: *you are my God* (1), *this is our God* (9).

The lone singer of verses 1–5 is best taken as Isaiah himself, whose gloom has at last been dispelled by the glorious prospect with which his vision in chapter 24 ended.[73] We all know what it is like to be transported into the heavens by a magnificent song of praise, so that, for a few precious minutes, our present struggles are left far behind and we stand with the angels and the redeemed people of God around the throne and join their song. That is Isaiah's experience here. He is impressed by the sheer power of the Lord's deeds (they are *wonderful*),[74] but even more by their purposefulness and moral character (*perfect faithfulness . . . things planned long ago*, 1b). The *city* of verse 2, like that of the previous chapter, represents the world as a whole organized in opposition to God. He destroys it, not for any spiteful satisfaction he may have in doing so, but in order to bring the *nations* to their senses (3) and to deliver those who have been the victims of their misuse of power (4–5). God always has been and always will be on the side of the *poor* and *needy*. It is something that we who profess to believe in him would do well to remember.

This focus on the poor and needy in the opening song makes it particularly appropriate that final salvation should be pictured in verses 6–8 as *a feast* at which, by implication, the food is free (cf. 55:1). That food is the very finest of fare, and the host is *the Lord Almighty* himself (6).[75] Like the vision of 2:1–5, this one too has both an inclusive and an exclusive aspect: it is for *all peoples* (or 'nations', RSV), but it is provided at only one place, *on this mountain* (Zion). The onus is on the nations to come there if they wish to partake. In view of this, *his* [the Lord's] *people* in verse 8

---

[73] Cf. Young, 2, p. 184.

[74] Like those of the exodus period; cf. Ps. 78:12–16, where 'did miracles' translates a word with the same root.

[75] As generally in the NIV, 'the Lord Almighty' = *Yahweh sĕbā'ôt*, 'Lord of hosts' (armies). The Lord presides as a victorious military commander. The pun (on 'hosts') exists only in English translation!

cannot be restricted to faithful Israelites. It includes all who come to the feast, from whatever nation.

It is, of course, a victory celebration, but in the description of the feast new dimensions of that victory are revealed. It will be total victory because it will include victory over the ultimate enemy – *death* itself (8a; cf. 1 Cor. 15:26). Hence the destruction of the *shroud* or *sheet* in verse 7, which represents the universal sorrow that death has brought into the world, and the wiping away of *tears* in verse 8a. The syntax does not establish any clear time sequence. It simply asserts that the Lord will do all these things: he will make a feast, he will destroy the shroud, he will swallow up death, and he will wipe away all tears. Chapter 55 sheds a little more light (the rich food is abundant pardon), but we have to turn to the New Testament for the full picture. The banquet consists of the blessings of the gospel, of which all are invited to partake (Luke 14:15–24), the decisive victory over death is won in the death and resurrection of Jesus (2 Tim. 1:10), and God's people enter fully into that victory when Jesus returns. It is then that death is finally 'swallowed up' for ever (1 Cor. 15:25–26, 51–57), pain and sorrow (Isaiah's shroud) are removed, and tears are wiped away (Rev. 21:4).[76] Isaiah's words, as always, are pregnant with gospel truth (cf. 1 Cor. 15:26).

But final judgment is just as much an aspect of gospel truth as final salvation, and it is this solemn note that is struck as we move from the end of the banquet scene into the second song. The people of God have waited long for their *salvation* (9), and during this time they have been objects of derision (*disgrace*, 8) in the world. But the *day* of which Isaiah speaks here will see a complete reversal in their fortunes: they will *rejoice and be glad* (9) while their proud enemies (represented by Moab) will be cast down and experience utter humiliation (10–12). The singling out of Moab in this context is at first surprising in view of the felt kinship which seems to underlie the laments of chapters 15 and 16, and the apparent recognition there by at least some Moabites (16:1–5) that their only hope is in Israel's God.[77] But perhaps that is just the point. In the end there will be a great gulf fixed between those who are at the feast and those who are not. It will not suffice to have belonged to a group close to the kingdom, to have stood on its very threshold, or to have known some who entered. Either repentance will bring you to the feast or pride will keep you away, and the

---

[76] The 'curse' of Rev. 22:3 may be a further extension of the 'shroud' image.

[77] We know of at least one Moabite who did in fact cross over at an earlier time (Ruth 1:16–17).

consequences will be unsullied joy or unspeakably terrible judgment. The alternatives which the gospel sets before us are as stark as that.

c. Waiting for the glory that shall be (26:1 – 27:1)

We have seen Isaiah depressed by the painful realities of the present (24:16b) and exultant at the glorious prospect of the future (25:1–5). But between these extremes lies the settled disposition of patient, trustful waiting to which the people of God must return again and again. It is to be their hallmark as they live out their lives in the world as it is. This note, which was struck in 25:9, is now developed at some length in a song which captures beautifully the tension between the promise of the 'then' and the pain of the 'now'. It begins with anticipatory celebration (1–6), turns back to reflect on the pain of waiting (7–19), and concludes with an oracle which confirms the final victory (26:20 – 27:1).[78]

The formula *In that day* runs like a refrain through these chapters (24:21; 25:9; 26:1; 27:1, 2, 12), and it is full of the certainty born of faith. No matter how perplexing or painful the present might be, Isaiah was confident that the whole of human history was converging on a single point which had been determined by God in advance. And then God's people would have much to celebrate. The first stanza of the present song (26:1–6) is about two cities. The *strong city* of verse 1 is the new Zion, the city of God of the future that will rise above the ruins of *the lofty city* (5), the human city which God will have destroyed by his judgment (cf. 24:10; 25:2). He will destroy the false only to raise up the true.[79] While this city is *in the land of Judah* (1; see on 19:17), it should not be understood in narrowly nationalistic terms, for its *gates* are *open* (2), and the one qualification for entrance is a steadfast *trust in the LORD* (3–4).[80] This truth is gloriously filled out for us in the New Testament. We, as the people of the new covenant, have already become citizens of the heavenly Jerusalem (Heb. 12:22) which will one day become an earthly reality (Rev. 21:2). *The righteous nation* of verse 2 is in fact a new people of God drawn from all over the earth (2:3; 24:14–16; 25:6; cf. Rev. 21:24–25). They are the *oppressed* and *the poor* whose righteousness consists simply in this: they have cast themselves wholly upon the Lord for their salvation (6).

---

[78] 27:1 is linked to 26:21 by the key word *punish*. It is the climax of the oracle. Cf. Oswalt, p. 490.

[79] So Oswalt, p. 470.

[80] *The Rock* (4) is a favourite metaphor for the Lord as faithful protector in the Old Testament, e.g. Deut. 32:4; Ps. 18:31; Isa. 30:29.

The keynote for the reflection which follows the song is struck in verse 8: LORD . . . *we wait for you*. While they wait for the final day to dawn, the righteous are perplexed by the perversity and blindness of the wicked who surround them on every hand (10–11). Such people do not understand kindness; the longer the Lord delays the worse they get. Hence the longing for him to act decisively to establish *righteousness* (9, 11b).

More perplexing, however, is the apparent harshness with which the Lord treats the very ones who are looking to him to save them. He chastises them so severely that they twist and turn like *a woman* in labour (16–17). And the result? Nothing but *wind* (18a)! Their commitment to the Lord brings them nothing but frustration and a sense of complete failure (18b). There is surely an acute crisis of faith here which must issue in either despair or a breakthrough to a new understanding of God's ways. It is a testimony to the resilience of Old Testament faith that such crises always do, in fact, turn out to be occasions for fresh light to break through, and that is certainly the case here. The groundwork has already been laid earlier in the song. The Lord has come to the rescue of his people time and again in the past (13–14) and he will certainly do so again (15).[81] But there is one further perplexity to be faced before the breakthrough can come, and it is implicit in verse 19. What about those who die in the time of waiting, who have put their trust in the Lord but experienced no fulfilment? Will they suffer the same fate as the wicked, described in verse 14, and miss out on the triumph to come?[82] Verse 19 issues a resounding 'No!' Their waiting will not be in vain. They will be raised from death to share in the final victory. Here again is that victory over death already glimpsed in 25:8.

The short oracle of 26:20 – 27:1 adds the capstone to the theme of waiting in language that recalls the experience of the Israelites in Egypt. Like them, Isaiah's contemporaries are told to go into their houses and hide themselves until God's *wrath* is past (20; cf. Exod. 12:22–23). That wrath, as the next two verses make clear, will be directed not towards them but towards their enemies, as it was in Egypt. Then there will be an accounting for every crime; nothing will escape his justice (21). The whole

---

[81] With Oswalt and others I take the perfects here to be prophetic, expressing the certainty of what is still future. See verse 12: 'O LORD, you will ordain peace for us' (NRSV).

[82] The word translated 'shades' (NRSV) is common to verses 14 and 19 (*spirits* and *dead* in NIV). 'Though the dead live on in Sheol, the body has been left behind . . . and therefore what survives is less than a whole person.' A. Motyer, *The Message of James: The Tests of Faith* (London: IVP, 2021), p. 43.

monstrous sum of the world's evil, represented by *Leviathan ... the monster* [dragon] *of the sea*,[83] will be vanquished at last (27:1), just as Pharaoh's army was slain in the sea (Exod. 14:27; 15:1).

Isaiah's contemporaries could not put the world to rights any more than their ancestors could, nor were they expected to do so. All the Lord required was trustful waiting. To them the wait seemed long; to him it was only *a little while* (20). So too for us. The truths which break through the clouds in this chapter are trumpeted from the housetops in the New Testament. There the certainty of our own resurrection is signed and sealed by the resurrection of Jesus (1 Thess. 4:13–18), and we are encouraged to count the troubles of the waiting time as nothing compared with the glory that awaits us (Rom. 8:18).

d. Israel in God's ultimate purposes (27:2–13)

As the apocalypse of chapters 24–27 draws to a close, and with it the whole second part of the book, *Israel* comes back into focus as the nation which stands at the centre of God's purposes for the world.[84] Verse 6 sums it up. That notion, of course, is basic to the whole book: God has a plan which embraces all nations, and Israel is destined to play a central role in that plan. But before it can fulfil its calling it must be cleansed. In bringing that central idea back into sharp focus this passage is a fitting climax to chapters 13–27. It ends, as the book does, with the Lord being worshipped on his *holy mountain in Jerusalem* (13b; cf. 66:18–23).

In terms of its structure this chapter follows the same pattern as the previous one. It begins with the future (2–6), swings back to the present (7–11), and ends by returning to the future (12–13). It also continues the theme of the previous chapter: the pain that must be endured before the joy of fulfilment comes.

i. The new song of the vineyard (27:2–6)

This song must be read in the light of the earlier song of the vineyard in 5:1–7. A whole series of contrasts is developed, as shown in the table overleaf.

---

[83] A mythical monster known by various names in Ancient Near Eastern texts dealing with creation. The same 'dragon' imagery is used with reference to the exodus in 51:9. See C. G. Gordon, 'Leviathan: Symbol of Evil', in A. Altmann (ed.), *Biblical Motifs* (Cambridge, MA: Harvard University Press, 1966), pp. 1–9.

[84] *Israel* is not the northern kingdom here, as opposed to Judah. A future situation is in view in which the ideals involved in the original constitution of Israel as a holy nation (Exod. 19:5–6) will be fully realized. For more on 'Israel in the book of Isaiah' see the comment under this heading, above, pp. 22–23.

First song (chapter 5)	Second song (chapter 27)
no fruit	fruit
no rain	rain
abandoned (wall removed)	guarded
thorns and briers	no thorns and briers
overrun	spreads out

In essence this song announces that eventually (*In that day*, 2) the judgment proclaimed in the first song will be totally reversed. Formerly the Lord was angry with Israel and invited her enemies to overrun her. But the time will come when his wrath against her will be spent (4a). Then her enemies (*briers and thorns*) will encroach no more. At the end of the song the Lord speaks like a lover whose love for his beloved is so intense that he almost wishes someone would attack her so that he might have the satisfaction of defending her (4)! But the impression left is that the nations will in fact choose the wiser course of reconciliation (5). The song finishes in verse 5, but verse 6 then makes the great reversal plain. The world will no longer invade the vineyard; the vineyard will invade *the world*, filling it *with fruit*. Here at last will be the fulfilment of the promise made to Abraham in Genesis 12:2–3.

It should not escape our notice that the Lord himself is the singer in this final song of the apocalypse. His people sing to him (24:14–16; 25:1–5; 26:1–6) and he sings over them. The Lord and his people are one, and their joy is complete (Zeph. 3:17).

ii. Conclusion (27:7–13)

In Isaiah's day, however, Israel (represented, after the fall of the northern kingdom in 722, by Judah and Jerusalem)[85] was very far removed from the ideal situation envisaged in verses 1–5. She was in the midst of the cleansing process, when the Lord had broken down the wall of his vineyard and allowed it to be overrun, as graphically described in chapter 1 (especially verses 7–8). So verses 7–11 jolt us back, in Isaiah's characteristic fashion, to present realities. We find ourselves back in the painful waiting period with which so much of chapter 26 was taken up – painful because of the judgment the Lord is bringing to bear. Three things are said about this judgment. First, it is less severe than that which the Lord has already

---

[85] See the comment on 'Israel in the book of Isaiah', above, pp. 22–23.

exercised against Judah's enemies (7; see 7:1–9).[86] Second, it is carefully controlled ('measure by measure', 8, RSV), with no more severity than is required to achieve the desired end.[87] Third, that end is atonement – the removal of what is offensive to God so that forgiveness can become possible (9). The pagan altars referred to here were particularly offensive to the Lord because they represented disobedience to the very first commandment (Exod. 20:3). They indicate that Judah was looking to other things – pagan gods and the nations whose gods they were – instead of to the Lord. King Hezekiah tried to get rid of them, but it is clear from the account of Josiah's reforms, less than a century later, that many remained (2 Kgs 18:4; 23:4–6). The sense of verse 9b seems to be that the *full fruit* of the Lord's cleansing judgment would be seen when, and only when, such objects were totally removed. *The fortified city* of verse 10 may be Jerusalem, but more likely it is representative of the many such fortified cities in Judah which were overrun by the invading Assyrians in the eighth century (cf. 1:7).[88] The Lord had temporarily to withdraw his *compassion* and turn against his people before he could forgive them (11b). The vineyard had to be ravaged before it could become fruitful again. And why? Because the people of Judah were *without understanding* (11; cf. 1:2–3). They could not see the wisdom of entrusting themselves to the only one who could save them. Chastisement is the hard route to fruitfulness. What it produces is good, to be sure (Heb. 12:11), but there is an easier and better way to go if only we will take it (see 1:18; cf. 1 John 1:9).

Two images are used in the closing paragraph (12–13) to express the final destiny of God's people. The first is agricultural. When the threshing (judgment) is over, the precious grains *will be gathered up one by one.*[89] There is great tenderness here, and strong reassurance. The grain will not be destroyed with the chaff. Not a single one of those who have relied on the Lord will ultimately be lost (cf. John 17:12). The second image is cultic (having to do with organized worship). The *great trumpet* of verse 13a is both a proclamation of liberty (Lev. 25:9–55)[90] and a call to *worship* (Num.

---

86 Possibly a reference to the fall of Damascus in 732 and Samaria in 722.

87 The 'measured' exile of this verse is probably not the fall of the northern kingdom but the deportation of many southerners by Sennacherib in the time of Hezekiah. See 1:9 and cf. *ANET*, p. 288.

88 Sennacherib claimed to have destroyed forty-six such 'strong cities'; *ANET*, p. 288.

89 The ideal land once promised to Abraham (see Gen. 15:18) is here envisaged as one vast threshing-floor. This is complemented by the picture of verse 13 in which exiles are gathered from beyond the traditional borders.

90 The arrival of the so-called Year of Jubilee (the fiftieth year) was announced by the blowing of a loud trumpet. It was specifically a time for the cancelling of debts and the freeing of captives. Cf. 1 Thess. 4:16.

29:1–6). As the freed captives of long ago assembled at Mount Sinai to worship the Lord, so will those of the future assemble at *the holy mountain in Jerusalem* for the same purpose (13b). Then and then only will they be the blessing in the midst of the earth that they were always meant to be (6; cf. Exod. 19:5–6).

A fuller picture of that end-time assembly emerges from elsewhere in Isaiah and, of course, from the New Testament. It will not be restricted to saved Israelites but will include people of all nations (2:2–4; 25:6–8). For ultimately the one qualification for inclusion among the people of God is the acknowledgment that salvation is to be found nowhere else than in the God of Israel (45:22).

All the strands of the second major segment of the book, then, converge on this single point: worship – God being acknowledged for who he is. Such worship is not an escape from reality but a return to it, and it is in returning to reality that the world, so long out of joint, will finally be made whole (66:22–23).

Isaiah 28 – 35

3. Human schemes and God's plan

The key issue in chapters 28–35 is whether Judah, and in particular its leaders, will rely on Egypt or on the Lord in the face of the growing threat posed by the ever-increasing power of Assyria. Chapters 30 and 31, which stand more or less centrally within the unit, are wholly taken up with this issue, with 31:1 providing perhaps the most pointed and succinct statement of it. This is not a new issue, of course. We have already met it in passing, so to speak, in chapters 18–20 of part 2. But it is appropriate that it should surface again here as a central issue because of the position of chapters 28–35, immediately before the account of Sennacherib's invasion of Judah in chapters 36–37. As we saw in the Introduction,[1] that invasion was a punitive action taken by Sennacherib in response to a revolt led by Hezekiah. He had refused to pay any further tribute to Assyria and had annexed all the Philistine cities as far south as Gaza, cities which, like Judah, had been part of the Assyrian empire (2 Kgs 18:7–8). It was a foolhardy move, and one which he would almost certainly never have taken without the assurance of military backing from Egypt. When the inevitable showdown came, the Egyptians did in fact take to the field against Sennacherib, but were defeated, leaving Judah to bear the full brunt of Sennacherib's wrath (37:9).[2] Much of Judah was devastated and it was only by a miracle that Jerusalem itself escaped (36:1; 37:36). Hezekiah almost destroyed Judah by listening to those at court who counselled him to rely on Egypt. Chapters 28–35 show how strongly and

---

[1] See pp. 5–6.

[2] Assyrian records refer to an earlier defeat of the Egyptians at Eltekeh; *ANET*, pp. 287–288. The attempted intervention by Tirhakah referred to here appears to have been no more successful.

consistently Isaiah had opposed this foolish counsel in the deepening crisis that led up to the events recorded in chapters 36 and 37.

But how is this third part of the book constructed? We will first observe some particulars and then try to grasp the broader picture. A series of woes spans chapters 28–31, in which the leaders of the nation are denounced for their faithlessness (28:1; 29:1, 15; 30:1; 31:1). One further woe appears in 33:1, but its import is different because it is directed against the 'destroyer' (Assyria) rather than against Judah itself. It signifies a shift from judgment to salvation as the focus of the message as the unit unfolds and begins to move towards its climax. That climax comes in chapter 35 with the joyful return of the Lord's redeemed people to Zion (see especially verse 10). As they go on their way the wilderness blossoms into a garden about them (1–2). But chapter 35 is really paired, in terms of its imagery, with chapter 34, for there a contrasting picture has been presented. The lands of those nations which have set themselves against the Lord are reduced to a sterile desert under his judgment (1–4, 8–10). So chapters 34 and 35 together present, in a climactic way, the twin themes of judgment and salvation which have run through the unit as a whole. The overall structure can be neatly summarized as shown in the table below.[3]

	Chapters	
A.	28–29	The crisis: foolish leaders and false counsel
B.	30–31	False solution: dependence on Egypt
	32–33	True solution: the reign of the Lord as king in the midst of his people
C.	34	The 'desert' which will result from trusting the nations
	35	The 'garden' which will result from trusting God

We are now in a position to explore the message of this major unit in more detail by looking at each of its parts in turn.

1. Foolish leaders and false counsel (28:1 – 29:24)

These two chapters are full of scorn for leaders who have been too arrogant and self-indulgent to heed the warnings that God gave through people like

---

[3] Cf. Oswalt, p. 505.

Isaiah. In chapter 28 the spotlight falls first on the leaders of the northern kingdom (1–13) and then on their southern counterparts (14–22). This chapter ends with a poem (23–29) about the peasant farmer who, in his simplicity, is wiser than the nation's leaders because *His God instructs him and teaches him the right way* (26–29). Chapter 29 then outlines in general terms the measures that the Lord will have to take to bring the nation and its leaders to their senses. It begins with an announcement of judgment on Jerusalem (1–4), and ends with a prediction that eventually

> Those who are wayward in spirit will gain understanding;
>> those who complain will accept instruction.
> (24)

a. The drunkards of Ephraim (28:1–13)

Ephraim here is the northern kingdom, Israel (cf. 7:1–9; 11:13), at least what was left of it after the severe mauling it received from the Assyrians in 733 (2 Kgs 15:29).[4] Its capital city, Samaria, was ideally situated at the head of a fertile valley (1) which extended westward to the Mediterranean Sea. In its heyday it was a beautiful city, and breathtaking views can still be enjoyed from the hill of Samaria where its ruins remain to this day. The *Woe* pronounced on it here (1) anticipates its imminent fall, an event which in fact occurred in 722 (2 Kgs 17:1–6). It is likely, then, that the oracle of verses 1–13 was originally delivered just prior to that date. In its present position in chapter 28, however, it serves as a preface to the oracle against the leaders of Jerusalem (14–22) who were the real targets of Isaiah's preaching in the crisis which led up to Sennacherib's invasion. It seems best therefore to see in verses 1–13 the re-employment of an earlier oracle for rhetorical purposes. The warnings given to Samaria's leaders had been tragically fulfilled. *Therefore* (14a) let their counterparts in Jerusalem take careful note and change their ways while they still have the opportunity to do so.[5]

Isaiah's indictment of Samaria's rulers moves from the more superficial aspects of their reprehensible behaviour to its more profoundly serious

---

[4] Cf. Bright, p. 274.

[5] It is possible that the pronouncements against Jerusalem in chapters 28 and 29 were delivered at the same time as the original denunciation of Samaria (Oswalt, p. 506), but the polemic against dependence on Egypt, implicit in chapters 28 and 29 and explicit in chapters 30 and 31, strongly suggests that it is the later situation, leading up to Sennacherib's invasion in 701, which is in view.

and disturbing aspects. Drunkenness, of course, is serious enough in itself, especially when it is indulged in at a time of national crisis by those who should be providing the steadying hand of firm and godly leadership. Like the revellers of 22:13, they respond to the prospect of imminent disaster (in reality God's judgment, 2) by drinking themselves into a drunken stupor (7–8), clutching at whatever pleasure they can extract from life while it lasts. Such escapism has been the way of fools from time immemorial. It simply postpones the hard encounter with reality which inevitably becomes the more devastating the longer it is avoided. The *wreath* ('proud garland', NRSV) of verse 1a is the beautiful city of Samaria, but it probably also contains a secondary allusion to garlands worn by the drunken revellers within it. Both alike *will be trampled underfoot* by the invading Assyrians (3); the party will suddenly be over (4b). Particularly disturbing was the involvement of the *priests and prophets* (7). These men, if any, might have shed the light of divine revelation (*visions*) on the situation and contributed to the making of the right, if hard, *decisions*.[6] But they, too, had chosen the pathway of irresponsible self-indulgence. Isaiah's disgust at their behaviour knows no bounds (8). What hope is there for a nation when even its spiritual leaders have given themselves over to debauchery?

But now Isaiah presses beyond drunkenness to something even more profoundly disturbing in the behaviour of these leaders, namely, the contempt they show for any who dare to speak the truth to them from God.[7] There has already been a hint of this in the almost casual way the word *pride* has been used twice in verses 1 and 3. Now it is unpacked: the proud city has proud, unteachable leaders. Through the prophets he had sent to them the Lord had offered them *rest* (*měnûḥâ*, 12a) – a word which represents the sum total of all that was promised to Abraham and confirmed to Israel at Mount Sinai, but especially a secure and peaceful existence in the land he had given them (see e.g. Deut. 12:9; 1 Kgs 8:56; cf. Ps. 95:11). *But they would not listen* (12b). That is the fundamental reason the northern kingdom came to grief – the refusal of its leaders to *listen* to the word of God which should have been the very foundation of their national life.

---

[6] For the role of priests in decision-making see Deut. 17:8–13.

[7] Perhaps including Isaiah himself, but it is doubtful that he ever addressed the northern leadership personally. More likely Isaiah is referring to the way they responded to prophets such as Amos and Hosea. See Amos 6:4–10; Hos. 7:5–7.

Verses 9 and 10 (in quotation marks) represent their typical response. They are insulted. They consider themselves to be the nation's teachers and resent being treated (as they see it) as *children* (9). The Hebrew text of verse 10 repeats two short expressions (with a linking preposition) four times each: *tsav latsav tsav latsav, qav laqav qav laqav* (cf. also verse 13). The NIV translates *tsav (ṣaw)* as *do* (from *tsvh [ṣwh]*, 'to command') and *qav (qaw)* as *rule* (possibly related to *qawqāw*, 'might').[8] But in fact the lines in question are quite obscure and there is no consensus among scholars about how they should be rendered.[9] Most likely *tsav* and *qav* are not words at all, but artificial syllables used for teaching infants the letters of the alphabet (in this case *ts[ṣ]* and *q*).[10] The drunken leaders mock the word of God through the prophet as infantile nonsense, childish prattle. *Very well*, says Isaiah, since they will not listen to the Lord when he speaks to them through the simple, clear message of the prophets, he will *speak to* them through the 'prattle' of foreigners (the invading Assyrians), and the result will be not rest but ruin (11, 13).[11] They will have what they have chosen. We may put ourselves above the word of God if we will, but there will be a price to pay; God is not mocked (Gal. 6:7). The tragedy, of course, is that when it is leaders who sin it is the whole community that suffers. Isaiah will have nothing of the currently fashionable separation of public and private morality, with its corollary that the private lives of public figures are entirely their own affair, for which they should not be called to account. Nor, at a later time, would John the Baptist. That doughty warrior lost his head for confronting a powerful political figure with the truth about his private conduct (Matt. 14:1–12). Jesus, too, humanly speaking, sealed his fate by his uncompromising exposure of the hypocrisy of the Jewish leaders of his day (Matt. 23:8–36). Our own relative silence on such matters today probably springs more from cowardice and unfaithfulness than from any careful reflection on whether such costly confrontation is required of us. But before we move out into the world we would do well to make sure that our own house is in order, for it is the leaders of God's

---

[8] See BDB, p. 876. *Qawqāw* occurs in the phrase 'a nation *mighty* and conquering' in 18:2, 7 (NRSV). Cf. NIV's 'an *aggressive* nation'.

[9] NRSV's better-known 'precept upon precept . . . line upon line' is more plausible, given the possible occurrence of *tsav (ṣaw)* as 'command' in Hos. 5:11 (RV), and the use of *qav (qaw)* as 'line' in, e.g., 1 Kgs 7:23 and Ezek. 47:3. But even this is, at best, an educated guess.

[10] See the NIV footnote and cf. Clements, p. 228, who cites Fohrer in support of this suggestion.

[11] Cf. 1 Cor. 14:21–22, where Paul quotes this passage in support of his assertion that 'tongues . . . are a sign, not for believers but for unbelievers'. The Corinthians should not jump to the conclusion that an abundance of 'tongues' is a sign of God's approval!

people whom Isaiah calls to account here. How can the church be effective in demanding integrity of secular leaders unless its own leaders take seriously the need for it?

On the whole, the atmosphere in this section is heavy. Light does break through briefly at one point, however. Corrupt leadership will not ultimately ruin God's people. The day will come when a *remnant* will recognize that the Lord is Israel's true *crown* of glory and her only sure defence (5–6). These two verses were probably placed here rather than at the end because they complete the 'wreath/crown' theme of verses 1–4.[12]

b. The covenant with death (28:14–22)

Like a skilled orator, Isaiah has approached his target group indirectly (cf. Amos 1 – 2), but now he unleashes on them the full force of his inspired rhetoric. *Scoffers*, in verse 14, is a strong indictment indeed, since scoffing, in Old Testament thought, is the very last degree of ungodliness (Ps. 1:1). The rulers in Jerusalem are, if anything, worse than those in Samaria had been. The words attributed to them in verse 15 are highly ironic. They themselves would hardly have described their alliance with Egypt in these terms, but Isaiah puts into their mouths words which show the real import of what they have done.[13] They have in reality *entered into a covenant with death* and *made an agreement* with *the realm of the dead* (Sheol; see on 14:9 and 26:19). If they think God's judgment will pass them by as it did their ancestors, they are mistaken.[14] The promise of effective support which the alliance offered was a false hope, and the faithless diplomacy by which it was constructed was therefore a 'refuge of lies' (17, NRSV). Like the fool's house in Matthew 7:26–27, it would be swept away. Or to put it another way (in one final change of metaphor), having made their *bed* they will have to lie on it, but they will find that it is *too short*; it will not give them any comfort or protection (20).[15]

These were not idle threats, as Jerusalem's leaders were soon to learn to their great loss. But neither did they represent the Lord's normal attitude to his people or his way of relating to them. Much more typical were his

---

[12] *And these also* (7) then resumes the indictment of the leaders, as we have seen. Cf. the similar placement of verse 16 within verses 14–22.

[13] Cf. Oswalt, p. 517.

[14] The allusion is to the coming Assyrian invasion on the one hand (the *overwhelming scourge*; cf. 8:8; 10:26), and to the escape of the Israelites when the Lord 'went through' the land of Egypt on the other (Exod. 12:23). The connection with Exod. 12:23 is clearer in the NRSV.

[15] Verse 20 probably quotes a popular proverb.

actions at *Mount Perazim* and *Gibeon* referred to in verse 21. At Perazim he gave victory to David by breaking through his enemies like a bursting flood (2 Sam. 5:20), and at Gibeon he defeated Israel's enemies by raining down hailstones upon them from heaven (Josh. 10:11). That is how he would prefer to act now, and that is why he appeals to his people in verse 22 to stop their scoffing.[16] But since they will not listen, he must turn his judgment, pictured as flood and *hail* in verse 17, against his own people and use their enemies as his instrument to punish them. It is the very reverse of the way things used to be, and not at all the way the Lord desires them to be. Like a loving father who must discipline his rebellious son, he does what he must do (*his strange work . . . his alien task*) with a heavy heart (21b; cf. 1:4–6). A parent who acts in this way does so with an eye to the future – to the good that will come if what is hard but necessary is done now.

The same basic thought underlies the image of the *precious corner-stone*, the *sure foundation* (16), which stands centrally within the unit and is in many ways the key to the whole. The Lord demolishes what is false only that the true may rise in its place. He acts in the interests of the long term. His ultimate aim is not the destruction of Zion but its renewal. Demolition is a necessary, if distasteful, prelude to rebuilding. And the Lord is already laying the foundation for that new Zion of the future (*See, I lay . . . a sure foundation*). There has been a great deal of discussion among scholars about the identity of the stone,[17] but it seems best to view it in context as another image of the faithful remnant who were even then gathering around Isaiah (see on 8:16). The stone bears an inscription which gives the hallmark of this community: the one who trusts will never be dismayed.[18] It represents collectively those who, very much against the current trend, placed their whole confidence in the Lord and waited quietly and confidently for him to act. It was from among this faithful remnant that the Messiah finally came, which is why the New Testament writers see this verse fulfilled ultimately in Christ (Matt. 21:42; Luke 20:17; Rom. 9:33; Eph. 2:20; 1 Pet. 2:4–6).

---

16 The double reference to scoffing and mocking (from the same Hebrew root) in verses 14 and 22 forms a literary bracket around the unit.

17 For the various alternatives that have been proposed, see Oswalt, p. 578.

18 Taking the last line of verse 16 as an inscription. Cf. the quotation marks in NRSV. It was common in the Ancient Near East, as it is today, for foundation stones to be inscribed. For some examples see *ANET*, pp. 653–665.

c. The parable of the farmer (28:23–29)

Just as Jesus often used parables to illustrate his teaching, so Isaiah does here. It may be an already existing parable which he presses into service,[19] but whether it is his own creation or not it certainly serves his purposes well. It relates to what he has just been saying in at least two main ways.

First, it illustrates God's various ways of working in history. Sometimes he deals harshly with his people, and sometimes he acts with great tenderness towards them. Sometimes he saves them from their enemies; sometimes he gives them over to their enemies. Why do his ways change so much? The parable gives the answer. A *farmer* changes his manner of working according to the materials he is working with and the stage he is at. So too the Lord changes his manner of working in history. But his ways are not haphazard; he is working according to a plan. Most of the processes described in the parable suggest pain – ploughing, threshing, grinding – but all contribute to the final good of food production. In a similar way the Lord's severe dealings with his people are directed towards a good end which he constantly has in view, as we have seen (16, 21).

The second connection is via the theme of *wisdom*, to which our attention is pointedly drawn at the end of both sections of the parable (26, 29). In acting as he does the farmer is simply putting into practice a wisdom that he has received from God.[20] That is why his work is so productive: he is open to God's wisdom and willing to be guided by it, unlike the proud, foolish leaders of Jerusalem. Like many of Jesus' parables, this apparently gentle and reassuring picture of rural life has a sting in its tail.[21]

The issue of the folly (i.e. false wisdom) of the nation's leaders is taken up and developed further in the next chapter; so the parable points forwards as well as backwards. Again and again Isaiah has reminded his hearers that in the short term the fate of Jerusalem hangs on the way its leaders respond to the warnings he has sounded, but that its final destiny is secure because of the Lord's unswerving commitment to make it the centre of a renewed earth (see 1:18–20; 2:1–4; 3:13–15; 4:2–6; and so on).

In chapter 29, Isaiah deals first with the city (1–8) and then with its leaders (9–16). In both sections the short-term prospects, which are bleak,

---

[19] Cf. the proverb in verse 20.

[20] Perhaps through others who taught him to farm. The point is that all such wisdom comes from God, whatever the channel.

[21] Cf. the response of the religious leaders of Jesus' day to the parable of the vineyard: 'they knew he was talking about them' (Matt. 21:45).

are presented first, followed by the long-term prospects, which are good. A renewed Zion will finally have leaders who, like the farmer in the parable of this chapter, 'will accept instruction' (29:24; cf. 28:26).

d. Fire in the fireplace (29:1–24)

There is no doubt that *Ariel* in verses 1, 2 and 7 is a code word for Jerusalem, described in more familiar terms in verse 1 as *the city where David settled* (cf. 2 Sam. 5:6–10) and in verse 8 as *Mount Zion*. In fact, it is this sustained focus on Jerusalem/Zion which unifies this first part of the chapter. But Ariel appears to be a term which Isaiah has used for his own purposes at this point, since it is not used as a name for Jerusalem anywhere else in the book or, for that matter, in the entire Bible. It must bear, in a very pointed way, on the specific message which Isaiah is delivering in these particular verses. It means 'a hearth' or, more specifically, 'an altar hearth' – the flat surface of the altar on which a fire was lit to consume the sacrifices (Ezek. 43:15). It alludes to Jerusalem as the religious centre of the nation, the place where the temple was situated and the Lord was worshipped, especially through the offering of sacrifices (note the reference to the annual *cycle* of religious *festivals* in verse 1b). But the word as Isaiah uses it has a terrible barb in it, for it also foreshadows the judgment that the Lord is going to bring on the city: *Yet I will besiege Ariel . . . she will be to me like an altar hearth* (2).[22] That is, the Lord is going to light another kind of fire in Jerusalem, the fire of his judgment (cf. 4:4), and when he does so the entire city will be like one vast blazing altar hearth. Hence the opening *Woe* (1; cf. 28:1; 29:15; 30:1; etc). Jerusalem was heading for flaming judgment because it was on a collision course with the Lord.

Sometimes we need to hear old truths in a new way if they are to shock us out of our complacency and stir us to needed action. The foolish notion that the externals of religious observance can of themselves protect us from God's judgment is one that the Old Testament prophets attack again and again. Isaiah has already done so in 1:12–17, and will do so again later in this chapter (13–14). He is not saying anything new here, but hammering home a familiar message in a particularly vivid manner. False religion is the very worst kind of pride because it attempts to make God our servant instead of recognizing that we are his. Isaiah predicts that the effect of the

---

[22] See NIV footnote.

Lord's judgment will be to reduce proud Jerusalem to the most abject weakness and helplessness (4)[23] before he at last turns his judgment (*flames of a devouring fire*) against her enemies (5–8).

So much for the city. Now the focus sharpens again so that we can take a closer look at its people. The picture that is drawn is damning: they are *blind*, *drunk* and *stunned* (9–10)[24] – and this is both their own choice and God's judgment on them (cf. 6:9–10). The *vision* or revelation of God's purposes that has been given to them through Isaiah has become like a *sealed . . . scroll* to them (11–12; cf. 8:16), and for all of this it is the religious leaders who are principally to blame. In view of what has gone before we might have expected Isaiah to single out the priests. Instead he lays the major blame at the feet of *the prophets* and *the seers* (10, 14). These were the people who, in a crisis situation, should have been able to bring a contemporary word of revelation or wise counsel to bear (cf. 28:7 and comment). But instead of being people of insight who might have cut through to the heart of the problem, they had deliberately fallen in with the establishment and pursued a course which they knew the Lord disapproved of. This is why they *hide their plans from the LORD* and do their work in the dark where they foolishly pretend that God cannot see them (15). In order to justify their actions they have to deny God's right to tell them what to do and, by implication, claim that it is they who are wise and he (their Maker!) who *knows nothing* (16): all of this (take note) while retaining their religious titles and the meticulous observation of the externals. It is truly astounding what depths of inconsistency religious people are capable of, especially in positions of leadership, where backroom decisions and policies all too often belie the faith in God that is professed in the pulpit. The *Woe* of verse 15 will be picked up in 30:1 and elaborated in terms of the determination to pursue an alliance with Egypt. This is the faithless plan which the leaders of Isaiah's day were hatching in the dark.

To rectify the situation the Lord will have to take drastic action, and this is exactly what is signified by the *Therefore* of verse 14: *Therefore once more I will astound these people with wonder upon wonder*. This kind of language is regularly used in the Old Testament of the mighty acts of God, works of such a nature that only God himself could be the doer of them

---

[23] The picture is of a captive grovelling in the dust before the conqueror.

[24] Cf. NRSV: 'in a stupor'.

(e.g. Judg. 6:13; Ps. 78:11). The miracles which accompanied his rescue of the Israelites from Egypt were such acts (Exod. 3:20; 15:11), and there is an allusion back to those events here in the phrase *once more*. What the Lord will do about the present situation will be just as 'wonderful' as his deliverance of the Israelites from Egypt. But it will be far less pleasant for the present generation, for it is not a foreign tyrant that they are enslaved to but their own foolish *wisdom*. That is what the Lord must destroy if they are to be free (14b), and we have already seen earlier in the chapter the means that he will use. The outcome, as Isaiah describes it in verses 17–21, will be a complete reversal of the present situation. The *deaf* will hear and the *blind* will see, so that the *scroll* of divine revelation will no longer be sealed (18; cf. 11–12). The proud will be abased and the meek exalted, and instead of the empty, insincere worship of verse 13 there will be heartfelt, joyful praise to the Lord, *the Holy One of Israel* (19–21). The final paragraph sums up[25] the great reversal and points to its significance: it will mean that everything that the Lord had in mind when he *redeemed Abraham* (by calling him out of pagan idolatry) so long ago will finally be a reality. God will be honoured and worshipped by a people who no longer trust their own wisdom but humbly rely on his (23–24).

Certain details of this chapter seem to point to the events of 701 when Sennacherib invaded Judah – especially the sudden reversal suffered by Zion's enemies (3, 5–8; cf. 37:36). Others seem more relevant to the events of 587 when Jerusalem was literally set ablaze by Nebuchadnezzar (2; cf. 2 Kgs 25:9). But clearly *the hordes of all the nations that fight against Mount Zion* in verse 8 (and cf. verse 7) includes more than either Assyria or Babylon, and the great reversal of verses 5–8 and 17–21 is more wide-ranging than anything that was accomplished in either 701 or 587 BC. The chapter as a whole is a *vision* (11) which presents the long view of God's plan for Zion. The events of 701 and 587 were but two significant steps in its implementation.

The *very short time* ('a very little while', NRSV) of verse 17 is not to be taken literally. As in 26:20, it represents God's perspective on history rather than the perspective of those who experience the historical process at ground level, so to speak. The great truth that Isaiah affirms again and again is that God is behind the process, directing it to a glorious end. If that end seems distant to us and we cannot see how God is at work in

---

[25] This is the force of the *Therefore* of verse 22; Oswalt, pp. 539–540.

contemporary events, that is simply because we are not God. He has shown us enough of his character and ways, however, to provide a firm basis for our wholehearted trust and obedience. We shall not achieve a better end or get there more quickly by rejecting God's wisdom and living by our own, as the leaders of Judah in Isaiah's day did.

2. A false solution: dependence on Egypt (30:1 – 31:9)

Chapters 30 and 31 must be read together if their message is to be grasped properly. They both begin by denouncing the alliance with Egypt in the most explicit terms (30:1–5; 31:1–3). In the latter parts of both chapters, however, different but complementary emphases are developed. Chapter 30 focuses on the grace which the Lord longs to show to his people (30:18ff.), while chapter 31 centres on the repentance that needs to be forthcoming before that grace can be extended (31:6ff.). In the crisis which subsequently developed, Hezekiah did in fact turn wholeheartedly to the Lord, who saved Jerusalem at the last moment by his gracious intervention (37:1, 14–20, 36). So these two chapters are closely connected in both their setting and their themes. Like chapters 28–29, they reflect the impassioned preaching of Isaiah in the worsening situation leading up to Sennacherib's invasion of 701.

Chapter 30, then, revolves around the contrasting notions of rebellion and grace. The first keynote is struck in verses 1 and 9 (*obstinate children, rebellious people*) and the second in verse 18 (*Yet the LORD longs to be gracious . . .*).

a. Rebellious children (30:1–17)

Talk of rebellion necessarily had political overtones in the eastern Mediterranean world of Isaiah's day. The small states of the region were all chafing under Assyrian control. Rebellion, in the political sense, was very much in the air, and the alliance with *Egypt* was part and parcel of just such an act of rebellion by Hezekiah, as we have seen (2 Kgs 18:7). But while these political overtones are certainly present, the primary reference here is to rebellion against God. This is clear from the word *children* (literally, 'sons'), which points at once to the special relationship between the Lord and those who are addressed here (cf. 1:2), and it becomes even clearer from the way in which their rebelliousness is subsequently described. Like the 'rebellious son' of Deuteronomy 21:18–21, these 'rebellious sons' (Isaiah uses the same two Hebrew words) are un-teachable; they 'will not hear' (NRSV) the instruction of him whose sons they are (9).[26] Their determination to rebel against Assyria (with Egyptian support) is the political expression of a rebelliousness which runs far deeper.

It may be strange to modern ears to hear politics and religion so intimately connected, but for the people of God in Old Testament times life was not compartmentalized into the sacred and the secular as it all too often is with us. The one Lord was Lord of all, and whether or not you respected his lordship was inevitably reflected in the way you made political decisions, just as in any other sphere. And as far as going *down to Egypt* was concerned, either to seek *protection* (2) or to acquire *horses* (i.e. for battle, 30:16; 31:1), the issues of obedience and disobedience were particularly clear, for the Lord had declared his mind on the matter long ago (Exod. 13:17; Deut. 17:16), and had now confirmed it in no uncertain terms through the preaching of Isaiah. It was forbidden.[27] The Lord had demonstrated his superiority over Egypt and its gods at the exodus and had been known to Israel ever since as 'the LORD your God, who brought you out of Egypt' (Exod. 20:2). Theologically speaking, to go down to Egypt for help (2) was to commit apostasy. But it was also just plain bad defence policy in terms of contemporary political realities. Egypt had failed to give effective support to Ashdod only ten years earlier (see on 20:1–6); why should Judah's leaders place such confidence in her now, especially with so much at stake? It is this proven ineffectiveness of Egypt which lies behind the jibe of verse 7: *Therefore I* [the Lord] *call her Rahab the Do-Nothing* (cf. 51:9).[28]

But it is not the way of rebels to listen to reason. The series of short oracles which comprises verses 1–17 reveals the determination and speed with which the nation's leaders pressed ahead with their *plans* (1) despite Isaiah's entreaties. Judah's envoys had already reached *Zoan* and *Hanes* in the Nile Delta (4); pack animals pressed southward through the wild and desolate *Negev* region of southern Judah, carrying treasures to buy Egypt's help (6); pressure was being applied to the nation's prophets to tone down their preaching and toe the official party line (10–11) and, with complete

---

[26] In particular, the term for 'rebellion' is *srr*, as in Deut. 21:18. A different word, *mrd*, is used in 2 Kgs 18:7.

[27] Cf. Oswalt, p. 544.

[28] Rahab was a mythical monster representing the powers of chaos, and sometimes, as here, used as a symbolic name for Egypt. See Clements, p. 245, and my comments on Leviathan at 27:1.

lack of reality, *swift horses* (from Egypt) were being promoted as the panacea for all the nation's ills (16). All of this has about it the marks of an indecent haste which is the very antithesis of that confident waiting on God which is the hallmark of those who believe (18b; cf. 28:16). And Isaiah could see only too clearly where *this sin* (13) was leading – to disaster, compared in verses 13 and 14 to the collapse of a *wall* and the shattering of a clay pot. One day there would be nothing left of the rebels' grand plan: the Assyrians would stand at the door with all Judah in ruins behind them.[29] Jerusalem itself would stand isolated and forlorn in the midst of a ravaged land, *like a flagstaff on a mountaintop, like a banner on a hill* (17; cf. 1:8).

b. Gracious Lord (30:18)

Now, however, comes the turning point of the chapter and with it the profound irony which lies at the heart of its message. *The LORD longs to be gracious*, and his eagerness to be so is expressed by the fact that *he will rise up* to do it. He stands on tiptoe, so to speak, ready to extend his mercy to the rebels. But since he is also *a God of justice* he can bless only those *who wait for him*. Sadly, the leaders of Judah refuse to do this and insist on rushing headlong to disaster. Therefore, since they will not wait for him, he must wait for them.[30] The picture is like that of the loving father in Jesus' parable of the prodigal son (Luke 15:11–32). And just as the father's grace to the returned prodigal is extravagant in the parable, so is the Lord's grace to the rebels of Judah here as soon as they 'cry' out to him (19), and it is with this that the balance of the chapter is taken up. Thus verse 18 points forwards as well as backwards. It is the pivot on which the whole chapter turns, and gives us a profound insight into the heart of God: he is the God who waits.

How thankful we should be for this! God is patient with his people still, no less than with rebel Judah of old or the prodigal in Jesus' parable. But such grace gives us no licence to become lax. Note carefully the words of the apostle: 'Or do you despise the riches of his kindness and forbearance and patience? Do you not realize that God's kindness is meant to lead you to repentance?' (Rom. 2:4, NRSV). To be given time to repent is a great mercy which should be grasped with profound gratitude.

---

[29] Oswalt, p. 554.

[30] Cf. the NRSV of verse 18a: 'Therefore the LORD waits to be gracious.' This important play on 'wait', which accurately reflects the underlying Hebrew, is unfortunately obscured in the NIV.

c. Grace in action (30:19–33)

The grace that the Lord will show towards his people when they repent is depicted here under three images: the Lord the teacher (19–22), the Lord the healer (23–26) and the Lord the warrior (27–33).

It would be easy to press the picture of the Lord as the waiting God too far and see him as purely passive up to the point where repentance is manifested. But the complementary picture which Isaiah now presents, of the Lord as the teacher,[31] shows that this is not so. He disciplines his people (20a), reveals himself to them in their suffering (20b), and gently shows them the way out of it (21). That is, as teacher he actually encourages and makes possible the response for which he waits. His grace is at work before repentance as well as after it. Of course, the Lord had always been Israel's teacher (see 30:9), but her people, and especially her leaders, had been too blind – wilfully so – to recognize him as such (29:9). Verses 20 and 21 of the present passage indicate how this situation will finally be reversed. In the midst of the *adversity* and *affliction* which he will bring upon them, the Lord will reveal himself afresh to them as their teacher, and this time they will recognize him as such and be willing to be taught by him. The *voice behind you* of verse 21 points to the new, delightful intimacy which will then exist between God and his people. The casting away of idols, in verse 22, is the natural consequence of this. For idols speak of divided loyalties, and there can be no place for that among those who have returned wholeheartedly to the Lord as their teacher. His very first commandment is: 'You shall have no other gods besides me' (Exod. 20:3; see NIV footnote).

In an economy largely based on agricultural production, the welfare of the people was intimately bound up with the state of their land. Thus, from the restored relationship between the Lord and his people (19–22), Isaiah goes on at once to speak of the restored fruitfulness of their land (23–26), and it is in this context that he speaks of the Lord as the healer, who *binds up the bruises of his people and heals the wounds he inflicted* (26b). What is envisaged here is a complete reversal of the situation presented in the opening chapter of the book. There the Lord's discipline had left Judah devastated, and her land devoured by aliens (1:7). Metaphorically she is described as bruised and bleeding, with her wounds unbandaged (1:6). Here, in chapter 30, the wounds are bound up and the

---

[31] The plural noun *mōrêkā* ('your teachers') is used with a singular verb *lōʾ yikkānēp* ('will not be hidden'), suggesting that the plural is honorific rather than literal, referring to Yahweh as the supreme Teacher (see NRSV).

land restored. Abundant, God-given rain ensures bumper crops and prosperous herds, and working animals that are strong because of their rich fare (23–24). If chapter 1 refers to the devastation caused by Sennacherib's invasion, this present passage refers to the recovery that would follow it, by God's grace. But at the same time it also envisages something greater, of which the immediate recovery would be but a foretaste. For Isaiah goes on, in verses 25 and 26a, to speak of a transformed cosmos in which streams will flow on the tops of mountains and the sun will be seven times brighter! Clearly, at this point Isaiah leaves the plane of history and fires our imagination with images of paradise – a world too beautiful for words to describe or finite minds to grasp (cf. Rev. 21 – 22). The same long-range perspective is implied by the ominous reference in verse 25 to *the day of great slaughter, when the towers fall* (cf. 2:15). Something far more terrible than Sennacherib's invasion must befall the world before the new, perfect age of God's blessing can come – a truth which Isaiah constantly holds before us (2:12–22; 13:6–16; 24 – 25). The world must be purged of its evil by God's judgment before, finally and for ever, 'the sun of righteousness will rise with healing in its rays' (Mal. 4:2).

The third picture, of the Lord as the warrior (27–33), has the same double focus that we have seen in the previous image. In the foreground stands the coming overthrow of *Assyria* (31; cf. 37:36).[32] But in the background stands the final, universal judgment, when the Lord's wrath will fall on *the nations* (28). The unit contains a mixture of metaphors (notice the *sieve* and *bit* in verse 28), but by far the dominant one is that of the warrior (see especially verses 30, 32, and cf. 27–28a).

The Israelites first came to know the Lord as warrior at the exodus when he delivered them by overthrowing the Egyptians in the Red Sea and bound them to himself in the covenant at Mount Sinai (Exod. 15; 19 – 20). Much of the imagery of water and fire in the present passage is drawn from that exodus background, and the general context here, as there, is the gracious action of God for his people. During their history, the Lord has from time to time had to fight *against* them in order to discipline them, but finally he will show them his grace again by fighting *for* them and overthrowing their enemies.[33] The coming defeat of the Assyrians will

---

[32] The same Hebrew verb, *nkh*, 'to smite', 'to slay', is used in both places.

[33] The curious expression *The Name of the Lord comes* in verse 27 probably alludes to the revelation of his name (i.e. character) at the time of the exodus (Exod. 3:15; 6:2). He will display in his future actions the same character that he displayed at the exodus.

be a foretaste of that final victory. And just as the Lord's victory at the Red Sea was celebrated in song (Exod. 15), so will his final victory be (29).[34]

But is it proper to celebrate something as terrible as what is described here? (See especially verse 33 with its talk of *fire* and *burning sulphur.*)[35] The unhesitating reply of Isaiah and of the Bible as a whole is, 'Yes!' The singing, joyful hearts which God's people will have when God overthrows their enemies will be his gift to them (29). There will be no regret or wishing that things were other than they are, for God's judgment will be seen to be the absolutely just and right thing that it is (Rev. 19:1–3). The Lord's action as warrior is the final expression of his grace to those who have cried out to him for salvation (19). There can be no salvation, however, without judgment, and in the end the choice is ours. The Lord is the warrior, and we must all finally meet him as either deliverer or destroyer.

d. Reasons for repentance (31:1–5)

With the transition to chapter 31, Isaiah is approaching his climactic appeal in 31:6: 'Return, you Israelites, to the One you have so greatly revolted against.' But in building to that climax, like the good preacher that he is, he reiterates his two main points: Egypt's help is worthless (1–3; cf. 30:1–17), and in any case unnecessary, for the Lord himself will fight for Zion and overthrow the Assyrians (4–5; cf. 30:19–33). This latter point is then repeated in verses 8–9, after the appeal of verse 6, as if to underline the fact that while grace is promised before repentance (and is therefore a ground for it), that same grace can be fully experienced only when repentance has taken place.[36]

The first reason for repentance is the threat of impending judgment. The *Woe* of verse 1 is the last pronounced on Judah in this part of the book (cf. 29:1, 15; 30:1), and may well have been sounded later than the others when Sennacherib was on his final approach to Jerusalem. By then the

---

[34] *The night you celebrate a holy festival* is almost certainly an allusion to the Passover, which began at night and celebrated the exodus. By Isaiah's time it involved pilgrimage to Zion (Deut. 16:1–8; 2 Chr. 30). In verse 29 the joyful celebration of the Lord's final victory is pictured as a great, final Passover. Cf. also the *tambourines* of verse 32 with those of Exod. 15:20.

[35] *The king* (i.e. of Assyria) is pictured as burning on a huge funeral pyre. *Topheth* ('a burning place', RSV) was a place of pagan worship, sometimes involving the incineration of children, in the Valley of Hinnom, just south of Jerusalem (2 Kgs 23:10). The fire is not to be taken literally here, however, any more than in verses 27 and 30. Sennacherib was not in fact burnt at Topheth, but returned to Nineveh and died there (37:37). Rather, the verse uses poetic language to depict the terrible, final judgment which awaits those who set themselves against God, of whom the king of Assyria was a prime example. Cf. Mark 9:44–48.

[36] Cf. Oswalt, p. 576.

futility of looking to Egypt for help had become fully apparent and it was clear to all that disaster was imminent. It was no time for mincing words or pulling punches, and Isaiah certainly does not do so; he is nothing if not hard-hitting in verses 1–3. There is a hint in the past tenses of verse 1 (unfortunately not reflected in the NIV or NRSV) of past decisions whose consequences have now come home to roost. He speaks of those who trusted in *chariots*, but did *not look to the Holy One of Israel*, and did not *seek help from the LORD*. And there is biting sarcasm in the opening words of verse 2: *Yet he too is wise and can bring disaster.* Those who thought they were wiser than God (5:21) are about to learn otherwise. *That wicked nation* ('the house of the evildoers', NRSV) is Judah (cf. 1:4) and *those who help* them the Egyptians, and the Lord has passed judgment on both alike: *all will perish together* (3). A contrast is developed in verse 3 between *mere mortals* and *God*, *flesh* and *spirit*. It is clear that it is an unequal contest; human beings cannot fight against God and win. Judah appears to be facing certain ruin, especially in view of the second line of verse 2: *he* [God] *does not take back his words*. But it is not so. As verses 4–5 immediately make clear, another possibility still exists. The point of verses 1–3 is that unless there is a radical change on Judah's part, the Lord will fully implement his threat, and nothing that people can do will stop him. We have to know that God cannot be manipulated before we are ready to throw ourselves upon his mercy.

The second reason for repentance is the promise of salvation or, more precisely, of a Saviour – a true, effective one instead of the false, worthless one that Egypt had proved to be. That Saviour is of course the Lord, pictured as *a lion* in verse 4 and as *birds hovering* in verse 5. And the two are complementary. As Saviour the Lord is both strong and determined (like the lion) and solicitous and protective (like the birds). It would of course be possible to press the word *prey* too far and to take verse 4 in a negative sense: Judah will be devoured and nothing can save her.[37] But the way verse 5, which is clearly positive, follows immediately and without explanation speaks strongly against this. It is the strength and determination with which the lion stands guard over what is its own that are the point.[38] The logic of verses 1–5 as a whole seems to be as follows: *Woe to those who go down to Egypt* . . . (1–3), for the Lord, and he alone, is

---

[37] Cf. Young, 2, pp. 377–378.
[38] Cf. Oswalt, p. 574.

Jerusalem's true Saviour. What the two pictures of verses 4 and 5 amount to is a promise that the Lord himself will fight for[39] and protect Jerusalem. That promise still stood when Sennacherib's envoys were finally at the gates (37:35), and Hezekiah then had, at last, the wisdom and humility to claim it.

e. Repentance and its fruits (31:6–9)

Repentance is radical. It is not just giving up this or that sin, but a complete turnabout in our stance towards God, and it goes right to the root of our sinfulness. As for the prodigal son, it is a recognition that we are rebels, and a return to the One we have so deeply offended (6; cf. Luke 15:18–19). Its consequences, too, are radical: all other gods have to go (7) in order to clear the way for the full enjoyment of God's blessing (8–9).

For Isaiah, idolatry was the ultimate outward sign of rebellion against God. Idolatry had taken hold long before the alliance with Egypt was conceived (2:8; cf. Exod. 32:1–6). It was, we may say, the cancer which lay at the root of all the nation's ills, for it showed that the Lord no longer had his people's undivided loyalty. It is natural, therefore, that in calling for radical repentance, Isaiah should again point to the casting away of idols as the evidence that will confirm it (cf. 2:20; 17:7–8).

The final two verses (8–9) put the seal on this call to repentance by reiterating God's promise to deal decisively with the Assyrians (cf. 30:27–33). But now a new element is added: the Assyrian shall be destroyed by *a sword*, but not a *human sword . . . not of mortals* (8). That is, the people of Jerusalem will not even have to fight. The Lord will intervene miraculously, and they will receive his promised salvation as a gift. Such is his grace to those who repent. The fulfilment is recorded in 37:36.

Again, however, as so often in this book, the immediate horizon of unfolding events does not exhaust the prophet's vision. For in the last half of verse 8 and the first part of verse 9 the figurative sword of verse 8a gives way to a literal one, and what seems to be in view here is the final collapse and destruction of Assyria – an event which did not occur until 612, with the fall of Nineveh. And the closing lines of verse 9, which speak of the Lord's *fire . . . in Zion*, also embrace more than the overthrow of Sennacherib's army in 701. For the fiery presence of the Lord in Zion has

---

[39] Oswalt (p. 574) points out that while ṣābā' 'al elsewhere means 'fight against', there are only four such references in all, and so this evidence is hardly conclusive. The NIV's *do battle on Mount Zion* (i.e. as its saviour) is more likely in this context.

already acquired, from such passages as 4:2–6 and 29:5–8, connotations of the Lord's future reign, when all Zion's enemies will be destroyed. The Lord's fire in Zion will then be (for Judah) no longer the fire of his judgment, but the fire of his saving presence: the complete reversal of the Ariel oracle of 29:1–5 (see 27:7).[40] This future, glorious reign of the Lord in Zion is explicitly taken up in chapters 32 and 33 which immediately follow.

In view of all this, the expression *in that day* in verse 7 must be allowed to point beyond the events of 701 (wonderful as they were) to something more distant and more perfect, as it so often does elsewhere in the book (e.g. 17:7–9; 27:1–2, 12). There was no perfect repentance or perfect salvation in 701. But God's gracious goodness to his people when they cried out to him then was a foretaste of something far greater and more glorious which he has in store for all who turn to him for salvation (Rom. 10:12–13; 1 Cor. 2:9; 1 Pet. 1:3–5).

3. The true solution: divine government (32:1 – 33:24)

These two chapters are unified by their sustained focus on the theme of good government – government which is grounded ultimately in the presence of the Lord among his people and the recognition by them of his kingship. This theme is introduced at once in the opening line of chapter 32 (*See, a king will reign in righteousness*), and the climax is reached towards the end of chapter 33 with the affirmation that

> the LORD is our judge,
>   the LORD is our lawgiver,
> the LORD is our king;
>   it is he who will save us.

For the most part Isaiah is looking forward in these chapters to a future, ideal situation – the dawning of a new age (32:1, 15–16; 33:5–6, 17–22). But the context from which he speaks is anything but ideal. It is a situation in which the complacent are having to come to terms with stern reality (32:9–10), when a destroyer is on the move (33:1), and when diplomacy has failed and the nation's leaders are distraught (33:7–8). Perhaps the clearest

---

[40] The imagery in both 29:1–2 and 31:9 is based on the ever-burning altar fire in the temple, which symbolized God's presence.

indication of the specific background is given in 33:18–19, which speaks of the presence of an enemy *whose speech is obscure* (cf. 28:11) and to the counting and weighing of tribute (see NRSV). This almost certainly refers to Hezekiah's last-ditch attempt to buy off Sennacherib by sending him extravagant tribute, even emptying the temple treasury and stripping the gold from its doors to do so (2 Kgs 18:13–16). It was a humiliating climbdown by Hezekiah (especially since the rebellion had begun by his refusal to pay tribute; 2 Kgs 18:7), but it was not enough to appease Sennacherib. He soon afterwards sent envoys to demand that Jerusalem's gates be thrown open to him, with all that that entailed (2 Kgs 18:17, 31–32). In these circumstances the people of Jerusalem were faced with the utter bankruptcy of government based on human wisdom. It is against this background that Isaiah pointed to the only alternative that could secure the nation's future: government grounded in the kingship of God. Hezekiah reverted to this kind of government at the eleventh hour of the Assyrian crisis (2 Kgs 19:14–19), but Isaiah looks in these chapters to the day when this will be the habitual stance of leaders and people alike. Then indeed a new age will have dawned. This is the state of affairs we pray for in the words of the prayer Jesus taught us: 'Your kingdom come, your will be done, on earth as it is in heaven' (Matt. 6:10).

Isaiah develops his theme in four main movements. The first (32:1–8) sets out the nature of good government and the results that flow from it. The second (32:9–20) shows that there is no shortcut to this ideal; it can come only through judgment (9–14) and the outpouring of God's Spirit (15–20). The third movement (33:1–6) summarizes in more specific terms the steps by which the new age will be ushered in: the Lord will arise, destroy the destroyer, and establish his rule.[41] The fourth and final movement (33:7–24) then fills out this summary by repeating each of its elements, but in a more expansive fashion. Central to both third and fourth movements is the confession that the Lord alone can save (33:2, 22). The new age will not come about by political manoeuvring. It will not be a human achievement at all, but a divine gift.

a. Good government (32:1–8)

The *king* of verse 1 is unspecified. In 11:1–9 (a passage which has a lot in common with this one) the king who will establish perfect government is

---

[41] Cf. Oswalt, p. 591.

the Messiah, a divinely empowered human ruler. In 33:22 it is the Lord himself. Of course, standing where we now do in the history of salvation we can see that there is no contradiction between the two, for Jesus, in whom these prophecies will ultimately be fulfilled, is both the Messiah and God himself. But the issue in this present passage is not so much the identity of the ruler as the quality of government that will characterize his rule. Isaiah looks to the dawning of a new age in which both the ruler himself (the king) and those associated with him (*rulers*) will rule with *righteousness* and *justice*. That is, they will reflect, in the way they exercise their rule, the very character of God himself (5:16).

The results of such government are then spelt out in verses 2–5. The first is security, conveyed by four images from the natural world in verse 2. Instead of being exploited by their rulers (see, e.g., 1:23; 29:21), the common people will be defended and cared for by them. The second result is the restoration of sight, hearing, good judgment and clear speech (3–4). Since Isaiah is apparently speaking here about a reversal of the conditions that prevailed in Judah in his own day, it is best to take the blindness and deafness of verse 3 in the same metaphorical sense as in 29:9, 18, namely, unresponsiveness to the word of God – especially among the nation's leaders. In the age to come, because of the totally different character of the leaders, responsiveness to God's word will characterize the people as a whole, so that ignorance and confusion about God and his ways will give way to insight and clarity.[42] The final result is a natural consequence of this, namely, that people will be seen for what they really are and judged accordingly (5). *The fool* and *the scoundrel* of verse 5 are then each described in turn in verses 6 and 7 before the contrast with *the noble* person is drawn in verse 8. This little discourse is in the style of the wisdom literature of Proverbs, and undoubtedly reflects what was happening all too often in Judah in Isaiah's day. Because of the topsy-turvy morality of the times, fools and knaves were able to exploit the poor and still pass themselves off as noble[43] people (5:20–23). But good government will put an end to that. Moral confusion will end and each person will be seen for what he or she really is.

So much, then, for what good government is. But how will it be established? By what process will the existing state of affairs give way to the new? That is the issue that Isaiah begins to take up in verses 9–20.

---

[42] The longer-range allusion is to 6:9–10 and to the reversal of the judgment announced there.

[43] The Hebrew has the same double meaning as the English. It refers to both social status and moral character.

b. Complacent women (32:9–20)

Let no-one charge Isaiah with being a misogynist! It is men, not women, who bore the main brunt of his stern preaching. They, after all, were the wielders of power and the ones chiefly responsible for the state of the nation. But here, as in 3:16–24, he focuses on the women, partly because of their shared responsibility as wives and partly, perhaps, because their demeanour was a particularly sensitive indicator of prevailing attitudes. There is a further reason here, however. Isaiah is going to issue a call to mourn and lament, and such calls were customarily addressed to women as those who would be touched most deeply by the suffering that was anticipated.[44] But whereas in chapter 3 the women are berated for specified forms of misconduct, here their only fault seems to be their apparent assumption that the present state of affairs can go on indefinitely. They evince the false security of those who have not taken the prophet's warnings of coming judgment sufficiently to heart. The people of Noah's day displayed the same attitude and so, according to Jesus, will those who live in the last days before his return (Matt. 24:38–39). Complacency is a perennial problem, and it is the way of perverse humanity to indulge in it even when disaster is staring them in the face. It is a way of avoiding the necessity of coming to terms with reality. The particular occasion for it here may have been the alliance with Egypt, in which so much false confidence was based, or, at a later stage, the prospect of a last-minute reprieve which Hezekiah's payment of tribute to Sennacherib seemed to offer.[45] In any case, such complacency was inappropriate in the extreme, for *in little more than a year* harvests would fail (10), once-cultivated land would be *overgrown with thorns and briers* (13a; cf. 5:6) and Jerusalem would become a joyless city (13b). In short, Judah and Jerusalem would experience the full impact of Sennacherib's invasion (cf. 1:7–8). That is the immediate reason for the lamentation that Isaiah calls for (note the threefold *for* of verses 12–13). But something even more terrible looms up behind it in verse 14: *the fortress will be abandoned* and *the noisy city deserted*. This did not happen until the fall of Jerusalem to Nebuchadnezzar more than a century after Sennacherib's invasion (2 Kgs 25:1–12), but Isaiah sees the two events as parts of one process of judgment. The

---

[44] Cf. Clements, p. 262. The stripping of the upper body and the beating of *breasts* (11–12) were likewise traditional for women in these circumstances. Cf. Oswalt, p. 585, who cites the pictorial evidence of *ANEP*, nos. 459, 636, 638.

[45] See the introductory comments to chapters 32–33 (pp. 122–123).

Lord would begin the work of establishing good government by dismantling the bad government represented by the whole existing establishment. It was to be a protracted affair, but it began in 701, and before he died Hezekiah was told in quite explicit terms how it would be completed (39:5–7).[46]

In verse 14 the outlook is very bleak, with the words *for ever* (*'ad-'ôlām*) apparently excluding all hope. But this is immediately qualified, paradoxically, by the *till* of verse 15. The change is so abrupt that many scholars have questioned the unity of the passage.[47] But this is quite wrong-headed. The expression *'ad-'ôlām* does not always have the absolute sense 'for ever' in the Old Testament. It can equally mean 'for a very long time',[48] and must clearly be taken in that sense here. The desolation brought by God's judgment will last a long time (cf. Hos. 3:4–5), but will eventually give way to a new era of blessing, inaugurated by the pouring out of the Spirit. In fact, as John Oswalt has noted, verses 9–20 as a whole constitute one finely balanced unit with the pattern: false security, disaster, restoration, true security.[49]

The new age of God's blessing will be an age of material prosperity (15, 20) and true and lasting security (17–18)[50] grounded in *justice* and *righteousness* (16) which, as we have seen, are the foundational characteristics of good government (1). It will be inaugurated by the pouring out of *the Spirit . . . from on high* (15), which is another way of saying that it will be wholly God's doing and God's gift.[51] The Spirit (*rûaḥ*) is associated throughout the Bible with God's kingly rule either directly, as in creation, or indirectly, through his chosen representatives, such as judges and kings (Gen. 1:2; Ps. 104:30; Judg. 3:9–10; 1 Sam. 16:13). In chapter 11 the Spirit is particularly associated with the rule of the Messiah. The present passage complements this by showing that the Spirit will not be limited to the Messiah but will be poured out on the people of God as a whole (*us*, 15). It is this universal bestowal of the Spirit that will make God's rule fully effective in the lives of his people (see Joel 2:28–29). This new age of the Spirit was inaugurated at Pentecost (Acts 2:16–18) and will be here in its

---

[46] 'Nothing will be left' in 39:6 corresponds perfectly to the prediction of 32:14.

[47] E.g. Fohrer, Schoors, Kaiser and Wildberger. See Clements, p. 263.

[48] Cf. Young, 2, p. 399, who cites 1 Sam. 1:22; 1 Kgs 1:31; Neh. 2:3; Dan. 2:4; etc. This usage is hyperbolic.

[49] Oswalt, p. 584.

[50] This time *for ever* (17) has no qualification. See verse 14 and comments.

[51] Cf. the new birth (literally 'from above') in John 3:3. The pouring out of the Spirit here represents the reversal of the pouring out of (literally) 'a spirit of deep sleep' in 29:10 (NRSV).

fullness when Jesus the Messiah – who is both Spirit-endowed and the one who bestows the Spirit (Acts 2:33) – returns in power to reign (Rev. 11:15–17).

My people (18; cf. 13) has a very intimate ring to it. In the Old Testament it undergoes refinement from Israel as a whole (Exod. 3:7) to the faithful remnant who truly fear the Lord (Mal. 3:16–17). In New Testament terms it is those (both Jew and Gentile) who come to Jesus the Messiah for salvation (1 Pet. 2:4–10). It is these who will enjoy the blessings of which Isaiah speaks. They will at last enjoy the *peace* (*šālôm*, 17) that only God's good, perfect government can provide.[52]

c. The destroyer destroyed (33:1–6)

There is much in chapter 33 which reflects the last-minute turning to the Lord which took place in Jerusalem, led by Hezekiah, when Sennacherib's envoys were at the gates. The treachery of the *destroyer* in verses 1–3 probably refers to Sennacherib's treachery in accepting Hezekiah's tribute and then preparing to attack.[53] The weeping of 'the envoys of peace' (Judah's envoys) in verse 7 reflects this same situation, while verses 2 and 14 respectively reflect the repentance of the people of Jerusalem who now look to the Lord alone to save them and yet tremble because they know themselves to be 'sinners' who deserve his judgment. But Isaiah, who had promised that God would be gracious to them when they cried out to him (30:19), now assures them that he will indeed arise to save them (10–12). It is because of the changed attitude of the people that in the *Woe* of verse 1 God's wrath is finally directed towards their enemies (contrast 28:1; 29:1, 15; 30:1; 31:1). Isaiah speaks in this chapter of both the immediate blessing of deliverance from the Assyrians (although they are not explicitly named) and of the final blessedness of Zion when all his purposes for her will be fulfilled (5–6, 17–24). The one is a foretaste of the other and, in characteristic fashion, the two are merged in Isaiah's prophetic vision.

The general sense of verses 1–6 is clear when viewed in this wider context. A few matters, however, are worthy of particular comment.

First, in view of the prediction in verse 1 that the *betrayer* would himself *be betrayed*, it is noteworthy that Sennacherib, after his return to

---

[52] Verse 19, which strikes a discordant note in the RSV (but contrast NIV), probably refers metaphorically to the destruction of human pride which is the necessary concomitant of God's rule (cf. 2:11).

[53] Cf. RSV, 'you treacherous one' (1), and see introductory comments to chapters 32–33 (pp. 122–123).

Nineveh, was treacherously slain by his own sons (37:38).[54] It is an expression of God's moral government that evil should rebound, sooner or later, on the heads of those who practise it.

Second, during war the *morning* was a time of particular danger since it was then that the enemy was most likely to launch a fresh attack. Hence the prayer in verse 2, *Be our strength* [literally, 'arm'][55] *every morning*. The people of Jerusalem are asking God to be their constant defence. As John Oswalt has rightly observed, *we long for you* (literally, 'wait for you') represents a dramatic reversal of the attitude expressed in chapters 29–30.[56]

Third, the image of verse 4 is of the people of Jerusalem stripping the bodies of their enemies, whom the Lord has slain, like *locusts* stripping bare a forest or field. They certainly had the opportunity to do this in 701 (see 37:36). But the picture is broader than this, for verse 3 speaks of *peoples* and *nations*. Verses 3 and 4 together speak of the total victory over all its enemies that Zion will finally enjoy (cf. 29:5–8).

Fourth, verses 5 and 6 list the gifts which the Lord, as the exalted, reigning king, will bestow on his people: *justice, righteousness*, a *sure foundation, salvation, wisdom* and *knowledge*. And then the final line identifies *the fear of the Lord* as the supremely precious thing (*the key to this treasure*) which crowns and sums up all his other gifts.[57] The fear of the Lord is the key to all blessing, but we do not have it except as a gift. Salvation is by grace from beginning to end (Eph. 2:8–9).

d. The Lord is king (33:7–24)

In this final movement of chapters 32 and 33 the theme of divine government receives its most elaborate treatment. As noted above, it is essentially an expansion of the summary outline already given in 33:1–6, but there are some new elements.

The lament in verses 7–9 shows the need for divine government by expressing the total bankruptcy of the human alternative. The answering oracle of verses 10–13 proclaims the Lord's total adequacy (and intention) to deal with all who challenge his own authority and the welfare of his people (cf. verses 3–4). Here is the negative aspect of divine rule: judgment. But this causes some anxious heart-searching among the people of

---

[54] Cf. *ANET*, p. 288.

[55] The 'arm' here is the warrior's strong arm. Cf. 51:9; 52:10; etc.

[56] Oswalt, p. 592.

[57] It is the crowning quality of the Messiah in 11:2–3.

Jerusalem themselves. For in view of their past conduct, may not some of them, too, be classified as enemies (14)?[58] Verses 15–16 respond to this by calling for the amendment of life which is the necessary accompaniment of repentance, for ultimately only those who reflect God's own character *can dwell with* him.[59] Verses 17–24 then present the positive aspect of divine rule: the blessings that will flow from God reigning in the midst of his people (cf. verses 5–6).

The treaty is broken (8) may refer to a particular act of treachery on the part of the Assyrians (cf. verse 1), though no details are given. The verse as a whole, however, reflects a far deeper problem than this, namely, the basic lack of morality in human affairs without which all agreements are meaningless and lasting peace is impossible. Those who have no regard for God finally have no regard for their fellow human beings either (*no one is respected*), and no stratagem can provide security in such a world. In striking contrast, the very 'foundation' of the government which God will finally establish is 'justice' and 'righteousness' (5).

If it is not immediately clear that *the king* of verse 17 is none other than the Lord himself, it soon becomes so as the chapter moves to its climax (21–22; cf. 5–6). That is not to say that Isaiah has no place for a human Messiah in his vision of the coming kingdom of God; he clearly does (11:1–9). There are tensions here which are completely resolved only in the New Testament. But in the present passage the stress falls on the ultimate truth that the Lord himself is king and that his people will one day *see* him reigning personally and gloriously in their midst. And if we turn our attention for a moment from the king to his subjects, we find them dwelling in a spacious, peaceful land, musing on vanished foes and scarcely able to comprehend the full extent of what God has done for them (17–18). The reference to *Jerusalem* as *a tent* whose *stakes will never be pulled up* (20) points to journey's end (cf. 4:5–6). The imagery of verse 21 (*a place of broad rivers* where *no galley with oars will ride*) is less perspicuous, but can be grasped easily enough if it is remembered that the rivers that adorned and enriched the life of such great cities as Nineveh and Babylon also gave access to their enemies. Zion under the Lord's rule will have all the glory of such cities (and far more!) but none of their vulnerability.

---

[58] Cf. Isaiah's own reaction to God's holiness in 6:5.

[59] This passage (33:14–16) is in the form of a Torah liturgy, based on the question-and-answer pattern used by pilgrims seeking admission to the temple and a priestly response to this; Clements, p. 268. Cf. Ps. 24:3–6.

After the climax of verse 22 two final touches complete Isaiah's vision of the coming age. The first is a reminder to his contemporaries that they are utterly unable of themselves to bring it about. They are like a stricken ship, totally at the mercy of forces beyond their control (23). Any share they may finally have in the promised blessings will be due to grace alone.[60] The second is closely related to this, namely, the assertion that the fundamental truth about all who inhabit the ideal world to come is that they *will be forgiven* people (24).[61] So after the climax has been reached in the confession of verse 22 (*the* LORD *is our king*), the chapter does not degenerate into inconsequential addenda, but returns us to fundamentals. Only grace can get us from where we are to where we need to be. The blessings of God's rule are for those who know that they are sinners in need of God's forgiveness more than anything else. That is just as true for us as it was for Isaiah's original audience.

4. Final judgment (34:1–17)

Judgment is not a comfortable subject. Even the Lord himself finds it 'strange' and 'alien' (28:21). But it is an indispensable part of the Bible's teaching about the last things. And the reason is obvious, if we quiet our feelings long enough to give it careful thought. Judgment is the natural corollary of the fact that God is king (chapter 33). A king must rule, or he is no king at all, and that means that rebellion must finally be put down. The fact is that God is almost unbelievably patient, but Isaiah is clear that his just anger is a reality to be reckoned with, and we delude ourselves if we think otherwise. Hence the urgent call to listen in verse 1. God has put the world on notice that he will not tolerate insurrection for ever.

God's wrath is expressed every day in a thousand ways (Rom. 1:18ff.) Every morning's newspaper provides more tragic evidence of the terrible price that the world is even now paying for its rejection of God. But this is nothing compared with what is to come; it is like the tremors that precede an earthquake. And it is the earthquake itself, the final shaking of every-thing, that Isaiah sets before us. The language is concrete and vivid. Divine judgment is no theological abstraction here, but destruction,

---

[60] The second part of the verse makes the same point using a different image: *even the lame* will take the prey.

[61] Their physical condition (*No one living in Zion will say, 'I am ill'*) will then completely match their spiritual condition. Cf. Rom. 8:18–25.

slaughter, stink and *blood* (2–3). It is *the sky* rolling *up like a scroll*, and stars falling from the heavens like *leaves* from winter trees (4). The end of the world is a reality which we instinctively push to the back of our minds because we find it too difficult to cope with, like the fact of our own approaching death. But the Bible will not allow us to evade these realities; it forces us to face them and live in the light of them.

God is king; that is the bedrock truth on which judgment rests. But he is also a warrior, and in verse 5 we meet his *sword*. It swings in a mighty arc from heaven to earth and finds its mark in *Edom*, Judah's southern neighbour. It is a strange target, we may think, for the Edomites and Israelites were blood relatives.[62] What could Edom have done to be the object of such fury on God's part? What heinous crimes had it committed? Only one: it had set itself against the people of God. Much had followed, but this was the root from which all else sprang. It was partly the memory of old wrongs (see Gen. 27:36), partly territorial jealousy, and partly pure greed and vindictiveness, but no nation is so consistently hostile to Israel throughout the whole Old Testament as Edom (see, e.g., Num. 20:18; 1 Sam. 14:47; 1 Kgs 11:14; Pss 60:8–12; 83:5–8; Lam. 4:21; Mal. 1:4).

Edom is representative here, then, not of the nations in general, but of the enemies of Israel. And once we have grasped that, we are in a position to see clearly the purpose of God's judgment. It is *to uphold Zion's cause* (8). The *vengeance* and *retribution* which this involves are expressions of God's commitment to those he has chosen to be his people.

There is no direct correspondence, of course, between this and the tragic political and territorial conflicts in the Middle East today. There are certainly distant echoes of the ancient hostilities, but, rightly understood, that is all they are, however powerful their influence might be. The line between God's people and their enemies is quite differently drawn this side of the cross, as the rest of the book will make abundantly clear. *Zion's cause* in this passage is a quite different thing from modern Zionism. However, there are theological principles which do still apply. From the moment God chose Abraham, the crucial question for others was how they would respond to him. They would be blessed if they blessed him and cursed if they cursed him (Gen. 12:2–3). Their fate was in their own hands; they could choose their response, but not its outcome. It is the way God

---

[62] Edom ('red') was originally an alternative name for Esau, derived from the red stew for which he exchanged his birthright (Gen. 25:19–34).

has always worked, and still does today. Only the particulars have changed. God now works through Christ and his people, but the same basic choice faces the world as faced ancient Edom.

The judgment on Edom is pictured as a terrible *slaughter*, but also as *sacrifice* (6),[63] which alerts us to something very significant about judgment as the Bible understands it. It is not just God acting to vindicate a particular group of people. Sacrifice is about recognizing who God himself is and giving him his due. Judgment is not just a judicial or military act; it is a religious act. It is God acting to claim at last the honour that is due to him as creator and ruler of the world. That is why the Bible ends with a great outburst of praise to God for his righteous judgments, for they mean not only the vindication of his people, but the vindication of God himself (Rev. 19:1–2). This is what we ask for when we pray, as Jesus taught us, 'Your kingdom come, your will be done.' In its most profound sense it is a prayer for the end of the world.

The weighty subject matter of this chapter makes us restive, and anxious to hurry on to more cheerful things. But Isaiah will not let us go until he makes one final point, and the time he takes over it is no doubt calculated to impress us with its gravity: there will be no reprieve from that last and terrible judgment. Edom is set before us as a smouldering ruin, gradually overrun by *nettles*, *brambles* and wild *creatures*, and never rebuilt (9–17). It is a picture of utter finality. The *smoke* of destruction rises for ever here (10), just as it does in the New Testament (Rev. 14:11). Try as we will, there is no escaping the Bible's teaching on the fate of those who persist in their rebellion against God. Their fate is fixed by God's determined purpose; it is written in his book,[64] and *his mouth* has already *given the order* (16). Isaiah never shrinks from his responsibility to set this terrible truth before us. The very last verse of the book returns us to it again, for we need it to spur us into action. In the last analysis, Isaiah's vision is a missionary vision, and every great missionary movement has derived its urgency from this truth: the world is in rebellion against God, and without the gospel people will be lost, utterly and eternally.

Now it is time to move on, however; for judgment may be necessary and right, but it is not what God delights in, or the goal he is working towards.

---

[63] *Bozrah* was the ancient capital of Edom.

[64] *The scroll of the LORD* (16) is probably a reference to the book of destiny, a concept which was familiar to the Jewish people (cf. Pss 40:7; 139:16; Mal. 3:16; Dan. 7:10; Rev. 20:12). 'The author is assuring the reader that all of this is certain; it is written in God's book' (Oswalt, pp. 617–618).

5. Final salvation: the joy of the redeemed (35:1–10)

In chapter 35 it is as though a brilliant shaft of light breaks through the clouds and all is bathed in splendour again. Arid wastes *burst into bloom* as *the glory of the Lord* comes down like refreshing showers, and the whole earth shouts *for joy* (1–2). It is a vision to steady trembling hands, strengthen weak knees, and lift fearful hearts (3–4).

The people addressed here remember the sights of home – *the glory of Lebanon*[65] and *the splendour of Carmel*[66] (2) – but they are far away, and powerless to return. They have been conquered and brutalized, and their anguished hearts cry out for *vengeance, retribution* and deliverance (4). But they have no strength to right the wrongs they have suffered or to bring those responsible to account. They are *blind, deaf, lame* and *mute*; they have no power to help themselves; only God can save them. And the good news of this chapter is that he will do just that (5–7). He will raise up *a highway* for them and bring them home. *They will enter Zion with singing . . . sorrow and sighing will flee away*, and they will be overtaken (glorious conquest!) by a *joy* that will never end (8–10).

Clearly, a situation of exile and return is in view here, something that will be developed at length in the second half of the book.[67] But just as clearly, this chapter reaches beyond that to something else. The *everlasting* joy of this chapter corresponds to the everlasting destruction of the previous one. Beyond the judgments and blessings of history lie the final 'everlastings' of salvation and damnation. These are the ultimate realities we have to reckon with. There are foreshadowings of them within history, but in Scripture something greater always looms up behind.

We, of course, would like to have only one of these realities: blessing without curse, salvation without judgment, heaven without hell. And we are always in danger of rewriting the rules, so to speak, to suit our own inclinations. But the biblical revelation has a stubborn shape to it that resists all manipulation of this kind. It forces us to decision: we must have it as it is or not at all; accept it or make up our own religion. No quarter

---

[65] Probably a reference to Hermon, a mountain in the Anti-Lebanon Range, and easily the highest in Palestine. 'Snow usually lies on the top all year round . . . in contrast to the parched land of that region' (*NBD*, p. 478).

[66] A mountain ridge on the Mediterranean coast in northern Israel, noted for its luxuriant growth (see Song 7:5).

[67] In particular, we meet again the motifs of the exiles as *the blind* and *the deaf* (42:18; 43:8) and the *highway* through the desert (40:3).

is given, either by the biblical writers or by Jesus himself. On the last day, some will go away to eternal punishment, and some to eternal life (Matt. 25:46).

But let us concentrate for a moment on the *highway* of verse 8. It is the way to everlasting joy. It is the way to Zion, the city of God, and all that it symbolizes. In New Testament terms it is the highway to heaven (Heb. 12:22–24). And it is *the Way of Holiness*, which puts us in touch again with a major theme of the book. For Isaiah, holiness is the defining characteristic of God himself. Above all else, God is holy (6:3), so the way of holiness is not just the way to Zion, or the way to heaven; it is the way to God. It is not the golden streets or the pearly gates that make heaven what it is, but the presence of God. To be in heaven is to be with God for ever, in totally joyous, unspoiled fellowship. And the way to heaven is provided by God himself. It is for those who have been *redeemed*, or ransomed (9–10). These terms refer to powerful and costly deliverance.[68] They have their roots in the exodus from Egypt, and find their final significance in the work of Christ, by which God rescues us from the power of sin and Satan. These acts of judgment and deliverance are the expressions par excellence of his holiness. Look at them, and you will see his holiness in action. The way of holiness is the way of salvation that God provides.

But it is also the way that we must choose; it is not for *the unclean* or for *wicked fools* (8). It is for those who have chosen holiness as their way of life and renounced other ways. And what a glorious picture of holiness this chapter gives us! The way of holiness is the way of *singing*, *joy* and *gladness* (10). No drabness here! The pursuit of holiness is the pursuit of God himself, and the face that is set towards God will open to joy and gladness like a flower opening to the sun.

With this we have reached another resting point in our journey through Isaiah's vision. And as we pause and catch our breath, where do we find ourselves? At home, joyful and at rest in the presence of God. It is where we long to be, and the only place where we will ever be totally content to

---

[68] On 'ransomed' (NIV *rescued*; root *pādâ*) see the note on 1:27. Here it is combined with *redeemed* (root *gā'al*), anticipating a major strand of the theology of chapters 40–66. '*Redeemed* . . . stresses the person of the redeemer, his relationship to the redeemed and his intervention on their behalf. The participle *gō'ēl* is the technical term for the next-of-kin who has the right to take his helpless relative's needs as his own (Lev. 25:25; Num. 5:8), and is often used of the "avenger" of a murdered person . . . In its classical expression the work of "redeemer" was a right which no other dare usurp (Ruth 3:12; 4:1–6). It was a right rather than an inescapable duty, calling for willingness. It speaks here, therefore, of the LORD as the only one who can redeem his people, identifying with them as their next-of-kin, willingly shouldering, on their helpless behalf and in their place, all and every one of their needs, paying their price (Lev. 27:13, 19, 31).' Motyer, p. 275.

stay. For we too are exiles (1 Pet. 1:1–2), and our hearts cry out for home (2 Cor. 5:1–9). We cannot save ourselves, but the way has already been raised up for us, and we have already set out on it. Like the prodigal, we are on the way home, but we know far better than he did the welcome that awaits us. And this part of Isaiah's vision is like a refreshing oasis on the way, where we can pause and gather strength for what remains of the journey. Joy and gladness and God himself are up ahead, and with that certain knowledge we can rise above our weariness and set out again.

Isaiah 36 – 39

4. In whom shall we trust?

As we saw in the Introduction,[1] these chapters are in effect the pivot on which the book turns, and appear to have been designed to act as a bridge between its two halves.

Likewise, the issue that these chapters throw into sharp relief is absolutely central to the book's total message. It is the issue of trust, and where that trust should ultimately be placed. It is explored first against the backdrop of an Assyrian invasion that brought Judah to the verge of extinction, and then in the context of a diplomatic initiative from Babylon which appeared to offer Judah everything it needed. It was hard to believe, in these circumstances, that Judah's security was in the Lord alone, and even harder to act on it. Ironically, it was the Assyrian invader who put the issue most succinctly: 'On whom are you depending?' (36:5). It is a question which the book of Isaiah forces us to ponder again and again, and with good reason, for our response to it will determine the whole shape of our lives.

1. The enemy at the gates (36:1–22)

Chapter 36 bounces us back with a sudden jolt from the glorious vision of the end to the very inglorious and frightening world of the here and now, or at least the here and now that Isaiah and his contemporaries had to wrestle with. True religion is always like that; It leads us not away from reality, but more deeply into it. It arms us with the knowledge of what will

---

[1] In the section 'The book of Isaiah', p. 12.

be, so that we can confront what is (however frightening it may be) with renewed courage and steadiness of purpose.

The invasion described so concisely and dispassionately in verse 1 was a devastating blow for Judah.[2] Hezekiah had become embroiled in anti-Assyrian activity, and Sennacherib was determined to make him pay for it. He would teach the small states of the region a lesson they would never forget, and establish once for all the unassailable supremacy of Assyria in Palestine. As a key player in the recent unrest, Hezekiah was a special object of Sennacherib's wrath. And the proud Assyrian arrived at the gates of Jerusalem with abundant proof of his invincibility. He had already swept across the north, down the Mediterranean coast and inland and northwards to Lachish. On his triumphant way he had *attacked all the fortified cities of Judah and captured them* (1), and was in the process of doing the same to *Lachish*, Jerusalem's last line of defence.[3]

Sennacherib's field commander presented Hezekiah's men with powerful arguments for surrender. Egypt is in no position to help (6); it is no good looking to the Lord, because Hezekiah has destroyed most of the places where he was worshipped (7); even if the Assyrians themselves were to *give* little Judah *two thousand horses* (they are taunting her now), she still could not defend herself (8–9); and in any case it is the Lord who has sent the Assyrians; they are his instrument to punish Judah, so what point is there in resisting (10)? This speech is a classic study in the satanic art of sowing doubt and unbelief through subtly twisting the truth. Egypt was weak at this time, and in any case, the fall of Lachish would effectively cut off any Egyptian advance. The field commander's warning about relying on Egypt echoes that of Isaiah himself (19:14–16; 30:7; 31:3).

---

[2] There is considerable controversy about the dating of Hezekiah's reign. There is general agreement that verse 1 of this chapter refers to Sennacherib's invasion of 701 BC, which would put Hezekiah's accession in 715 (701 + 14). But 2 Kgs 18:1 puts it in the third year of Hoshea of Israel (the northern kingdom), which is approximately 727. The most likely solution is that he was co-regent with his father Ahaz from 727 and ruled in his own right from 715. This would mean that the invasion occurred in either the fourteenth or twenty-sixth year of his reign, depending on the method of calculation. But since he reigned twenty-nine years from the beginning of his co-regency (2 Kgs 18:2), his death must be placed at approximately 698 BC (727 minus 29), and his serious illness fifteen years earlier, in 713 (38:5). The visit of the envoys from Babylon, which happened shortly after this, would have been in approximately 712 (39:1), eleven years before Sennacherib's invasion. For a full discussion, with reference to opposing views, see Oswalt, pp. 674–675. My own conclusions are in substantial agreement with Oswalt's.

[3] Sennacherib himself claimed to have conquered forty-six of Judah's 'strong cities, walled forts, and . . . the countless small villages in their vicinity', and to have shut Hezekiah up in Jerusalem 'like a bird in a cage'; *ANET*, p. 288. Cf. 1:8. Lachish, 26 miles south-west of Jerusalem, had particularly strong fortifications, but it was no match for Sennacherib. His siege and capture of Lachish are portrayed in a relief sculpture from his palace in Nineveh, now in the British Museum. It was completely razed, leaving an ash and destruction layer over the whole site. *NBD*, p. 669.

Hezekiah's destruction of outlying shrines in the first year of his reign must have left a legacy of doubt and disaffection among many of his subjects (2 Kgs 18:1–4). Judah was indeed desperately short of fighting men, and (the most powerful argument of all) Assyria was in fact the rod of the Lord's anger (10:5). The speech is so persuasive precisely because it contains so much that is true. But its basic premise is false: namely, that the Lord has forsaken Judah, and therefore that trust in him is futile. It is always Satan's way to make us think that God has abandoned us, and to use logic woven from half-truths to convince us of it. This speech is so subtly devilish in character that it might have been written by Satan himself. The truth is that the Lord had brought Judah to the end of her own resources so that she might learn again what it meant to trust him utterly. But he had not abandoned and would not abandon her.

Since the leaders appeared to be standing firm (no doubt to the field commander's surprise), he decided on another ploy. He had always meant the bystanders to overhear what he had to say; that was why he had used Hebrew instead of Aramaic.[4] But now he addressed himself directly to them (13–20), and this time he is less subtle: they should forswear their allegiance to King Hezekiah (who is powerless), and entrust themselves to *the great king, the king of Assyria*, who will guarantee their prosperity (13–17).[5] None of the gods of the other nations have been able to save them,[6] so they should not listen any longer to Hezekiah's lies about the Lord saving Judah (18–20). But the common people are not as easily swayed as the Assyrian expects them to be: they remain silent, as *the king* (Hezekiah) had commanded (21). There are times when silence is the most eloquent testimony to whose we are and whom we serve (53:7; 1 Pet. 2:23).

So the ball is firmly back in Hezekiah's court (22). The people will follow where he leads; in a sense, the lives of them all are in his hands. What will he do, and what resources can he call on at this fateful moment?

---

[4] See verses 11–12. Aramaic was the language of international diplomacy, and was understood only by the educated elite.

[5] The Assyrian does not disguise the fact that they will be deported (this was standard Assyrian practice for conquered peoples), but puts the best possible face on it.

[6] *Hamath* was a major Syrian city on the Orontes River, 275 miles north-east of Jerusalem. Sargon II destroyed it for rebelling against Assyria (*ANET*, p. 285). *Arpad* was another Syrian city, 85 miles north of Hamath. The location of *Sepharvaim* is unknown. Samaria, the capital of the former northern kingdom of Israel, fell to the Assyrians in 722 BC. Sennacherib's envoy apparently thought that Samaria and Jerusalem served different gods.

2. The tables turned (37:1–38)

a. The power of God's word (37:1–13)

There was no denying the seriousness of the situation, and Hezekiah's torn clothes and sackcloth showed that he had no intention of pretending that things were other than they were. But he had three great resources: the Lord (1), the Lord's prophet (2) and prayer (4, 15). And Hezekiah resolved at once to use them all. He resorted to the temple of the Lord, he informed Isaiah of the desperate situation, and he both asked for prayer and prayed himself. This was perhaps Hezekiah's finest hour. He was not perfect. In fact, the mess he was in was largely of his own making. But in the last analysis, he knew that the Lord reigned, and therefore nothing was impossible or hopeless (cf. Matt. 19:26; Gen. 18:14; Jer. 32:17). The pressure of circumstances had stripped him back to basics.

Isaiah's response was immediate: *This is what the LORD says . . .* (6). Isaiah is the channel by which God's word enters the situation and begins to transform it (cf. 55:11).[7] Sennacherib's envoy had expressed himself in very similar terms: 'This is what the king . . . says . . .' (36:16). But now a greater king has spoken. It is not just Hezekiah or the people of Judah whom Sennacherib has demeaned, but the living God (4, 6), and in so doing he over-reached himself. Isaiah saw very clearly that pride is the worst of all sins (2:11, 17). It is the purest form of defiance possible; it is ousting God from the throne of our lives and putting ourselves in his place (14:12–15). It is the sin of Adam and Eve (Gen. 3:4–5), and before them of Satan himself (Gen. 3:1; Rev. 20:2). It is the primal sin from which all others grow. And it was especially, in this case, the sin of the king of Assyria, the 'great king' (36:13; 37:23). Isaiah had spoken in 10:12 of 'the wilful pride of his heart and the haughty look in his eyes' and declared God's intention to punish. Now that threat is fleshed out and confirmed: he will *return to his own country, and there I will have him cut down with the sword* (7). In the last analysis, it is the word of the Lord that will prevail, not the word of Sennacherib.

The word which has entered the situation like leaven gradually begins to have its effect. Isaiah had spoken about God unsettling Sennacherib and of him hearing a *report* (7).[8] Unease is suggested by the fact that when the

---

[7] As we shall see, the power of the Lord's word is a major theme of chapters 40–55.

[8] On the expression *I will make him want to . . .* , Oswalt (p. 647) has the following helpful comment: '[This] reflects God's complete control of the situation . . . Things as ephemeral as a vague uneasiness or a distant rumor are all that is necessary to remove the emperor from before Jerusalem . . . God is going to dispose Sennacherib to leave.'

envoy returns, he finds that Sennacherib has temporarily broken off the siege of Lachish and is *fighting against Libnah* (8). Is he perhaps expecting an attack from Egypt (cf. 36:6), and moving so that he will have a consolidated defensive position to work from?[9] If so, his suspicions are soon confirmed; he receives a *report* that an Egyptian force has indeed begun to move against him (9).[10] What happened next is unclear; neither the Bible nor Sennacherib's annals throw any light on it. But since he continued to threaten Jerusalem (33ff.), it is unlikely that the Egyptians had much success. Perhaps they never even materialized. But Sennacherib had been given something to think about. He had been forced to withdraw from Lachish and to halt, for the moment, his diplomatic offensive against Jerusalem (8–9). He had to reckon with the possibility of more harassment of this kind. It had been a long campaign, and he was still far from his home with a lot of men to feed and his supply lines exposed. There was always the nagging concern, too, about what might be happening back in Assyria in his absence (verse 38 suggests he had good reason to be worried about this!) In short, despite his successes, it was clearly in his own best interests to wind up proceedings in Palestine as quickly as possible. But what was to be done about Jerusalem? If it could not be frightened into surrender, the Assyrians could either mount a full-scale siege (which might last eighteen months or more)[11] or decide that Hezekiah had already been taught a salutary lesson and leave him to lick his wounds. Sennacherib may well have been considering these options as Hezekiah went to prayer (14).

b. Hezekiah looks up (37:14–20)

What a magnificent prayer! And how feeble it makes our own prayers seem by comparison! It begins and ends with God, and its overriding concern is that God might be glorified in the situation. Hezekiah has gone up to the temple and spread out Sennacherib's letter before the Lord. And now, as he begins to pray, he recalls who it is he prays to: *Lord Almighty, the God*

---

[9] The location of *Libnah* is uncertain, but most think it was to the north of Lachish, making the suggestion of a tactical withdrawal probable. Oswalt, p. 649.

[10] *Tirhakah*, an Ethiopian, did not actually become king of Egypt until 690 BC, eleven years after Sennacherib's invasion. This has led to speculation that the biblical account combines elements from two distinct Assyrian campaigns; Bright, pp. 298–309. Alternatively, and more likely in my judgment, the writer simply uses Tirhakah's later title here for convenience, much as we might now speak of 'President Clinton' when referring to events in his life both before and after his inauguration; K. A. Kitchen, *The Third Intermediate Period in Egypt (1100–650 BC)* (Warminster: Aris and Phillips, 1973), pp. 161–162.

[11] This is how long it took the Babylonians to bring Jerusalem to its knees more than 100 years later (2 Kgs 25:1–4).

of Israel, enthroned between the cherubim (16a).[12] This is no distant, unknown God, but the God who has revealed himself to his people and is present among them. But neither is he just a local, national God. He is creator of *heaven and earth* and sovereign *over all the kingdoms of the earth* (16b). Hezekiah's prayer is so magnificent because it arises from a deep and true understanding of who God is, and is fundamentally an act of worship. Such praying lifts people out of themselves and into the presence of God. And in that context, present problems are not lost sight of; they are just seen from a new perspective, and the cry for deliverance becomes a cry that God's kingdom may come and his will be done (20).[13] The context of worship purges the cry of all pathetic self-interest and binds together the one who cries and the one who hears in a common desire and a common purpose. If only we could learn to pray like this, what times we would have on our knees, and what a difference we would see in the progress of the gospel in the world!

c. Sennacherib's fall (37:21–38)

Such prayers do not go unheeded. Even as Hezekiah has been praying, God has been revealing his word to Isaiah, so that Hezekiah scarcely has time to rise from his knees before he receives an answer (21). *Because you have prayed*, God says, *this is the word the LORD has spoken* . . . (21–22). We must not miss this, because it is part of the Bible's strong teaching about prayer. Because someone has prayed, God steps in and changes the course of history. It is a breathtaking truth, and at first sight a worrying one, because it appears to put humans rather than God in control. But this is an illusion. There is no conflict between God's absolute sovereignty and the power of prayer, because, quite simply, this is the way God has chosen to work. Through prayer he draws us up into his purposes and involves us in what he is doing. What a privilege! Even the desire to pray is his gift (Rom. 8:15).

The first word that Hezekiah receives is a judgment oracle against Sennacherib (22–29).[14] The victories which Sennacherib has boasted about

---

[12] The Lord, whose glory had filled the temple when it was dedicated (1 Kgs 8:10–11), was thought of as *enthroned* on the two *cherubim* above the ark of the covenant, which contained the two tables of the law (Exod. 25:10–22). The symbolism was clear: the Lord was present with his people and responded to their prayers on the basis of the covenant which he had made with them at Mount Sinai.

[13] One might almost think that Hezekiah had had the Lord's Prayer revealed to him in advance and modelled his own prayer on it (Matt. 6:9–13).

[14] The opening words of the oracle, *Virgin Daughter Zion*, already anticipate the theme of verses 33–35: Zion will not be violated. The boast of verse 25b, *I have dried up all the streams of Egypt*, goes far beyond the facts; Sennacherib did not reach the Nile Delta.

as if they were his own were really God-given; he has merely been an instrument in God's hand (26–27).[15] Now his proud boasting is to be brought to a sudden end. God will break him as someone breaks a wild horse, and lead him home humiliated and exhausted (29). There he is eventually to meet his end at the hands of his own sons (38). This word is for Hezekiah's ears rather than Sennacherib's. It is not meant to bring Sennacherib to repentance; he is beyond that. He has gone too far, and God has already passed judgment on him. Hezekiah has nothing more to fear from him.

The second word is a *sign* for Hezekiah himself (30). The removal of Sennacherib will be only a means to an end, and Hezekiah will know that it is indeed the Lord who has done it by the positive things that flow from it (30b–32). The land will yield its *fruit* again. Agricultural activity will be resumed and community life will flourish. In short, from the 'death' of the present crisis will spring new life: *out of Jerusalem will come a remnant.* And Hezekiah's guarantee is the Lord's total commitment to bringing this about: *The zeal of the* LORD *Almighty will accomplish this* (32). Once again we are in touch with a major theme of the book; God comes to chastise his people, not to destroy them. And for those who trust, blessing comes through discipline, prosperity through suffering, life through death (1:21–26; 28:16; cf. Heb. 12:4–13).[16]

The third and final word for Hezekiah again concerns Sennacherib: he will not be allowed to take Jerusalem. The Lord will defend it for his own sake and for the sake of David his servant (33–35). For all Hezekiah's piety, the plans of God do not revolve around him, but around God himself, and his servant. Hezekiah is saved, not for his own sake, but for the sake of another. As the book moves on, of course, David will be dwarfed by a far greater Servant of God (42:1–4), and the question how (on what basis) God saves his people will be explored at a far deeper level. At every point in Isaiah's vision we find ourselves in contact both with the details of a particular situation and with the great principles that undergird all God's saving work. As in a marvellous tapestry, every thread contributes to the glory of the whole.

All that is needed to draw this chapter to its close, however, is the brief, almost matter-of-fact report that God did what he said he would do. He

---

[15] *Have you not heard? Long ago I ordained it* (26) anticipates a major theme of chapters 40–55 (see, e.g., 41:21–29; 44:6–8; 45:21; 46:8–11).

[16] For a thorough examination of the remnant theme in the book as a whole, see my article 'Zion in Transformation', in D. Clines et al. (eds.), *The Bible in Three Dimensions* (Sheffield: JSOT Press, 1990)..

broke the morale of the Assyrian force with a single blow (36),[17] where-upon Sennacherib obediently *broke camp* and headed for home (37),[18] and eventually met precisely the fate that the Lord had said he would (38; cf. 7).[19] The towering tyrant is despatched in just three verses! All Hezekiah had to do, like his ancestors of old, was to 'stand still, and see the salvation of the LORD' (Exod. 14:13, AV). It brought king and people back to the exodus roots of their faith.

3. Hezekiah's illness (38:1–22)

The opening phrase, *In those days*, is deliberately vague, and gives only a general indication of the time frame of the narrative. In fact, as we observed earlier, this chapter and the next are effectively a flashback to something that happened before the events that have just been described. Note, for example, verse 6: *I will* [future] *deliver you and this city from the hand of the king of Assyria. I will* [future] *defend this city.* But the deliverance of Jerusalem as pronounced here has already taken place in the previous chapter. And, as we have seen, the reception of ambassadors from Babylon in chapter 39 was part of Hezekiah's anti-Assyrian activity which led up to Sennacherib's move against him in 701 BC. So we have stepped back in time, and back from the broad canvas of international events, to pick up something far more intimate and 'private': *In those days Hezekiah became ill and was at the point of death* (1). It is the crisis behind the crisis, so to speak.

For an individual, of course, sickness can be just as much a crisis as an invasion is for a nation. Illness, especially if it is serious, brings us face to face with our mortality, and can put our trust in God on a razor's edge. This is precisely the situation in which we find Hezekiah in this chapter. He is ill – very ill – and the word from Isaiah is that he is *going*

---

[17] Verse 36 is commonly regarded as legendary, a blend of fact and pious fiction. The most common 'natural' explanation is a sudden outbreak of bubonic plague. The main force may have been in the vicinity of the Nile Delta, where such an event would be much more likely than in Palestine. Herodotus refers to a plague of mice which caused Sennacherib to withdraw from Pelusium (on the edge of the Delta; 1.141). However that may be, the account as we have it is strongly reminiscent of the slaughter of the firstborn in Egypt (Exod. 12:29–30), and we are clearly meant to understand that God intervened suddenly and dramatically, whatever the means. For a fuller discussion see Oswalt, pp. 668–670.

[18] Sennacherib's own annals tacitly admit that he left Palestine without taking Jerusalem; *ANET*, p. 288.

[19] The final irony is that Sennacherib is killed while praying to his god in a temple, just as his intended victim Hezekiah had done twenty years earlier. Cf. Oswalt, p. 668.

to die (1).[20] Hezekiah is deeply shaken by the news. He turns *his face to the wall* and weeps *bitterly* (2–3). It is a helpful reminder that monarchs are human too. We are far too inclined to put leaders on a pedestal and forget that they are subject to the same weaknesses as ourselves. It can be very lonely at the top.

But Hezekiah is not alone, and his faith is not utterly extinguished. He does not just weep; he prays (3). It is a far cry from the robust prayer of 37:14–17 (it is harder to be strong in a personal crisis than in a national one), but it is a prayer none the less, and shows that his face is turned, not just to the wall, but also to God. There is no praise, no pious resignation to the divine will, no expressed desire that God may be glorified – just a muted cry for help: *Remember, Lord, how I have walked before you faithfully* . . . It is not much of a prayer, but it is all he is capable of at this moment. But this is precisely the kind of backdrop against which God's splendid grace shines to fullest advantage. And that is certainly the case here. Hezekiah is granted not only what he asked for, but much, much more. The Lord *will add fifteen years to* Hezekiah's own *life* – and he will also *defend* and deliver Jerusalem (5–6).[21] No wonder Hezekiah prayed with more robust faith next time! He learnt something in this crisis which strengthened him for the next.

But here we must digress slightly, for we have stumbled on another important clue to the significance of chapters 38 and 39 as a whole. A parallel is being drawn between king and nation, Hezekiah and Jerusalem (which is effectively all that is left of Judah). Both are in crisis, and both have been given a reprieve. But there is more than a hint that, just as Hezekiah's reprieve was temporary (fifteen years), so will Jerusalem's be. In short, the fall of Jerusalem in 587 BC is already beginning to loom up on the horizon of the narrative; it will come into direct view at the end of chapter 39, and dominate the scene from there on. Chapters 38 and 39 are not (as they might at first appear) a digression from the main drama, but an introduction to its second major movement.

---

[20] *Šĕḥîn*, translated *boil* in the NIV of verse 21, is of uncertain meaning. It is related to *šāḥan*, 'to be hot, inflamed' (BDB, p. 1006), and was used in ancient times of a wide range of skin diseases. In the Old Testament it is used of Job's illness (severe eczema?) and the sixth plague of Egypt which affected both people and animals (some kind of pox?), as well as of Hezekiah's illness (possibly an abscess, boil or carbuncle). In a personal communication, John Marsh, a retired surgeon, has pointed out to me that carbuncles could be fatal in earlier times. For a technical discussion see F. Rosner, 'The Illness Schechin [*sic*]', in *Biblical and Talmudic Medicine* (New York: Hebrew Publishing Company, 1978), pp. 339ff.

[21] *And seen your tears* is a nice touch in verse 5. God not only hears our prayers but sees us cry. One day he will wipe away every tear (25:8; Rev. 21:4).

In 38:7–8 Hezekiah is given a *sign* to assure him that the Lord will indeed do as he has promised. According to verse 22 he had requested such a sign, an indication that his faith had not yet reached a point of confident rest. But at least he was *disposed* to believe, in contrast to Ahaz, who had refused to accept a sign when one was offered (7:10–13).[22] There is all the difference in the world between someone who is disposed to believe and someone who is not. It is the difference between light and darkness.[23]

Hezekiah recovered as the Lord said he would. It is rather surprising, however, after the astonishing nature of the sign, to be told that recovery itself was accomplished by something as mundane as the preparation and application of *a poultice* (21)![24] But if we are surprised it is because of a defect in our own theology rather than anything incongruous in the text. For there is no disjunction in Scripture between miraculous and natural healing, as though God were involved in one and not the other. He is as much Lord of the soothing poultice[25] as he is of the moving shadow, and perhaps our eyes would be more open and our hearts more thankful if only we could grasp this simple and sane biblical truth more firmly.

In a sense, by the time we reach verse 9 of this chapter everything of importance has already happened. But in fact what follows is the most significant part of all, for here Hezekiah reflects, with the benefit of

---

[22] The fact that the sign is associated with *the stairway of Ahaz* (8) makes the comparison inevitable. The 'stairway' may have been a normal outdoor set of stairs or a stepped sundial of some kind.

[23] The nature of the sign itself is in one sense straightforward (the backward movement of a shadow) and in another sense very problematical (how could it happen without convulsing the entire earth?). 2 Chr. 32:31 suggests that in other places it was heard about rather than directly experienced, so it appears that we are dealing with a local phenomenon rather than a global one. Anything beyond this is pure speculation. Oswalt suggests that 'some sort of refraction of light was involved' (p. 678). But the precise timing and exact extent of the shadow's movement exclude any purely natural explanation.

[24] The endnotes in verses 21 and 22 appear as an integral part of the parallel passage in 2 Kgs 20. Most scholars believe that the Kings account is primary, but in that case one would expect to find the two notes in the same place in both. And there are larger issues to be considered. As we saw in the Introduction (p. 17), 2 Kgs 18:13 – 20:19 as a whole is parallel to Isa. 36 – 39, but the chronological arrangement of the material makes sense only in terms of the book of Isaiah. This strongly suggests that Isaiah 36 – 39 as a whole is primary. The position of the endnotes in chapter 38 can be explained on the supposition that the Isaiah version of Hezekiah's illness was expanded slightly in 2 Kgs 20, and that the two endnotes were then added to Isaiah 38 to harmonize the two accounts. The implications for the date of the book of Isaiah are discussed in the Introduction, and in my article 'Zion in Transformation', pp. 70–71.

[25] Whether or not the *poultice* itself was an effective treatment is debatable. The use of *figs* as softening compresses in antiquity is clearly documented (Pliny the Elder, *Nat.* 23.63; Dioscorides Pedanius, *Mat. med.* 1.184). The rabbis, however, believed that figs were harmful for šĕḥîn, and that their healing effect in this case was miraculous (Rosner, op. cit., p. 342). In a personal communication, John Marsh, speaking as a medical professional, takes a positive view: 'Sugar solutions kill germs and drain pus by their strong osmotic pressure. People have used honey and such for years to clean infected wounds. Figs would be good. The poultice saved Hezekiah.'

hindsight, on all that the experience has meant to him (9–20). He remembers the numbed shock he felt first (10), his anger at God (*you made an end of me*, 12), his tearful exhaustion (14a), and his feeble cry for help as he lifted his *eyes*, at last, to heaven (14b). But then, with that upward look, it was as though the knife of his suffering was turned around, and he was able to grasp it by the handle instead of the blade. The fact that it was the Lord who had afflicted him (15a) became a cause for gratitude rather than anger (17). It gave him the opportunity to experience the saving power of God not only in his body, but in his spirit as well (16). And out of that came a new humility (15b), a deeper appreciation of God's love (17b), an assurance of forgiveness (17c), and a determination to *praise* God and tell others about him for as long as he was given the strength to do so (18–20). Such lessons are priceless, but often it is only by looking back, as Hezekiah does here, that we can see how suffering has been the means God has used to teach them to us (Heb. 12:11).

But now it is time for us to widen our perspective again, for although Hezekiah was a human being like ourselves, he was also the king of a nation which had a unique place in God's purposes. Because of this, his sickness and recovery could not be purely private affairs; they had the potential to change the course of history, as we now see in chapter 39.

4. Envoys from Babylon (39:1–8)

Enter *Marduk-Baladan* (1), and with him a whole new chapter in Israel's history. It may be difficult for us (knowing what subsequently happened) to think of Judah and Babylon as allies, but in 712 BC[26] it must have seemed the most natural thing in the world. Babylon had been trying to break free of Assyrian domination ever since Tiglath-Pileser III had conquered it in 745 BC, and Marduk-Baladan was the hero of the resistance. He had seized the throne in defiance of Sargon II in 721 BC, and was still clinging to it despite increasing Assyrian pressure. At the same time Hezekiah had become the de facto leader of the anti-Assyrian coalition in southern Palestine. What could make better sense than cooperation between them? It certainly made sense to the Babylonians, who had apparently been watching events in Palestine with keen interest. But would Hezekiah see things their way? There was probably no reason to

---

[26] See n. 2 above (p. 137).

suspect that he would not, but wisdom indicated that the most opportune moment should be sought for a major initiative of this kind. Hezekiah's sickness and *recovery* appeared to present just such a moment.

Envoys were despatched with *letters and a gift* (1), and they found Hezekiah in high spirits. His strength had returned, his storehouses were full, and his little kingdom was well armed and confident. He was flattered at being courted by one so famous, and did everything in his power to impress his distinguished visitors: *There was nothing in his palace or in all his kingdom that Hezekiah did not show them* (2). It was all very understandable, but hardly prudent, and even before Isaiah appears on the scene abruptly in verse 3, we have reason to suspect that something has gone badly wrong. Events have moved too quickly. Action that required careful thought and wise counsel has been taken precipitously from wrong motives and, worst of all, God has not been consulted. But it is a hard truth for Hezekiah to accept. We can sense his defensiveness in the tense exchange of verses 3 and 4, and by the end of the chapter he has descended into pure petulance (8). It is a sad fall indeed from the spiritual heights he had attained so recently (38:9–20). Fortunately he bounced back again, as we already know from chapters 36 and 37, where his very first thought is to seek God. He learnt valuable lessons from his fall from grace. But it was tragic none the less, as such events always are; they leave long memories behind them.

Isaiah saw only too clearly that in the long term Babylon would prove to be an enemy rather than a friend. The royal treasure which the Babylonians had seen they would eventually carry off as plunder, and with it the surviving members of the royal family (5–7).[27] It was a judgment not so much on Hezekiah's single lapse as on the kind of faithlessness that it exemplified. The full explanation of why the Lord finally withdrew his protection from Jerusalem and allowed Babylon to overwhelm it is told in the books of Kings, especially 2 Kings 17:7–20.[28] It came at the end of a long history of apostasy, rebellion, refusal to listen and, most of all, lack of trust: 'they would not listen and were as stiff-necked as their ancestors, *who did not trust in the* LORD *their God*' (2 Kgs 17:14, my emphasis). Hezekiah's hasty alliance with Babylon was as much symptomatic of that

---

[27] For the progressive outworking of this threat, see Dan. 1:1–5 (605 BC), 2 Kgs 24:8–17 (597 BC) and 2 Kgs 25:1–21 (587 BC). The subsequent reference to eunuchs in 56:4 suggests that some members of the royal family were literally castrated.

[28] Verses 18–20 refer explicitly to Judah.

lack of trust as the more blatant sin of idol worship which increasingly blighted the life of the whole nation. And Isaiah is relentless in hammering home the message that whatever we put our trust in, instead of God himself, will eventually turn on us and destroy us.[29]

If Hezekiah thought that the closing years of his life were to be marked by *peace and security* (8), he was in for a rude shock. Eleven years after his recovery, relentless Assyrian pressure reached its nerve-shattering climax with Sennacherib's invasion. And although Jerusalem escaped, most of Judah was a wasteland and Hezekiah himself an old man with only four of his fifteen years remaining. As he contemplated his approaching death and the future of his people, the words that Isaiah had brought to him from the Lord during those momentous years must have left him suspended between hope and dread. There had been talk of a remnant that would survive and blossom into new life (37:30–32), but also of plunder, captivity and exile (39:5–7). It was a puzzle that only a greater mind and a greater power than his own could solve. From a human point of view, Judah was once more on a knife-edge. The air was heavy with possibilities, for good or for ill.

In these circumstances the question of the succession was vital, and must have occupied Hezekiah's mind very much since his illness, and especially in his last four years. But it soon became apparent that Manasseh was no man of faith. It is likely that he was co-regent with his father for several years before assuming sole rule,[30] and if so Hezekiah must have already known before his death what Manasseh's intentions were. As soon as he was in a position to do so, he totally reversed his father's policy of religious reform and resistance to Assyria, and plunged Judah into one of the darkest and most shameful periods of its history (2 Kgs 21:1–18). In fact, the apostasy that took place in his reign was so bad that its effects were irreversible; God decided that Judah would have to be totally demolished (2 Kgs 23:26–27). And Babylon would be the instrument he would use.

As we come to the end of this crucial central section of the book, then, we are faced with the grim prospect of exile and the hard questions that

---

[29] Cf. Oswalt, p. 696.

[30] It is unlikely that he would have exercised sole rule at twelve years of age (2 Kgs 21:1), and, given the special circumstances (Hezekiah knew when he was going to die), a co-regency would have been a natural way of preparing for a trouble-free succession. Such co-regencies were common in the Ancient Near East at this time.

it would inevitably throw up. Was there any hope of recovery, or was judgment to be God's final word to Israel? Had the promises to David (2 Sam. 7:16) been cancelled or only put into abeyance? Who was really in control of history, the Lord or the gods of Babylon? Was trust in the God of Israel even possible any more? Paradoxically, it was precisely in this situation, where all the external supports of Israel's faith had been destroyed, that she was to learn in a deeper way than ever before what real trust in God was all about.

Isaiah 40:1 – 51:11

5. Comfort my people

In order to appreciate what follows, we need to pause at this point to reflect on the probable course of Isaiah's life in his later years.

The last time we hear of him engaged in public ministry is in 701 BC, at the time of Sennacherib's invasion (chapter 37). By then he would have been about sixty-nine years of age.[1] By the time Hezekiah died, three years later, he would have been seventy-two. But it is likely that he lived for several more years than this. Tradition has it that he died as a martyr during the reign of Manasseh, who had him sawn in two,[2] and there may well be an echo of this in Hebrews 11:36–37. At the very least we can be reasonably sure that he lived on for some years after his public preaching ministry had come to an end. What might he have done during this latter part of his life?

As early as 712 BC, as much as twenty years before his death, he could see that the Babylonian exile was coming (39:5–7). It must have weighed heavily upon him, but as far as we know he did not enlarge on it in his preaching. For most of the following fifteen years the more immediate Assyrian crisis demanded his attention and, with the accession of Manasseh and the fierce repression that came with it, it would have become impossible for him to preach at all. The nation and its leaders were no longer willing to listen. It would only be after they had reaped the full consequences of their apostasy that they would become teachable again,

---

[1] Assuming that he was about thirty years of age at the time of his call in 740 BC, 'the year that King Uzziah died' (6:1). See note 2 on p. 137.

[2] 'The Martyrdom and Ascension of Isaiah', chapter 5 in J. H. Charlesworth (ed.), *The Old Testament Pseudepigrapha* 2 (New York: Doubleday, 1985), pp. 163–164.

and then the word that they would need would not be one of judgment, but of restoration.

It is likely, therefore, as the movement from 39:5–7 to 40:1–11 implies, that in the latter part of his life Isaiah was called to a new task: to *comfort* God's people in words that his disciples would cherish and preserve in the dark days ahead until Israel[3] was at last ready to hear them (see 8:16–17).

1. Overture (40:1–11)

This opening part of chapter 40 is like the overture to a great musical composition. All the major themes which the following chapters will develop so powerfully get their first exploratory treatment here: *comfort* (1), atonement (2), *the way* of *the LORD* (3), *the glory of the LORD* (5), and the power of *the word of . . . God* (8), the city of God (9), and the might and tenderness of Zion's saviour (10–11). It leaves us full of expectation that a whole new movement in God's dealings with his people is about to unfold.

The first thing we hear is three stirring commands, like three trumpet blasts: 'Comfort . . . Speak . . . Proclaim!' (1–2). The tone is urgent, but it is not clear to whom these commands are directed.[4] It is as though we ourselves are being addressed, first by God himself (1), and then by the anonymous *voice* that rings out in verse 3. The Lord is about to visit Zion. His royal way will be across the desert, and it is imperative that appropriate preparations be made. *Cry out*, says another voice (6a). There is tension in the air, because an urgent call to action has been issued, and so far no-one has responded. Who of us cannot remember being in such a situation on countless occasions? It is the point at which people begin to squirm in their seats and everyone avoids the speaker's eye. Then at last someone speaks. *What shall I cry?* he says (6b). He is not so much volunteering as acknowledging that he is the one whom the speaker has had in mind all the time. These are his prophetic credentials. He has stood in God's council and heard God calling him to the specific ministry which he now takes up (cf. 1 Kgs 22:19–22; Jer. 23:18–22).

---

[3] After the death of Solomon, Israel in the political, national sense survived in fragmented form in the separate kingdoms of Israel and Judah. I follow Isaiah's own practice in chapters 40–66 in continuing to use 'Israel' for the descendants of Jacob/Israel, even when the situation in view is one in which Israel in the national, political sense has ceased to exist altogether (see, e.g., 40:27; 41:8; cf. Dan. 9:20; Ezra 2:70; 6:16; 7:7, 13). For more on 'Israel in the book of Isaiah' see above, pp. 22–23.

[4] The imperatives are plural. No single addressee is specified at this stage.

As we noted in the Introduction,[5] the identity of the unnamed prophet in this passage is provided elsewhere in the book. Isaiah's foundational call has already been described in chapter 6; this is his recommissioning for the second phase of his work. Once again he finds himself caught up into the presence of God, and hears not only the voice of God himself, but the cries of the mighty beings who surround his throne. His response here (*What shall I cry?*) is the counterpart of his earlier cry ('For how long, Lord?'). There he was summoned to a ministry of judgment; here to one of comfort. The former ministry was to continue 'until cities lie ruined and without inhabitant . . . until the LORD has sent everyone far away' (6:11–12). The present ministry is to be directed to those who have experienced the full outworking of that judgment. Like Elijah at Horeb (1 Kgs 19:1–18), Isaiah finds himself back at the source of his prophetic ministry, and is commissioned afresh for the second phase of his work.

Isaiah's new message is for people whose whole world has been shattered.[6] And for people like that, cheap comfort is not only a waste of time, it is cruel. Comfort that is not grounded in reality is no comfort at all. But the word that Isaiah is commissioned to bring to them is not like that at all; it is based on truth at every point.

The first truth is that they are God's people (1). The covenant that God made with their ancestors at Sinai still stands. He is not indifferent to Jerusalem's plight, in spite of the disasters he has allowed to come upon her. He still has plans for his people which are tied up in some way with that special place (2).[7] Like the prodigal in the far country, they are reminded that they still have a father who loves them, and a home to go to (Luke 15:17–20).

The second truth is that they have been forgiven (2). The penalty for their *sins* has been *paid* in full, and consequently they are to be released forthwith from hard labour. The royal pardon has come, the prison doors are flung wide open, and they are free! What good news this is – but how unexpected! No doubt the inner circle of Isaiah's disciples long treasured these words. But others, hearing them for the first time in exile, must have been startled by them, as a prisoner emerging from a dungeon blinks at

---

[5] In the section 'Unity and authorship', above, pp. 15–20.

[6] Ps. 137 poignantly captures how they felt.

[7] *Jerusalem* in verse 2 is parallel to *my people* in verse 1, indicating that the intimate relationship between people and city would survive the cruel separation foreshadowed in the previous chapter (39:5–7; cf. Ps. 137).

the light. How could this be? What was the explanation for it? Could fifty, sixty or seventy years of exile[8] pay for rebellion that had gone on for scores of generations? Could it atone even for the sins of those directly affected, let alone for those of their ancestors? The fact of the matter is that there is far more to this announcement of pardon than first meets the eye. There is a mystery here that will not be explained fully until chapter 53. But for now the simple announcement is allowed to stand alone in all its stark and bold splendour. You are forgiven! Your sin has been paid for! Your hard labour is over! What more comforting truth could there be for shattered people than that?

The third truth is that God will act to give concrete expression to the fact that he has forgiven them. He will not leave them where they are; he will bring them home (3–5). The processional way through the wilderness is not just *the way for the Lord* (3), but the way for his people too, for he is going to take them with him. He will tend, gather, carry and lead them as he brings them to Zion, like a *shepherd* caring for *his flock* (11). And as the watching world looks on, it will learn what kind of God he is; his *glory . . . will be revealed*, and all humankind *will see it* (5). A note is struck here which will recur more and more clearly as the book moves to its climax. The Lord is a missionary God; what he does for his own, he does not for their sake alone, but that all may come to know him. For the moment the focus is on the people of God themselves. 'Aliens and exiles' (1 Pet. 2:11, nrsv) they might be, but not for ever. There is solid comfort in that.

The fourth and final truth is that God's *word* can be relied upon. It does not decay and fade away as we do, but *endures for ever* (6–8). The person who cannot rest his or her whole weight on the word of God can never know peace, for in the last analysis it can be found nowhere else than in a trusting relationship with the God who made us and rightly claims us as his own. Reliance on the word of God is not fatalistic or superstitious. It is not trust in something impersonal like the stars or a good-luck charm. It is trust in a person who is committed to us and has all the resources necessary to care for us. It is *the word of our God* that Isaiah speaks of, a word or message that arises from a relationship. And the truth is that God's word has the same character as God himself. It is as unchanging and reliable as the God who speaks it.

---

[8] The deportation to Babylon took place in stages between 605 and 587 bc (Dan. 1:1–2; 2 Kgs 24:8–14; 25:1–12). The return began with the decree of Cyrus the Persian in 539 bc.

Such comfort is good news indeed, so good that it cannot and must not be contained. It must be shouted confidently and fearlessly from the mountain tops (9). The NRSV has captured the sense somewhat better than the NIV at this point; Jerusalem herself is to be the herald, and *the towns of Judah* are the ones to be told the good news. But *Jerusalem* here almost certainly refers to the exiled people of Jerusalem rather than the city itself, as in verse 1. The good news is for them first, but they are to share it quickly with their fellows still back in Palestine: the Lord is about to return to Zion! He will come with the strength of a warrior (no enemy will be able to resist him) and with the tenderness of a shepherd (the weak will not be left behind), and he will bring gifts (*his reward, his recompense*) that will make the sufferings of the exile vanish like a forgotten dream (10–11).

What news this is! It is in many ways the forerunner of the New Testament gospel,[9] just as John the Baptist was the forerunner of Jesus himself. It is no surprise to find, therefore, that when that fearless herald made his appearance in the wilderness of Judea centuries later, the Gospel writers could find no better way of describing what had happened than to say that it was the fulfilment of Isaiah 40:3, *A voice of one calling: 'In the wilderness prepare the way for the LORD; make straight . . . a highway'* (cf. Matt. 3:3; Mark 1:3; Luke 3:4; John 1:23). They did not mean that Isaiah's words had lain dormant until that point, but that with the coming of Jesus the Messiah they sprang to life again with deeper and fuller meaning.[10] The gospel of Jesus Christ is the gospel of Isaiah 40 transposed into a new, higher key. And it, too, is far too important to be contained. It must be shouted from the housetops, not just for the cities of Judah, but for all the world to hear (Matt. 10:26–33).

2. Majesty (40:12–31)

With this passage we leave the overture behind and are swept up into the first major movement of the composition. Its theme is a grand one, the majesty of God.

---

[9] Our English word 'gospel' corresponds to the Greek word *euangelion* (news, announcement), and in the LXX the related word *euangelizomenos* (herald) is used to translate the Hebrew word *mĕbaśśeret* (herald) in Isa. 40:9. But there is more than a verbal link with the New Testament gospel. All the same basic ingredients are here: atonement, forgiveness, the coming of God, release, reward. And as we shall see, the key to atonement in Isaiah is the Servant of the Lord, an Old Testament image of the Messiah.

[10] Although there was a partial return from exile in the years following 539 BC, spiritually the exile continued until the Messiah came. Only he could solve the deep, underlying problem.

a. The Incomparable One (40:12–26)

The reason the gospel is so powerful is that it is no mere human invention; it emanates from the very throne of God. It is powerful because it is God's gospel (Rom. 1:1), and what a God he is! Isaiah paints a breathtaking picture of him in verses 12–26. He created the universe as effortlessly as a skilled craftsman constructing a model on a workbench (12). He is infinitely wise (13–14), totally sovereign (15, 17),[11] worthy of more worship than we could ever give him (16), incomparable (18–20), and *enthroned above the circle of the earth* (22–24). *Lift up your eyes*, says Isaiah, and see who it is who has given you his word. There was plenty on the horizontal plane to discourage Isaiah and his contemporaries, and still more their successors who suffered the humiliation of defeat and deportation. But how could they give in to despair with a God like this? The danger, of course, was not that he would prove inadequate to their need, but that they would forget what he was like. That the God of Israel was the creator and Lord of the whole earth was not a novel idea; it was one of the most fundamental elements of their religious heritage. Their ancestors had seen the proof of it at the Red Sea (Exod. 14:21 – 15:12), and for generations they had affirmed it in public worship (Ps. 118:10–14). But such truth is not so easy to believe when our world is in ruins. In the midst of suffering we can become almost too numb to grasp it. Isaiah therefore clothes the age-old truth in vivid language so that it will penetrate the dullness of those who are almost past hope, take fresh hold of them, and lift them up.

b. Strength for the weary (40:27–31)

No sooner has the truth of God's *power* begun to take effect, however, than an insidious doubt about his goodness begins to assert itself. 'In view of all that has happened, can we really believe that God still cares for us? Isn't the message that he will move heaven and earth to save us rather too facile? Isn't the truth rather that we are too small to be of more than passing interest to him, and that if he ever really cared about us, surely he has long since ceased to do so?' (cf. 27). Isaiah knew that feeling only too well. He himself had doubtless been troubled by it many times in his own long pilgrimage of faith. But he had also learnt enough about God to know

---

[11] The NIV of 40:17 is somewhat misleading. The meaning is not that God is contemptuous of the nations, but that they are so small and insignificant compared with him that he is not in the least overawed or intimidated by them. They are totally subject to his sovereign control. Cf. North (1964), p. 85.

that it was a hideous lie.[12] The glory of God is not just, or even essentially, his power, but his servanthood; the fact is that no-one and nothing is too small to be important to him or worthy of his attention and care. He is not only strong in himself (28), but *he gives strength to the weary* (29). And therefore those who hope in him will never do so in vain: *They will soar on wings like eagles; they will run and not grow weary, they will walk and not be faint* (31).

3. God, his people, and the nations (41:1–29)

The nations have already come in for review in 40:15–17. To God they 'are like a drop in a bucket' or like the fine 'dust' on his 'scales'. But to the victims of imperial aggression, people who had become pawns in the ruthless power plays of the Middle East of their day, they had a very different aspect indeed. The nations inspired dread, and made trust in God seem absurd.

The fall of Jerusalem in 587 BC tested Israel's faith more profoundly than any other single event in the entire Old Testament period. But Isaiah, who clearly saw it would happen (39:5–7), never regarded it as calling God's sovereignty into question. Babylon, like Assyria, had a part to play in the drama of history, but it was the Lord, not they, who wrote the script. And after they had made their exit he would press other nations, too, into his service.

With this in mind he addresses those to whom Babylon's imperial might must have seemed an established and unassailable fact. He sets out to convince them of two things. First, events beginning to take shape about them, especially the rise and progress of the Persian king Cyrus (named explicitly in 44:28 and 45:1), are the Lord's doing (2–4, 25–27).[13] Second, they themselves, as the surviving remnant of Israel, are God's servant; he has chosen them and will not abandon them (8–10). Therefore they are to see the fear which has gripped them as the irrational, baseless thing it is, and not give in to it (10, 14).

The rise of Cyrus, king of Anshan (a city in Persia), was swift and impressive. When he came to the throne in 559 BC, Persia was subject to

---

[12] Comparable to the archetypal lie of Gen. 3:4–5.

[13] Although Cyrus is not named in the present passage, it is clearly he who is in view. He originated in *the east* (2) and made his final approach to Babylon *from the north* (25).

Media. By 549 BC, he was strong enough to rebel, kill the Median king Astyages, and found the Persian empire. In the next few years he pushed out its boundaries dramatically. He first moved west, conquering King Croesus of Lydia in 547 BC and subduing Asia Minor (now Turkey). Then he turned east to extend his rule into north-west India. By 540 BC he had brought much of the former Babylonian empire under his rule and was threatening Babylon itself. It fell to his general Gubaru without a fight in 539,[14] and seventeen days later Cyrus himself entered the city. There was no carnage; the previous king, Nabonidus, and his son Belshazzar,[15] had been deeply unpopular with the people of Babylon, many of whom regarded Cyrus as a liberator. For those who had been brought to Babylon against their will, the advent of Cyrus proved to be a particularly happy event, for by the standards of those times he was a very enlightened and humane ruler. He reversed the Babylonian policy of deportation and quickly embarked on a programme of repatriating displaced people and restoring their places of worship, the captives from Jerusalem being one of the first groups to benefit. The substance of his decree permitting their return is recorded in Ezra 1:2–4.

Most of this, of course, would have been quite unknown to the people in view in the present passage. All they would have been aware of was that another conqueror was on the move, with all the disturbing possibilities that this involved. They had no idea how things would turn out, or how their own fragile existence might be affected by the developing events. They felt themselves to be utterly powerless, like driftwood at sea, at the mercy of forces totally beyond their control. But in fact this was far from the case. The power shaping events was neither impersonal nor capricious. It was the powerful, purposive hand of God. But how could Isaiah convince them of this?

a. The nations on trial (41:1–7, 21–29)

He invites them to imagine God summoning the nations before him to prove, if they can, that they are the ones who shape history (1). But before

---

[14] As stated in the *Babylonian Chronicle* (*ANET*, p. 306). According to Herodotus (1.90–91), the Persians made a surprise attack along the bed of the Euphrates after lowering the water level by diverting the river into a nearby lake or marsh upstream from the city. The real explanation for the victory, however, as suggested by the *Babylonian Chronicle*, may be that the defenders had been alienated by the previous regime and simply offered no resistance.

[15] Nabonidus spent much of his time away from Babylon. Belshazzar was probably co-regent, and effectively sole ruler in his father's absence (Dan. 5). 'Darius the Mede' (Dan. 5:31) may be an alternative title for either Cyrus himself or his general Gubaru, whom he appointed governor. See the article 'Darius' in *NBD*.

the bar of God's judgment throne they have nothing to say. The rapid advance of Cyrus has made them all afraid (2b–3), and it is clear that their idols are powerless to save them, despite their pathetic attempts to pretend that it is otherwise (5–7). But is it Cyrus himself, then, who is the master of the world? 'No,' says the Lord, 'he is merely my instrument. I am the one who has *stirred* him *up*' (cf. 2a). It is an astounding claim, bold, powerful, and certain to sweep all before it – if it can be sustained. But can it? That is the crucial question. Bold claims unsupported by credible evidence are mere bluster; they carry no weight at all. Verses 1–7 leave us in suspense, with the crucial question of evidence unanswered. But in verses 21–29 the Lord takes up his dispute with the nations again, and this time his case against them is clinched. The proof that he and he alone is Lord of the historical process is that he announces beforehand what will happen, and then brings it to pass, as he has done in the present case, something that no human potentate or man-made idol could do. The rise and progress of Cyrus were no accident; they were foretold through Isaiah, and what the nations saw in due course was God putting his powerful word into effect.[16] More importantly, the exiles from Judah were in a position to see for themselves the correspondence between Isaiah's inspired predictions and the events unfolding before them, and to know for certain that their God, the God of Israel, was in total command of their world.[17]

b. Israel, God's servant (41:8–20)

But where did this leave them, and what was their response to be in the present circumstances? First, they were to remember who they were. They were collectively God's *servant*, just as their ancestor *Jacob* had been, and as *Abraham* had been before him (8–9). As the *descendants* of Abraham, they still shared in his calling to be a blessing to the whole earth (Gen. 12:1–3). They might feel themselves to be worms (14), to be *poor and needy* (17), and utterly insignificant (*little Israel*, 14), and so in a sense they were. Their significance did not reside in themselves, however, or in their circumstances, but in the fact that God had *chosen* them to serve him (8).

---

[16] The reference to Cyrus calling on the Lord's name in verse 25 need not imply worship (Cyrus in fact never became a worshipper of the Lord). The original Hebrew (literally 'to call by name') may mean simply 'to refer to something or someone by name'. According to Ezra 1:2–4, Cyrus did acknowledge the Lord to the extent of referring to him by name in his decree permitting the exiles to return to Jerusalem.

[17] Much of the force of the theological argument of these and other passages is lost if they are not genuinely long-range predictions, as advocates of the Second Isaiah hypothesis often conveniently overlook. See especially verse 26.

The form that their service would take is indicated by a startling meta-phor: *I will make you into a threshing-sledge, new and sharp, with many teeth. You will thresh the mountains* [a figure for worldly powers] *and crush them, and reduce the hills to chaff* (15). It is such a contrast to their present weakness that it is laughable. But two things must be borne in mind. First, a threshing-sledge was an instrument in the farmer's hands. Its effective-ness depended in the last analysis on the power and skill of the one who wielded it. This is much more a statement about what God will make them and what he will do with them than about what they themselves will achieve. And second, a threshing-sledge was an instrument for separating the corn from the chaff, for distinguishing between what was to be gathered into the granary and what was to be burned.[18] 'Threshing' is a metaphor for judgment. From the moment God called Abraham, the fate of nations depended on their response to him and his descendants: 'I will bless those who bless you, and whoever curses you I will curse' (Gen. 12:3). In a sense the threshing began at that point, and Isaiah wants those who have been carried off to Babylon to know that God still holds the nations accountable for how they treat his people. They, the surviving remnant of Israel, are still the touchstone by which the nations will be judged. In this sense they will fulfil their calling by simply being there, in the world, as the people of God.[19]

First, then, they are to remember who they are. And second, they are not to give in to *fear* (10, 14). They had plenty of external enemies, and God would deal with these in due course (11–12). Far more dangerous, however, was the enemy within. That could undermine their whole relationship with God, for it was a denial of everything God had called them to be. Fear was the very antithesis of the trust that had characterized their ancestor Abraham, the one in whom their own call to be the people of God had its genesis (8; Gen. 15:6). But in their present situation what grounds did they have for trust? Two very good ones. They had God's promise to *strengthen, help* and *uphold* them (10b). They also had the memory of how God had done just that for their ancestors. Verses 17–20 are full of allusions to the exodus from Egypt, when God sustained his people in the wilderness. The implication, of course, is that God's promises are not idle ones. What

---

18 A threshing-sledge was a heavy wooden board studded with metal teeth on its underside (cf. Amos 1:3). After it had been dragged around the threshing-floor, the grain and chaff were tossed into the air with a pitchfork and the chaff was carried away by the wind; North (1964), p. 99.

19 We are not far here from the New Testament images of salt and light (Matt. 5:13–16).

he has done before he will do again. The Lord, who was Israel's Redeemer from Egypt (Exod. 6:6; 15:13), will also be her Redeemer from Babylon (14).[20]

What a great preacher and pastor Isaiah was! He sustained the weary people of God by bringing them back to the great fundamentals of their faith: election, calling, redemption, the promises of God and the faithfulness of God. God give us such preachers today!

4. God's perfect Servant (42:1–9)

The 'servant of God' theme is one of the richest strands of Isaiah's thought, and it lies right at the heart of his message as it moves to its climax in this second half of the book. Of course, there have been several intimations of it before this point. Isaiah himself has been called God's servant (20:3), and so has the faithful Eliakim, Hezekiah's chief steward (22:20). More recently, those who were to find themselves far away from all the tangible signs of their election (land, temple, the throne of David, and so on) have been reminded that, in a corporate sense, they too are God's servant, since they still share in the call and mission of their ancestor Abraham (41:8–9).

However, the announcement at the beginning of chapter 42, *Here is my servant* . . . , suggests that a new and significant stage has now been reached in the development of this theme. Samuel used a similar expression when he presented Saul to the people as their new king (1 Sam. 10:24), and Pilate did the same when he presented Jesus to the crowds at his trial: 'Here is your king' (John 19:14). It is like a sudden blast of the trumpets or roll of the drums in an orchestral work. We immediately sense that a climax has been reached, or that a significant change in the tempo or direction of the work is about to take place, and this is certainly what happens here. The passage 42:1–9 is the first of a remarkable series (commonly called the 'Servant Songs') in which the servant theme is developed in a quite distinctive way and brought to a resounding climax.[21]

---

[20] Uses of the terms 'redeem' and 'redemption' and 'redeemer' (*gō'ēl*) indicate that the redeemer relationship depended on ties of kinship. A *gō'ēl* was a kinsman who had the responsibility of protecting the interests of his relative by every means in his power, whether by 'redeeming' him or his property during his lifetime, or by avenging his death if he had been murdered (Lev. 25:25, 48; Num. 35:16–21). See the note on 'ransomed/redeemed' at 35:9. The implication of the present passage is that the Lord's covenant bonds with Israel are as close as those which bind members of the same human family, and he will never repudiate his self-imposed obligations (North, p. 100).

[21] It was Bernhard Duhm (1892) who first identified 42:1–4; 49:1–6; 50:4–9; and 52:13 – 53:12 as the four Servant Songs. Most scholars today still follow his lead, but with some difference of opinion about the precise limits of the passages. I take the four Songs to be 42:1–9; 49:1–7; 50:4–9; and 52:13 – 53:12, and regard 61:1–3 as a fifth and final Song which brings the whole series to a climax.

Clearly, God himself is the one who makes the announcement in verse 1. But who is the servant he is referring to, and to whom is he speaking? One possibility, especially in view of 41:8–9, is that the servant is the surviving remnant of Israel, and that the announcement is made to the nations. 'Look,' God says, 'here is my servant – this apparently insignificant group of people! I will achieve my purposes for the whole world through them.' But on reflection this can hardly be the case. For one thing, whereas in chapter 41 the nations were addressed directly ('Be silent before me, you islands!' 41:1), here they are referred to indirectly: *he*, the servant, *will bring justice to the nations* (42:1b). And perhaps more significantly, the servant is far too ideal a figure to represent Israel in any direct sense. He fills God with *delight*, he is quiet and gentle, faithful and persevering; he does *not falter* or become *discouraged* (1–4). Israel, by contrast, is resentful and complaining (40:27), fearful and dismayed (41:10), blind, deaf (42:18–19) and disobedient (42:23–24). If Israel is to be found at all in the announcement of 42:1–9 it is in the *bruised reed* and the *smouldering wick* of verse 3 rather than in the servant of verse 1. In short, the servant in this passage seems to be a figure who embodies all that Israel ought to be but is not. He is God's perfect servant.

The announcement, then, is made to God's people themselves. The servant it refers to is not just an ideal they should aspire to but (as we shall see in due course) a real person who is God's answer to their weakness and failure. His identity is not clear at this stage, so for the time being we will follow the practice of most scholars and refer to him simply as the Servant of the Lord, or just the Servant (capital 'S').

There are three parts to this first Song. Verses 1–4 are addressed to Israel[22] with the Servant as the subject (*Here is my servant . . .*). Verses 5–7 are addressed to the Servant himself, with Israel overhearing what is said (*I, the Lord, have called you* [singular] *in righteousness*). Finally, in verses 8–9 Israel is once more addressed directly (*I am the Lord . . . new things I declare . . . I announce them to you* [plural]). The main topic of all three parts is the mission that the Servant is to carry out.

---

[22] See the note on 'Israel in the book of Isaiah', above, pp. 22–23. I have chosen to avoid the more common expression 'the exiles' for the addressees in contexts like this in chapters 40–55. While an exilic situation is certainly envisaged following 39:5–7, it is never simply, or primarily, a particular exilic community which is being addressed, but Israel as a whole as the elect people of God. This is made very clear by the way 'Jacob' and 'Israel' are used in 40:27 and 41:8 before we reach the first Servant Song of chapter 42. The Servant's ministry always has Israel as a whole in view, not just the Babylonian exiles (49:5).

The key term in verses 1–4 is *justice* (*mišpāṭ*). The Servant *will bring justice to the nations* (1); he will faithfully *bring forth justice* (3), and he will establish *justice on earth* (4). But we have to be careful here, for in the book of Isaiah *mišpāṭ* is a rather bigger thing than we normally think of as justice. In 40:14 it has to do with the order God has given to the whole universe by his creative acts.[23] In 40:27 it refers to the maintenance of Israel's position in the world as a nation in a special relationship with God,[24] and in 41:1 it has to do with the false claims of the nations and their gods being silenced, and the truth about the Lord's total sovereignty over history being established.[25] Viewed against this background, the mission of the Servant is a gigantic one. It is nothing less than to put God's plans for his people into full effect, and to make the truth about the Lord, Israel's God, known everywhere, especially the fact that he alone is the sovereign creator and Lord of history.

The same breathtaking mission is explained in verses 5–7 in terms of the Servant being *a covenant* and *a light* (6b). As creator, God is the one *who gives breath to* all *people* (5b). Moreover, the God who made the world is committed to its welfare; there is a 'covenant' between God and the human race implicit in the act of creation itself. And the Servant, as *a covenant for the people and a light for the Gentiles,* is to be the very embodiment of that covenant. It is through him that God's purposes for his world will be realized, by the opening of *eyes that are blind,* the freeing of *captives,* and the *release* of *those who sit in darkness* (7). In short, the Servant will undo all the horrendous and degrading effects that sin has had on the human race and restore to people their true freedom and dignity as sons and daughters of God.

Finally, in verses 8–9, the mission of the Servant is spoken of in terms of *former things* and *new things.* The correspondence between prophecies that had been made and events as they unfolded was to provide the captives in Babylon with significant proof of the Lord's uniqueness and sovereignty in their present experience (especially the rise of Cyrus). But the work of the Servant would open a new chapter in God's relationship with his people and with the world, in which his *glory* would be displayed in a new way, far surpassing anything that had happened previously. In fact, it would lead eventually to new heavens and a new earth (65:17; 66:22).

---

[23] 'The right way' there is literally 'the way of *mišpāṭ*'.

[24] 'My cause' is literally 'my *mišpāṭ*'.

[25] 'The place of judgment' is literally 'the place of *mišpāṭ*'.

The real wonder of the Servant's mission, however, lies not so much in its breathtaking scope as in the manner in which it will be accomplished. He will not be a military conqueror like Cyrus. The source of his strength will be the Spirit of God (1). The instrument of his rule will be the word of God (4b).[26] His manner will be gentle rather than overbearing (2, 3a), and there is more than a hint in the opening line of verse 4 that his mission will involve him in personal suffering.

This contrast between Cyrus and the Servant brings us back at last to the people in view in this passage. They were going to need two kinds of deliverance. They would need release from physical captivity, and God would use Cyrus to achieve that. But they would also need release from bitterness, blindness and spiritual *darkness* (7). Their deepest need would be for someone who could heal their broken relationship with God. And here God points them to the one who will accomplish that for them. The message of comfort with which chapter 40 opened has its deepest roots here, in the work of the Servant. This first Servant Song is good news for all people, but it was good news for Israel first of all. God's healing, saving work would begin with them, and then overflow to a waiting world (cf. Rom. 1:16).

5. Praise the Lord! (42:10–17)

What could be more appropriate after the tremendous announcement of the previous passage than a great outburst of *praise* to God! Like the apostle Paul, Isaiah cannot contain himself when the glory of the gospel grips him (cf. Rom. 11:33–36). The praise of other things – especially *idols* – is foolish and pathetic compared with the rich and strong praise of the Lord which we have here.[27] Unlike them, he can and will do what he has promised, and so the announcement of 'new things' in verse 9 leads naturally to the *new song* of verse 10.

Isaiah calls on the whole world to join him in praising God – sailors and desert-dwellers, sea creatures and human beings, islands and mountains (10–11) – and why not, since he is creator of all and Lord of all? But the song of these verses has a higher theme than this, which emerges in verses 13–16 as the praise reaches its climax in two bold and dramatic pictures

---

[26] The Servant's *teaching* (4b) is literally 'his *tôrâ*', which means 'instruction' or 'guidance' (rather than 'law', RSV). In the last Song (61:1–3), the Servant appears as a Spirit-anointed preacher of the gospel.

[27] Note how the passage is framed by reference to the vain worship of *idols* (8, 17).

of the Lord as the saviour of his people. *Like a warrior he* stirs *up his zeal* (13), and *like a woman in childbirth* he gasps and pants (14). Redemption is accomplished with tremendous effort and at great cost, and it is the glory of the Lord that he spares himself neither. He is totally committed to the welfare of his people, however blind they may be and however dark their circumstances; he *will not forsake them* (16). What a grand theme! This *new song* anticipates the song of the saints in heaven (Rev. 5:9).

6. Sinful Israel, the blind and deaf servant (42:18–25)

It is the way of great preachers to shock their audiences at times in order to shake them out of their lethargy and gain their attention. This is a 'shocking' passage in that sense. The words *my servant*, so recently used approvingly of the Lord's ideal Servant (1), are now applied to the Lord's people in the context of a stinging rebuke (19). How unlike him they are! And what a plunge this is from the anticipation of heaven in the previous song of praise! God's people are anything but full of praise. Israel has so given in to bitterness and unbelief that all they are capable of at present is complaint (40:27). The word *blind* is picked up from verse 16 of the previous passage, but now it is given a different edge. They are *deaf* to God's word, and blind to his purposes (18–19).[28] In this they are no better than their ancestors, whose stubborn rebelliousness led to the punishment of the exile (23–25). And this blindness is doubly culpable, since Israel, in contrast to other nations, had the benefit of special revelation. The Lord had made *his law great and glorious* among them (21).[29]

Isaiah is in full flight here, and quite unsparing of the feelings of his audience. Like a good pastor, he knows that they will never know the comfort of God and fulfil their mission to be his servant people until they have faced up to their sinfulness and repented of it. But at the same time there is no self-righteous denouncing of them from a position of assumed superiority. Note the *we* in *against whom we have sinned* (24). He has never forgotten that moment when he saw the exalted Lord and knew that he himself was as unclean and undone as everyone else (6:5). He speaks as

---

[28] *The one in covenant with me* (19) translates the single word *mĕšullām*. This is passive, and is related to *šālôm* ('peace'). It should probably be understood as meaning 'the one who has been granted peace' (cf. 54:10, 'my covenant of peace'). It is parallel to *the servant of the Lord* (Israel) in the last half of the verse.

[29] *Law* (Hebrew *tôrâ*, 'instruction') is probably more here than just the law of Moses, and includes also the teaching God had given through the prophets. Israel had despised this instruction, but it is God's intention to carry out his purposes. Young, 3, p. 134.

one who has discovered the wonder of forgiveness himself and longs for others to know it too.

Of course, there is a paradox here. In a sense they have already been forgiven (40:2). But what Isaiah is trying to elicit from them is the response that is necessary if they are to appropriate that forgiveness and live in the good of it.[30] So lest they be overwhelmed by his stern rebuke, he moves on quickly, in chapter 43, to assure them again of God's continued commitment to them.

7. Strong encouragement (43:1 – 44:5)

This long section is rather daunting at first sight because of its varied contents and complex structure. But fundamentally it is a reaffirmation of Israel's calling to be the Lord's servant. The fact that the Lord has pointed to another and greater Servant does not mean that Israel's own servant role has been abrogated. Quite the reverse. It is confirmed here in the strongest possible terms (43:10; 44:1–2).

The main thrust of the passage can be summarized in six great statements of encouragement, one for each of its six parts:

'Do not fear, for I have redeemed you' (43:1).
'You are my witnesses,' declares the LORD (43:10).
'I am the LORD . . . your King' (43:15).
'See, I am doing a new thing!' (43:19).
'I, even I, am he who blots out your transgressions' (43:25).
'I will pour out my Spirit on your offspring' (44:3).

a. 'Do not fear' (43:1–7)

The first section picks up the ominous word *flames* (2b) from the closing verse of the previous chapter (42:25), and counters it with the steadying exhortation *Do not fear* (1b). There are some of the tenderest words here that God ever spoke to his children: *you are mine; you are precious and honoured in my sight; I love you; I will be with you.* They are addressed to people far from home, still in the midst of fires and deep waters, with many more trials to face before they reach their final rest. There is no

---

[30] Perhaps the best analogy is that of someone who has been left a large inheritance but has never claimed. it.

promise here of a quick fix or a trouble-free future, but of God's sustaining presence right through to journey's end, come what may. They are words which we ourselves may appropriate and treasure with complete propriety, for as the old covenant opens out into the new, the people of God, even though they have the cross and the empty tomb behind them, remain aliens and exiles in a hostile world (1 Pet. 2:11; cf. Jas 1:1). And it is the faithfulness of the same God, who has promised never to leave them or forsake them, that will bring them home (Heb. 13:5–6).

The strong encouragement of this passage is anchored in the great truths of creation and redemption, and both are given fresh meaning in the process. In chapter 40 Isaiah directed the gaze of his hearers upwards to contemplate the power of the one who created and formed the universe. Now he tells them that this same God has *created* and *formed* them too, *for* his *glory* (1, 7). And the value he places upon them is translated into the concrete terms of *ransom* and *exchange*. The Lord will reward Cyrus for releasing his precious people by giving him a vastly expanded empire in exchange for them (3–4), not with the desperation of someone who is weak, but with the lavish generosity of someone who loves deeply and has the whole world at his disposal. People who are loved like that have absolutely nothing to fear (cf. Rom. 8:31–39).

b. 'You are my witnesses' (43:8–13)

Fear, of course, turns us in upon ourselves. It chills our heart and silences our lips, and is the greatest possible hindrance to effective witness. So it is not until he has dealt with the fear that was crippling Israel that he can move on in verses 8–13 to tell them of their call to be the Lord's *witnesses*. And the substance of their witness is to be this: 'There is no god, no saviour, but the LORD' (cf. 10–12). Imagine the scene which Isaiah sketches in so cryptically in verses 8–10. The Lord himself is on trial. He claims that he alone is God, but is accused of lying. His rivals, the pagan gods, have as *their witnesses* the many people who worship them. The Lord has only the *blind* and *deaf* captives (8). As they are led in to take the witness stand a hush falls over the courtroom. Surely the Lord's case is lost. But no; these feeble witnesses produce incontrovertible evidence of the truth of the Lord's claim: he alone *foretold* the things now taking place, especially the rise of Cyrus (9b).[31] Immediately the whole atmosphere in the court

---

[31] Verse 9b is cryptic. I take *them* to be the gods of the nations, and *It* to be the rise of Cyrus.

changes. The opposition is reduced to silence and the Lord's case is carried. And something else happens. The witnesses themselves are transformed. Their own blindness and deafness are swallowed up by a new assurance, and they leave the court with a firm tread and heads held high (10b).[32] That is why this call to witness fits so comfortably in a passage about assurance. The feeble people of God can and will be his witnesses! Truth is on their side, and as they rise above their fears and proclaim it, that truth will grip them and transform them. Witness is not an onerous burden, but an unspeakable privilege. It is a means not only of projecting the truth about God into the world, but of strengthening God's people themselves.

But here we strike a problem. How were those whom the enemy would herd off into exile to fulfil their calling to be witnesses? Isaiah has used a literary figure (the courtroom scene), but what reality corresponds to it? The deportees never did proclaim the truth about the Lord to the nations in the way that we normally think of witnessing today. They (or a significant number of them) simply returned to Jerusalem when God opened the way, and lived there again as his people. But the fact is that this itself was proof of the Lord's claim to be God, for it was the historical fulfilment of the word he had spoken concerning them through his prophets. He had done what no other god could do, and established his people like a lamp on a lampstand or a city set on a hill, bearing witness by their very existence to the truth about him (Matt. 5:14–16). But Isaiah also foresaw the day when witnessing would assume a far more active form; heralds would be sent out far and wide to proclaim the Lord's glory among the nations (66:19–20). This lay far beyond the horizon of Isaiah's own experience, or that of those who were to live through the dark days following his death, but it was part of the vision he gave them. They were to see what happened to them as laying the foundation for something far greater that God would bring to pass in the future, and take courage from that.

c. 'I am the Lord . . . your King' (43:14–15)

The third word of encouragement follows naturally from this. If Israel was to witness to the truth about the Lord by a return to Jerusalem, those for whom this might seem impossible would need assurance that the enemy

---

[32] Note the purpose clause (*so that* . . .) in 10b. The purpose of witness is not just to convince the world but also to confirm the faith of the witnesses.

that held them was not invincible. This is just what verses 14–15 affirm. This is the first time since comfort was announced in chapter 40 that Babylon is explicitly mentioned (14). It is as though the might of Babylon has been a reality too terrible to confront directly. But we will not necessarily overcome hostile realities simply by confronting them. If we are not equal to them they may very well overwhelm us, however brave we are. We can overcome them only when we face them in the certain knowledge that they are not absolute and that there is a greater reality that is for us (cf. 1 John 4:4).

In this short oracle mighty Babylon is framed and diminished by the greater reality of Israel's God: *the LORD, Redeemer, Holy One, Creator* and *King* (14a, 15b). As these terms cascade out, God's people (who have heard them all before; see, e.g., 41:14; 40:28; 6:5) are powerfully reminded of all that they know about God and his commitment to them. And to this is added a promise addressed to the specific situation of exile: *For your sake I will send to Babylon and bring down as fugitives all the Babylonians, in the ships in which they took pride* (14b).[33] How different the proud Babylonians suddenly appear – fugitives fleeing downstream as Cyrus, who has been sent by the Lord, enters the city from the north! Babylon was certainly a terrible reality, but the greater reality by far was the Lord's absolute sovereignty, and unswerving commitment to his people. How aptly the last line sums it up: *I am the LORD . . . your King.*

d. 'See, I am doing a new thing!' (43:16–21)

So much for Babylon. But for those who were to leave it at last, there would be other obstacles to be faced, including the desert and the long journey home – the subject of the next word of encouragement in verses 16–21. It is perhaps hard for us to appreciate fully what a frightening prospect this journey must have been to those who faced it. First, it was across unknown territory. Most of those who were young and fit enough to travel would have been born in exile, and although Babylon was not their true home it would have been the only place they knew. The wilderness represented a break with even that limited security. Second, Jerusalem was a long way off, between 500 and 900 miles, depending on the route. The returnees could expect to be travelling for at least four months through harsh

---

[33] Herodotus (1.194) speaks of ships that discharged their cargoes in Babylon. They were apparently small trading ships that sailed the Euphrates and the Persian Gulf. Cf. Young, 3, p. 153.

terrain, in which they would be vulnerable not only to exhaustion but also to attack by bandits (Ezra 8:31). The wilderness meant hardship and danger. And what could they expect on arrival? Not hearth and home and plenty, but a devastated land, and the arduous task of rebuilding their lives from scratch. In a sense the wilderness was just as frightening a thing as Babylon.

With this in view Isaiah speaks of *former things* and a *new thing* (cf. 42:9). Verses 16–21 are full of allusions to the exodus from Egypt centuries before, and the journey through *the wilderness* to Canaan – *former things* which were fundamental to Israel's whole existence as the covenant people of God. But then, paradoxically, having deliberately called them to mind, Isaiah diverts attention from them: *Forget the former things . . . See, I am doing a new thing!* (18–19). He knows human psychology only too well. The past can become an idealized world (the 'good old days') into which we retreat when the future becomes too frightening to face, or it can be a springboard from which we launch ourselves into the future with new strength. Isaiah does not want Israel to retreat into the past. He does want them, however, to remember that the wilderness has been conquered before and, armed with that knowledge, to go forward and to conquer it again. As they do so, they can be assured that the Lord goes before them to make *a way* for them through the desert, just as he made one for their ancestors (19). They can be the witnesses God has created them to be only by going forward with God, by grasping the *new thing* he has for them (21).

e. 'I, even I, am he who blots out your transgressions' (43:22–28)

The fifth word of encouragement at first sight seems to be nothing of the kind. It consists largely of an indictment of Israel for its corrupt worship. The opening words of verse 22 are emphatic in the original Hebrew: 'It was not *me* you called upon, Jacob.' In other words, Israel's worship was such a farce, such a misrepresentation of the truth, that the LORD did not regard it as worship of himself at all. It was utterly repugnant to him (cf. 1:10–17). So he consigned Israel and its leaders to destruction, and those who survived to the disgrace of exile (28).[34] The use of the old name *Jacob* in verses 22 and 28 (at the beginning and end of the passage)

---

[34] I follow the LXX in taking the verbs of verse 28 as past tense. Cf. NRSV: 'Therefore I profaned . . . the sanctuary, I delivered Jacob to utter destruction.'

emphasizes just how deep and persistent Israel's sin had been; throughout its whole history the nation had behaved just like its *first father* (27).[35] They had burdened the Lord with their sins and wearied him with their offences (24b)[36] until his patience had been exhausted. The generation that suffered exile to Babylon had a shameful past that haunted them. It was with them in the disgrace they suffered every day, for this was its bitter fruit. The past could not be exorcised by some psychological trick, by pretending that it had not happened, or that they themselves were a new breed of people utterly different from their ancestors. The truth was that they were 'Jacob' too. The only solution was to accept their past, with the verdict that God had pronounced on it, and then to reach out with both hands and grasp the forgiveness that he offered them. *I, even I, am he who blots out your transgressions, for my own sake, and remembers your sins no more* (25). Once spoken, this word of forgiveness totally dominates its context, like a shaft of brilliant light piercing a night sky. The dark sayings around it simply serve to throw it into sharp relief. At its deepest level, this passage is not about Israel's past at all, but about the forgiveness that releases her from it, a release she needed far more than release from Babylon. The word of forgiveness is the most encouraging message of all, and Israel, like us, needed to hear it again and again.

f. 'I will pour out my Spirit on your offspring' (44:1–5)

The chapter division at 44:1 is particularly unfortunate, because 44:1–5 is in fact the sixth and final word of encouragement that caps the whole series. And what an appropriate climax it is! All attention is now focused on the future, a future as different from the past as light is from darkness. As *water* poured on *thirsty land* causes it to burst into life again, so the Lord *will pour out* his *Spirit* on Israel's *descendants* (3; see 32:15; and cf. Ezek. 39:29; Joel 2:28; Zech. 12:10).[37] *They will spring up like grass in a meadow, like poplar trees by flowing streams* (4). So blessed will they be that total outsiders will join them, forsaking their paganism and gladly

---

[35] In the present context this must refer to Jacob rather than Abraham. The patriarchal narratives are quite candid about his sinfulness (e.g. Gen. 27:35).

[36] Note the sustained play on *burdened* and *wearied* in 22–24. The Lord had not burdened or wearied them by making excessive demands in the area of formal worship, but they had burdened and wearied him with their sins. *Calamus* (24), an eastern aromatic plant, was a luxury import. The mention of it here suggests that Israel's worship was outwardly extravagant, but hollow none the less.

[37] The image of 'pouring' links all these passages with the fulfilment which comes on the day of Pentecost (Acts 2:16–7). While he may be likened metaphorically to water, wind, breath, and so on, the Spirit himself is just as fully personal in the Old Testament as he is in the New. See especially 63:10, and cf. Eph. 4:30.

swearing allegiance to Israel's God. *Jacob* will no longer be a shameful name, but a glorious one, held in honour by all (5).[38]

All this, of course, is exactly what was promised to Abraham: a great name, many descendants, blessing overflowing to all the families of the earth (Gen. 12:1–3). How remote the fulfilment of that promise must have seemed to the small, humiliated remnant in Babylon! The purpose of this passage is to remind them, when they had reached the depths of that bitter experience, that God had not forgotten his promise to Abraham, or withdrawn his call from their descendants. Beyond the dark days of exile they would flourish again and become the blessing to the nations that he had always intended them to be. This final word of encouragement to Israel rests upon the bedrock of God's faithfulness, and strongly reaffirms his commitment to fulfil his promises to them and through them. There would be many twists and turns in the road ahead, but it would not be a dead end. All God's promises would eventually find their resounding 'Yes' and 'Amen' in Christ, to the glory of God (2 Cor. 1:20).

What, though, of the pitfalls along the way? In the next section Isaiah warns of one of the most dangerous of them.

8. Idolatry (44:6–23)

Idolatry is the worst sin of all, because it moves God to the periphery of our lives and puts something else in his place. It gives to something else the glory that should be God's alone. Chameleon-like, it constantly disguises itself so that we are scarcely aware of its presence, even when we are most in the grip of it. Greed, Paul tells us, is idolatry, because it turns us away from God towards things, and makes the pursuit of them the passion of our lives (Col. 3:5). The modern world is no less given over to idolatry than the ancient one; it is just that its cruder forms were more prevalent then.

Of course, idolatry was a peculiarly pagan practice; Israel was forbidden to have anything to do with it (Exod. 20:1–6). Yet it always held a fatal attraction for them, even in its crudest forms, because it seemed to work. It was not just primitive and backward people who practised it, but the

---

[38] *Jeshurun* ('upright one') in v. 2b is an honorific title that stands in sharp contrast to *Jacob* ('deceiver'). See Gen. 27:36; 32:28; Deut. 32:15; 33:5, 26.

cultured and powerful – the Egyptians, the Assyrians and the Babylonians. And of course they attributed their success to the power of their gods. How absurd, then, for their humiliated victims to maintain that their God, the Lord, was supreme and that the gods of their conquerors were mere nothings! At times they must have doubted it themselves, and yet they were called to be *witnesses* to precisely that fact (6–8).[39]

This is the context in which we must see Isaiah's broadside against idolatry in verses 9–20. Its purpose is to expose the real character of idolatry so that Israel will have no illusions about it. The truth is that idolatry is not only deeply offensive to God, it is also fundamentally absurd; those who indulge in it feed on *ashes* and their *deluded* hearts deceive them (20). Humans beings *make idols* (9), but the Lord has *made* Israel (21),[40] and *displays his glory* through her (23b). What an honour! And it is an honour that we have inherited as the people of God today (Matt. 5:13–16).

But such an honour calls for constant vigilance, for the danger of idolatry in one or other of its enticing forms is always with us. *Remember,* Isaiah says, remember the truth (21). Our eyes and ears are constantly bombarded with lies about God and attractive alternatives to serving him, and we will be swamped by them unless we constantly call the truth to mind. This is where meditation on Scripture is such a strengthening thing for us, for it is full of the greatness and glory and faithfulness of God. But what if we do stray, and slip into idolatrous patterns of thought or behaviour (and which of us does not from time to time)? *Return,* says Isaiah, to the one who *redeemed you* (22). We are all going to need a lot of forgiving on our way to our final rest, and the great news of the gospel is that it is available to us. The one condition is that we return and seek God for it whenever we stray (1 John 1:8–9). And finally, *Sing for joy* (23). This last exhortation is addressed to *heavens* and *earth, mountains, forests* and *trees,* and in a sense they do praise him; it is only humankind that is idolatrous (Ps. 19:1–4). But surely, of all created things it is those made in God's image who ought to praise him most, and, of them, the *redeemed* most of all. And those who do will find that the battle is won; it is impossible for idolatry to get a foothold in a joyful, praising heart.

---

[39] The *Rock* (8b) is a very ancient title for the Lord (Gen. 49:24; Deut. 32:4, 15, 18, 30, 31; Ps. 18:31), applied in the New Testament to Christ (1 Cor. 10:4).

[40] The same Hebrew word, *yāṣar,* is used in both verses.

9. Cyrus, the Lord's shepherd (44:24 – 45:13)

This important passage about *Cyrus* bursts upon us rather surprisingly and shockingly at this point. It is not that Cyrus is unknown to us; we have already met him as the 'one from the east' whom the Lord has stirred up (41:2). The surprise is that he should be spoken of as the Lord's *shepherd* (44:28) and his *anointed* (45:1), directly after a passage in which idolatry has been so comprehensively condemned. For Cyrus himself was a pagan idolater![41] As we shall see (45:9–13), the Lord's choice of such a person was to cause Israel considerable bewilderment, and quite understandably so. But surely there is an important lesson here which the very placement of this passage serves to drive home. God may disapprove of idolatry but use an idolater for some good purpose. The fact that he uses someone in a specific way does not mean that he approves of that person's total lifestyle. We should neither stand in judgment on God's actions nor draw wrong conclusions from them, but praise him for his sovereignty (45:8). His use of Cyrus to shepherd his people home was a stunning demonstration of that sovereignty.

a. Cyrus's mission (44:24 – 45:8)

There has been constant reference to creation and redemption in the preceding chapters. Now these two great themes are woven together in a powerful statement by the Lord of his total mastery of the historical process (44:24–28). In a sense nothing new is said here; it is more like a summary of all that is already 'on the record', so to speak. But the concentration and power of it are impressive, building to the climactic announcement of verse 28. That this pagan emperor, identified by name,[42] will fulfil so exactly what the Lord has announced beforehand will be the final proof that the Lord is indeed who he claims to be. And of course, from where we now stand, the fact that Cyrus did in fact do just that has become a matter of historical record (Ezra 1:2–4). The Lord's claims have been vindicated; he is indeed the creator and *Redeemer*, not just of Israel, but of the whole *earth*.

---

[41] See 45:4: *I . . . bestow on you a title of honour, though* [note this] *you do not acknowledge me.*

[42] Cf. 45:4. Most scholars have found it impossible to believe that Isaiah, inspired by God, actually named Cyrus 150 years before he existed, and this has been a key element in the argument for ascribing chapters 40–55 to an anonymous 'Second Isaiah' who prophesied when Cyrus was already on the move. We must insist, however, that such prediction is neither impossible for one inspired by God, nor unique in the Old Testament (cf. 1 Kgs 13:1–3).

While Cyrus himself is addressed in 45:1–7, the words are not primarily intended for him,[43] but for those who were to wait anxiously for his arrival in Babylon. These verses disclose exactly what is in God's mind concerning him: how God regards him, what help he will give him, and why. The captives from Judah must have been particularly startled by the title *his* [God's] *anointed* (1). In Hebrew it is *māšîaḥ* (messiah), a title normally reserved for Saul, Israel's first king, and for the kings of the line of David who followed him.[44] It refers to the human king who is the Lord's chosen representative, the one who stands at the very centre of his purposes for his people and for the world (see especially Ps. 2). It was an especially appropriate title for the kings of Judah because of the special promises God had made to David, from whom they were all descended (2 Sam. 7:1–17). It must have seemed to many, therefore, that by taking that title and giving it to Cyrus, God had washed his hands entirely of the house of David. From now on God's Messiah, through whom he would work out his purposes for his people and for the world, would be a foreigner, not a king of David's line. But it will become increasingly clear in the rest of the book that this is not so. Cyrus was only a temporary 'messiah', used by God for a very specific task at a time when the house of David was in total disarray.[45] It is the Servant whom we met at the beginning of chapter 42 who stands at the centre of God's longer-term plans for his people, not Cyrus, and Isaiah will eventually relate the ministry of this Servant to the 'faithful love promised to David' (55:3). We have come very close to the heart of Isaiah's marvellous vision, but we must be patient and allow him to unfold its riches gradually, in his own way. For the moment all we need to note carefully is that any alarm Israel may have felt at this pronouncement was without foundation; the promises to David had not been set aside.

This is confirmed indirectly by the nature of Cyrus's mission, for it was to be entirely centred on *Jerusalem* and *the temple* (44:28), both of which had the strongest possible associations with David. It was David who had conquered Jerusalem and made it the capital of his kingdom (2 Sam. 5:6–10). To build a temple for the Lord there had been the most cherished

---

[43] It is questionable whether this oracle ever came to his attention, although some knowledge of it, or at least its substance, may be suggested by Ezra 1:2.

[44] 1 Sam. 2:35; 12:3, 5; 16:6; 24:6, 10; 26:9, 11, 16, 23; 2 Sam. 1:14, 16; 19:10, 21; 22:51; 23:1; 2 Chr. 6:42; Pss 2:2; 18:50; 20:6; 84:9; 132:10, 17; Lam. 4:20.

[45] Zedekiah, the last Davidic king, had been blinded and carried off to Babylon in 587 BC (2 Kgs 25:4–7).

desire of his heart, and it was there that God had promised him a 'house' (a dynasty and a kingdom) that would last for ever (2 Sam. 7:1–16). God was going to use Cyrus to revive these hopes after exile, not to destroy them. Cyrus himself, of course, did not personally rebuild Jerusalem or the temple, but he created the conditions and gave the word that set their restoration in train.

Three further things are said about his mission in 45:1–7. It would be accomplished by God's help (1–3a); it would be accomplished for the sake of God's people (4); and it would be accomplished so that all people (6) – including Cyrus himself (3a) – might know that the Lord alone is God. In short, God was going to use Cyrus to put his people back in Jerusalem, so that from there, the place he had chosen to be the centre of his kingdom on earth, the truth about him might become known everywhere. In the longer plan of God, of course, it was to Jerusalem that Israel's true Messiah, the Son of David, eventually came to fulfil his mission, and it was from there that the gospel went out to the whole world (Matt. 21:1–11; Acts 1:7–8).

What an appropriate response is verse 8 to the announcement of Cyrus's mission! God commands the *heavens* and the *earth* to respond by bringing forth *righteousness* and *salvation*. This echoes the original creation commands of Genesis 1, but what is in view now is the new creation – the new heavens and the new earth – that will eventually emerge from what Cyrus will accomplish (65:17–19). The restoration of Jerusalem would be only the first step, of course, but God can see what it will lead to. No wonder he is enthusiastic!

b. The potter and the clay (45:9–13)

Sadly, though, God's people do not share his enthusiasm. They cannot see past the fact that Cyrus is a pagan, and because God's chosen way of working does not fit their own notions of what is proper they cannot rejoice in it. They are trapped in small-mindedness, like the Pharisees of later times. And God, we sense, can scarcely contain his exasperation with them: does it make any sense for *clay* to question *the potter*, or for a newborn babe to question its parents (9–10)? How absurd their narrowness of vision is! And how tragic, for it shuts them out from oneness with God and from the joy that should be theirs. We are reminded of the elder brother in Jesus' famous parable (he 'became angry and refused to go in'; Luke 15:28), or of Paul's sharp rebuke to the upstart theologians of his day ('Has the potter no right over the clay . . . ?'; Rom. 9:21, NRSV). It is often hard to move beyond theologizing to trusting, but we must do so if we are to exercise the kind of faith which God requires of us and without which we cannot please him.[46] Theological impertinence is the blight of religion in every age, and God is rightly angered by it. But he is not deterred by it. He stoutly defends his sovereign freedom as Creator to use anyone he pleases, and the rightness of his choice of Cyrus (11–13).[47] But how sad that he has to press on with his good plans for his people in the face of their complaints instead of to the joyful strains of their praise!

10. No other saviour (45:14–25)

We have now reached one of the grandest moments in the book. Cyrus fades into the background and the whole scene is dominated by the uniqueness and glory of the one who has chosen to use him. This magnificent poem reverts to the thought of 45:6–7 and develops it. The Lord alone is God, and salvation is to be found in no-one else. Cyrus's mission will demonstrate this fact, and one day people everywhere will acknowledge it. There are two speeches by the Lord in this passage, and two short responses by Isaiah.

The first speech, in verse 14, is addressed to Jerusalem, as indicated by use of the feminine singular pronoun *you*.[48] But here, as in 40:1–2, Jerusalem stands for the people of God – the citizens of Jerusalem – scattered by their enemies, but destined to return. And the astounding assertion of this speech is that they will rule the world! The rich agricultural *products* and other *merchandise* of the Nile valley will flow into Jerusalem, and the *tall Sabeans*, the inhabitants of its most remote upper regions, will come like prisoners in a victory parade, confessing that there is no God but the one who reigns in Jerusalem. Like the Magi who came to worship Jesus, they represent all that is remote and exotic in heathendom, while Egypt

---

[46] Heb. 11:6. In a private communication about this passage in Isaiah 45, Alec Motyer drew my attention to the difficulty Mary must have felt at the wedding feast in Cana, when what she needed was wine and Jesus was busy filling pots with water.

[47] *Not for a price or reward* (13) is at first sight hard to reconcile with 43:3–4. But the point here in chapter 45 appears to be that Cyrus will not be *motivated* by reward, or perhaps even be aware that the Lord will reward him. He will do what he does purely because the Lord in his sovereignty has constrained him to do it. The Lord is defending his *righteousness* in raising up Cyrus, and therefore the suggestion that he has enticed Cyrus with the prospect of reward is discounted.

[48] Cities are referred to in the feminine gender in Hebrew.

represents everything cultured, rich and oppressive.[49] And although the imagery is commercial and military, what is ultimately in view is a conquest that is intensely spiritual in nature, the final triumph of the truth about God. This victory, the Lord declares, will be achieved through 'Jerusalem', his people whom he is soon to restore to their homeland.

Isaiah's response (15–17) is like a gasp of amazement at the sheer audacity of God! No-one who saw the captives from Judah struggling to rebuild their shattered lives in Babylon would guess their significance. They were not a nation – scarcely even the remnant of one, since all their national institutions had been destroyed. God's purposes, for the present, were hidden in them (15), but would one day become visible. Then the tables would be completely turned; idolaters, presently so powerful, would be put to shame, while God's people, presently weak and insignificant, would *be saved* with *an everlasting salvation* (16–17). Jesus later made the same point in his teaching about the kingdom of God. It is like a treasure in a field, or yeast in flour, hidden from view, but destined to dwarf everything else into insignificance (Matt. 13:33, 44). 'The meek . . . will inherit the earth' (Matt. 5:5), or as Paul put it, 'the Lord's people will judge the world' (1 Cor. 6:2). It is something we do well to remember in our own day, when we might be tempted to lose heart at the 'hiddenness' of God. Things are not always as they seem!

But great care is needed in talking about the hiddenness of God. It can suggest that he has deliberately made himself and his purposes obscure, so that people are driven to seek him by superstitious, occult means. Nothing could be further from the truth, however, as the Lord's second speech makes absolutely clear (18–24a). Religious superstition in all its forms, especially idolatry, is quite inexcusable (20b), for God has spoken to his people (and through them to the world) truthfully and clearly, making possible an open and trusting relationship with him (19). He has also backed up his words through the prophets with actions, such as the raising up of Cyrus, that confirm his claim to be the only God and Saviour (21). So people everywhere have been put on notice; one day they will all have to bow the knee to the Lord and confess the truth about him (23–24a; cf. Phil 2:9–11). The question is whether they will do so now. The salvation he offers (22) must be understood in the light of verses 16–17. It is a share in everlasting salvation, the final state of blessedness he has in store for

---

[49] The Egypt of the pyramids had subjected Israel's ancestors to cruel bondage.

his people Israel, and escape from the everlasting *shame* and disgrace that will be the lot of idolaters. What an offer! Isaiah's final response (24b–25) is simply a quiet, respectful summary of it. The hidden God has revealed himself, and the implications are awesome.

The ultimatum that has come from the throne of heaven is universal in its scope (*all you ends of the earth*) and yet intensely personal in its reference (*every knee, every tongue*). And it contains a great imperative within it: such news must be published! The fate of men and women everywhere depends on it. In the final analysis, the vision of Isaiah is a profoundly missionary vision.

11. 'I will carry you' (46:1–13)

The development of this part of the book can be perplexing at times. There is a good deal of repetition. It seems as though the text keeps doubling back on itself. But each time a particular theme is returned to, something new is added to the treatment of it, and often there is a link word or phrase to indicate what exactly it is that is now to be picked up and taken further. Like a good pastor, Isaiah returns to basic issues again and again because he knows that it is around these issues that the fundamental, daily struggles of the believer's life are lost or won. This whole chapter is in effect an elaboration of the last two lines of 45:20, 'Ignorant are those who carry about idols of wood, who pray to gods that cannot save.' The key link word is *carry*.

Bel and *Nebo* (1) were pagan gods. Bel ('lord') was an alternative name for Marduk, the chief god of the city of Babylon.[50] Nebo ('speaker') was the son of Bel-Marduk.[51] He was the patron of wisdom and the art of writing, and his function was to write on the tables of destiny the fates decreed by the gods for the coming year. Every year at the New Year festival, he was brought from his own temple at Borsippa, south-west of Babylon, and carried in procession with his father Bel-Marduk through the streets to the great Esagila shrine. Nations like Israel, who were in diplomatic contact with Babylon, would have known about this festival,

---

[50] *Bel* is the equivalent of the Canaanite 'Baal'. It was used as an epithet for Marduk from the time of Hammurabi (approx. 1792–1750 BC). Cf. Jer. 50:2.

[51] *Nebo* (Babylonian *nabu*) is probably related to the Hebrew *nābî'* ('prophet'). It is probable that Nabu was the patron-god of the Babylonian-Chaldean dynasty, since its three most important kings, Nabopolassar, Nebuchadnezzar and Nabonidus, had names compounded with his. See North (1964), p. 163.

and at least some of those who were eventually taken there as captives would have witnessed it at first hand.[52] It was the greatest religious event of the year, the centre around which their whole pagan environment revolved; an impressive celebration, year by year, of the power of Babylon and its gods. But in Isaiah's inspired vision this festival is grotesquely transformed. Bel and Nebo *bow* and *stoop*. They are too heavy, and the exhausted animals that bear them stagger and fall. And instead of processing to the Esagila they stumble away into captivity (1–2).

There is no simple correspondence between this passage and historical events of the sixth century BC. There was no stampede to evacuate Babylon of its gods before it fell to Cyrus. Nor did Cyrus banish the idols from their temples. He restored the gods of Sumer and Akkad, which Nabonidus had brought into Babylon, unharmed to their shrine, and besought them all to ask Bel and Nebo to grant long life to him and to Cambyses his son.[53] If anything, Cyrus's conquest of Babylon enhanced the status of Bel and Nebo rather than diminishing it. But how different things are now! The greatness of Bel and Nebo is a distant memory, while the Lord is known and worshipped by millions. It is easy, of course, to see this in retrospect. It is much harder to take the long view when evil is in full flight. That, however, is exactly what Isaiah does here. He asks the exiles to look beyond the present to what will finally be the case, and paints a graphic picture of the shame and disgrace that await all man-made religion and those who trust in it (cf. 45:16).

But he goes further. In verses 3–7 he asks Israel to reflect again on the fundamental absurdity of idolatry and the contrast between it and their own covenant faith. 'Idolaters carry their gods,' says the Lord, 'but I carry you. I have carried you since you were born, and I will never stop carrying you until your days are done.'[54] There it is in a nutshell; false religion is based on works, true religion on grace. So it has always been and so it always will be (Eph. 2:8–9).

The last part of the chapter, though, comes as something of a shock (8–13). Surely if God carries his people in his arms he could be expected to use only affirmative, comforting language in his dealings with them. Not so! God's love is robust, not weak and indulgent. He cares for his

---

[52] Especially people like Daniel and his friends, who lived in Babylon itself.

[53] *Cyrus Cylinder*, lines 33ff., in *ANET*, p. 316b.

[54] The figure of the Lord carrying Israel occurs also in Exod. 19:4; Deut. 1:31; 32:11; Isa. 63:9, always with reference to the exodus. This is the point at which Israel as a nation was conceived and brought to birth.

people too deeply to deprive them of necessary rebuke. *Rebels*, he calls them, *stubborn-hearted*, and *you who are now far from my righteousness* (8, 12). We might think for a moment that he has turned his attention to the pagan idol-worshippers! But this is clearly not the case. *Remember this* in verse 8 is the sequel to *Listen to me, you descendants of Jacob* in verse 3. The audience is the same. But what then is the reason for the strong language the Lord uses?

The answer lies in his reference to Cyrus as *a bird of prey* in verse 11, probably reflecting again the shocked response which Isaiah expected the Lord's choice of Cyrus to evoke. How could it be right for God to choose such a man, and how could he have his people's best interests at heart in doing so? But such a response is tantamount to rebellion against God, for it calls into question not just his sovereign freedom, but his goodness – and that is to strike at the very heart of the covenant relationship. It was because he loved Israel that the Lord chose her in the first place (Deut. 7:8), and because of that same love that he had carried her ever since. How dare they doubt his goodness? The strong language is shocking, but it is the language of loving discipline rather than rejection. It is intended to jolt the people of God out of a very dangerous and sinful state of mind, and has their ultimate good in view. However many rough patches there may be in his relationship with them along the way, it is the Lord's grace rather than their sinfulness that will triumph in the end; he *will grant salvation* and *splendour* to his people (13).[55] The two problems that have to be overcome are their circumstances and, more importantly, their heart condition. Both are taken up afresh in chapters 47 and 48.

12. A tale of two cities (47:1 – 48:22)

Conceptually, chapters 47 and 48 form one large unit dealing with the fulfilment of the Lord's purpose to use Cyrus to free his people from captivity in Babylon (see 44:28 – 45:4). But while chapter 47 is one poem with a single theme (Babylon is to be judged), chapter 48 is more complex. It has four parts: verses 1–11, 12–15, 16, and 17–22, all addressed to the captives. The first three are introduced by calls to listen; the fourth by the

---

[55] There is a play on *ṣĕdāqâ* ('righteousness', 'victory') and *tĕšûʿâ* ('salvation', 'deliverance') in 12–13. The exiles are at present far from victory and deliverance because they are far from righteousness. It is a theme that will be developed at length in chapters 56–66 with reference to the situation that was to develop after the return.

announcement formula *This is what the LORD says* (17). This is the climax of the whole chapter, and what it amounts to is a rousing call to leave Babylon at once and set off for home.[56] Home, as we have been reminded in verse 2, is *the holy city*, Jerusalem, which stands in sharp contrast to Babylon, the wicked city doomed to destruction. The captives are portrayed here as residents of one city[57] but citizens of another, a tension between place and citizenship that can be resolved only by returning to where they belong. The logic of the whole unit is that Babylon is doomed (chapter 47); leave it, and set out for Jerusalem, your true home (chapter 48).

a. Babylon: defiant but doomed (47:1–15)

The portrait of Babylon in chapter 47 is a classic study in worldly power and arrogance. She is the *queen of kingdoms* (5) and believes that she will remain so *for ever* (7). She has an utterly false sense of security, which leads her into self-indulgence and complete indifference to the needs of the weak and vulnerable in her midst (8, 6). She considers herself so self-sufficient that all notions of accountability are excluded. She feels no need to acknowledge the claims, or even the existence, of anyone or anything other than herself (8b, 10b). She is proud of her *wisdom and knowledge* (10), and has perfected a form of religion (astrology) which enhances her sense of power over her own destiny without making any moral demands upon her (9b, 12–13).[58] She is the complete symbol of worldly success. But the message of this chapter is that she stands under the judgment of God, and is about to suffer a complete change of fortune. The virgin city will be violated, the queen of kingdoms will *sit in the dust* (1a), the pampered city will become a slave (1b–3), the mother will suddenly be widowed and bereaved (8b–9), and the witch will find that her spells do not work any more and all her masters of *magic* will be powerless to save her (12–15). In short, her sense of impregnability is a complete illusion. She is like the man who built his house on the sand (Matt. 7:26–27), or like the rich man who did not reckon on what the night would bring (Luke 12:20). Babylon is the city of destruction.

---

[56] Verses 20–21 present the escape from Babylon and the journey to Jerusalem as a new exodus. As God provided for his people on the first exodus, so he will do again.

[57] While most of the captives when the time of exile came were not literally resident in the city of Babylon itself (see Ezek. 1:1–2), they certainly lived in its shadow and were subject to its rule. We must allow Isaiah the normal liberties of poetic licence.

[58] Babylon was celebrated from ancient times for its practice of magic and divination. Cf. Dan. 2:1–4.

We must note two things carefully, however, before we hurry on. First, Babylon here is not merely the ancient city of that name, and the poem does not simply look forward to what was to happen to it in 539 when Cyrus conquered it. Like Jerusalem, with which it is contrasted, it is both a concrete historical reality and a symbol, and it is the symbolic significance of Babylon which is primary here. Second, the sin of Babylon is not simply its pride and self-absorption, but its self-deification (cf. 14:12–14). The twice uttered *I am, and there is none besides me* (8, 10) is a direct challenge to the Lord's identical claim in 45:5. And this defiance of God finds concrete expression in abuse of his people (6). As in 14:3–23, Babylon represents humankind organized in defiance of God – the kingdom of mere mortals, in contrast to the kingdom of God. In this sense 'Babylon' is still with us, and still stands under judgment of God (see Rev. 18). The historical Babylon of the sixth century BC was merely one manifestation of it.

b. 'Leave Babylon!' (48:1–22)

Now we are in a better position to understand the challenge of chapter 48, where the contrast between Babylon and Jerusalem is developed. The reference to Jerusalem as *the holy city* in verse 2 at once activates the symbolism associated with it also. By the sixth century BC it was to be little more than a forsaken ruin, its walls broken down, its temple destroyed, and most of its citizens in exile (Lam. 1 – 2). But for all that, it would continue to be the place God had chosen as the centre of his kingdom on earth, and the announcements concerning Cyrus in the previous chapters have made clear his intention to raise it up again. It would once again be 'the holy city', not just in the sense that no evil will be found in it (1:21–26; 52:1), but that God himself would return to it and rule from it (2:1–4). The holiness of Jerusalem was inextricably linked to God's choice to be present and manifest himself in it (12:6; cf. Ps. 46:4–5). For the captives from Judah, of course, this was to be something they looked and longed for rather than something they presently experienced. The holy city was to become the symbol of their future hope – the coming of God's kingdom. The challenge of chapter 48 is that they should live constantly in the light of that hope, expecting its realization at any moment.

But how are they actually depicted here? They certainly profess to be *citizens* of the kingdom (2a), but their lives give little evidence of it. Even as they call on God they harbour evil in their lives (1b). There is more strong language in this chapter, and most of it could be applied with equal appropriateness to their ancestors – *stubborn* (4), *treacherous* and rebellious (8) – the old sins live on; it is as though their suffering has taught them nothing (4–6). *The furnace of affliction* has produced disappointing results, and the Lord is tempted to discard altogether what is left (9–10). But no, for there is more at stake here than their own betterment; there is the honour of the Lord's name (11). The world must know that it is he, and not Babylon, Bel and Nebo, who rules the world, and for that reason he will press on, regardless of how his people respond.

There is anger in this chapter, but there is also sadness, and this brings us to the heart of Israel's sinfulness. It lies in their failure to listen: *Listen to this, you descendants of Jacob* (1), *Listen to me, Jacob* (12), *Come near me and listen* (16), and finally, *I am the LORD . . . who teaches you . . . If only you had paid attention* (17–18). God has opened his heart to them. He has given them his law; he has spoken to them through his prophets, but they have not listened, and they are still not listening! How different their history might have been, and how different their present relationship with God might have been, if only they had listened to his word (18–19)! And because this problem is still unresolved, their return to the land will not bring the fullness of blessing they hope for. They will spoil the next chapter in their history, just as they have spoilt all the previous ones. *'There is no peace,' says the LORD, 'for the wicked'* (22).[59] It is a tragic note on which to end, but it underlines powerfully the serious nature of failure to listen to God; it shuts us out from the peace of God. As in chapters 40–55 in general, Isaiah has been speaking here of a situation that was to emerge after his own lifetime.[60] As far as the basic sins and failures he describes are concerned, however, he may just as well have been looking about him, or even speaking directly to the church in our own day and age. We need no great imagination to recognize ourselves in his stinging rebukes. Sadly, the sins of the people of God do not alter.

What, then, is to be done? Clearly something more is needed here than a change of address, and that means that something more is required than the mission of Cyrus. With this issue hanging heavily in the air, the scene is set for the Servant of the Lord to take centre stage again in chapter 49. In fact, it is more than likely that his voice has already been heard here in chapter 48. For who else can it be who announces his presence in

---

[59] In this context *the wicked* must be the unbelieving exiles themselves. Cf. 57:21. *Peace* (šālôm) is complete well-being, the sum total of covenant blessings (Num. 6:22–26).

[60] Cf. the apostle Paul in Acts 20:29–30; 1 Tim. 4:1; 2 Tim. 3:1–9; 4:3–4.

verse 16 with the words *And now the Sovereign* LORD *has sent me, endowed with his Spirit*? Most scholars suggest that it is either Isaiah himself or an anonymous 'Second Isaiah'.[61] But the reference to the *Spirit* pointedly recalls the presentation of the Servant in 42:1: 'I will put my Spirit on him.' And the voice we hear in *the Sovereign* LORD *has sent me* sounds remarkably like the voice we are about to hear again in 49:1: 'Before I was born the LORD called me.' In short, the problem of the *spiritual* state of the exiles, which is highlighted as acute in chapter 48, is answered by the reappearance of the Servant of the Lord, at first enigmatically in 48:16, and then plainly in chapter 49.[62]

13. God's Servant and God's people (49:1–13)

First the Servant himself speaks in verses 1–6. Two messages to the exiles follow in verses 7–12, drawing out the implications of what the Servant has said. Then comes the grand finale in verse 13: *Shout for joy, you heavens; rejoice, you earth . . . For the* LORD *comforts his people*. The movement is from the Servant himself to the people of God who are associated with him. And with the return of the Servant the sharp rebuke of the previous chapter gives way, once more, to comfort.

Strangely, although the sinfulness of God's people is crying out for remedy, the Servant does not address them directly at all. He speaks to the world at large, the *islands* and *distant nations* (1). As we saw in 42:1–4, the Servant has been commissioned to make the truth about the Lord, Israel's God, known everywhere. It is not that he does not have a mission to the people of God themselves; verse 5 makes it very clear that he does. It is to bring them back to God, so that their relationship with him is right again,[63] and this aspect of his work will receive more and more attention in the following chapters. But the first essential for them is to be reminded that there is a whole world out there waiting to hear the truth about God. Healing begins when we stop focusing on ourselves and our arguments with God and start looking outward to the world that he loves and that needs to know about him (6b).

---

[61] So, e.g., North (1964), p. 182: 'The sentence is prose and the "me" can hardly be anyone but the Prophet [Second Isaiah].'

[62] Cf. Young, 3, p. 259.

[63] The regathering of verse 5 is spiritual in nature, since it is *to him* (the Lord), *to himself.* Cf. Lam. 5:21. The physical return of the exiles to the land is the mission of Cyrus, not the Servant.

a. A polished arrow (49:1–6)

But who is the Servant? Verse 1 teases us by referring to his *name* without disclosing what it is. It seems that at this stage we have to be content with knowing what *kind* of person he is. Is he perhaps a prophet, a priest or a king – or even all three? 'Justice' and 'law' (rsv) in the first Servant Song suggested kingship but, as we saw, these terms seemed to refer there to something bigger than the normal activities of a king (see on 42:1–4). Here in chapter 49 he looks rather more like a prophet. Like Jeremiah, he was called even before he was born (1b; Jer. 1:5). His weapon is the word of God that issues from his mouth like a sharp sword (2).[64] Like Jeremiah again, he meets with opposition which brings him close to despair[65] – but carries on anyway, trusting God to *reward* him (4). But just as we are beginning to think he must be Jeremiah or some other known prophet, he is referred to in a way which explodes all our categories and puts him in a class of his own: *You are my servant, Israel, in whom I will display my splendour* (3).

His name is *Israel*! But how can this be, since, as we have already seen, a key aspect of his mission is to restore Israel to a proper relationship with God (5)? We are forced back to the tentative conclusion we reached in chapter 42, that he is a figure who embodies all that the nation of Israel was called to be, and therefore one who is truly worthy of the name – God's perfect Servant. As such he is far greater than Jeremiah, or any other Old Testament prophet for that matter. He is the prophet par excellence. And if that does not satisfy us, we shall just have to wait, because for the moment he is 'hidden' in the *shadow* of the Lord's *hand*, and *concealed . . . in his quiver* like a *polished arrow* (2).

b. A new people of God (49:7–13)

As we move on to verse 7, however, the word *Israel* reverts to its normal sense,[66] and the focus shifts back again from the Servant of God to the people of God, the surviving remnant of the nation. We need not dwell on the details of what is said, for much of it is a repetition of previous

---

[64] Opinion is divided as to whether this is a prophetic or kingly (messianic) image. Both are possible. In 11:4 the messianic king 'will strike the earth with the rod of his mouth'. But the similarities to Jeremiah suggest a prophetic rather than a kingly figure, and note Hos. 6:5: 'I cut you in pieces with my prophets, I killed you with the words of my mouth.' Cf. Eph. 6:17. In the end, as we shall see, we will not have to choose between 'king' and 'prophet'; the Servant is both.

[65] Cf. especially Jeremiah's so-called 'confessions': Jer. 4:19–22; 8:22 – 9:1; 15:15–21; 17:14–18; 18:18–23; 20:7–12, 13–18.

[66] This is crystal clear from the use of the formula *the Holy One of Israel*, in which *Israel* always means the nation. See especially 47:4 and 48:17, where 'Holy One of Israel' is combined with 'Redeemer', as it is here.

promises: they are at present *despised*, but will one day be honoured; even *kings* and *princes* will acknowledge that God has *chosen* them (7; cf. 45:14). They will return to *the land* and *restore* it (8b), and on the way back the Lord will care for them as a shepherd cares for his flock (9b–12; cf. 40:11).

But there are also new things here, and the whole passage is significantly nuanced by its close relationship to the Servant Song which it follows. For example, the Servant was told in verse 6 that the Lord would make him 'a light for the Gentiles'. In verse 8 Israel is told that the Lord will make the nation *a covenant for the people*.[67] And of course, neither of these expressions is new to us; they were both used with reference to the Servant himself in 42:6 and, as we saw there, they refer to God's intention to extend his salvation to all peoples, to bless the whole world that he has created (see on 42:5–7). Now, by reusing the two expressions as he does here in chapter 49, Isaiah underlines the fact that God will achieve this great goal both through the Servant himself and through his restored people. As they are brought back into a right relationship with God, God's people become one with God's Servant in his worldwide mission.

This means that the very idea of the people of God begins to undergo a kind of metamorphosis. Those whom God restores to himself become a sign of his commitment to extend this same blessing to all people. Those already free say to those who are still captive, *'Come out,' and to those in darkness, 'Be free!'* (9a). And on closer examination the flock of God in 9b–12 is not simply those who have been carried off to Babylon and who are now coming back again, but a great throng from *the north, the west* and the south (*the region of Aswan*) – a massive flow of people into the kingdom of God.[68] The accent does not fall on the return of the physical remnant from Babylon, or even on their spiritual restoration to the Lord, but on the mission to the Gentiles that will flow from it.

---

[67] The NIV heading at verse 8 unhelpfully separates verses 7 and 8, both of which are introduced by *This is what the LORD says*. Motyer (p. 389) takes verses 7–8, like verse 6, to be addressed to the Servant himself, and has indicated to me privately that this is partly on the grounds that the same personal pronoun, *you* (masc. sing.), is used in all three verses. But this is inconclusive, given the use of the same singular pronoun for Israel/Jacob as God's servant in 41:8–9. *Servant* (sing.) is a metaphor which is sometimes corporate and sometimes personal. Only the content and context can determine how it is being used in any particular case. See also n. 66 above.

[68] 'The east' is conspicuous by its absence from verse 12, but probably this simply reflects the fact that direct approach from the east was blocked by the north Arabian desert. The exiles themselves would have approached Jerusalem from the north. *Aswan* (*sînîm*) is probably the *swn* of the Elephantine papyri. Cf. Ezek. 29:10; 30:6. There was a community of expatriates from Judah there from the late sixth century BC. But here, following *north* and *west*, it would seem to be the southern location of *sînîm* which is relevant rather than any known connection with a Jewish community. Given the all-embracing significance of *a covenant for the people* in verse 8, what follows cannot be limited to the return of dispersed exiles.

The *shout* of praise, then, in verse 13, is the 'Hurrah!' of mission accomplished – a cause of rejoicing to the whole earth. But by the time we reach that point the theme of 'comfort for the people of God' is no longer focused narrowly on the captives in Babylon. They may be its most immediate point of reference, but it reaches beyond them to embrace all people. And the key to all this is the Servant of the Lord. Israel is to understand that its entire future in God's purposes is intimately bound up with him.

But such grand, sweeping visions are very difficult to grasp in the midst of pain. Verse 14 ('But Zion said . . .') suddenly reintroduces us to the acute pain associated with the fall of Jerusalem, and the numbing effect it was to have on those who experienced it.

14. Zion and her children (49:14 – 50:3)

At last the particular issue of the Lord's choice of Cyrus has faded into the background, but a deeper tension in the relationship between God and his people remains to be worked through. How could God abandon Zion and still be committed to its people? As long as Zion lay in ruins, the sense of being abandoned by God would prove exceedingly hard to shake off. Some, like Daniel, would be resilient enough to rise above it. Most would sink into deep depression and find the struggle to believe and hope again long and difficult. This passage is about that struggle and the pain at the heart of it.[69]

a. Zion's lament – and the Lord's response (49:14–21)

Zion's lament in verse 14 is brief but poignant: *The Lord has forsaken me, the Lord has forgotten me* (cf. 40:27). By now, of course, we know the code that is operating. *Zion* is not just the city of that name, it is its people. Zion is not simply their home, it is their name, their identity. If Zion is ruined, so are they. If Zion weeps, so do they. And they will never be fully themselves again until Zion is restored to its former glory. It is hard for us to appreciate such a complete identification of people and city, and there is nothing quite like it in our own experience. No earthly city has the same significance for us that Zion had for the Old Testament people of God. 'Our citizenship is in heaven,' Paul tells us (Phil. 3:20), and that heavenly city certainly is not in ruins as Zion was. Nevertheless, it is at present hidden

---

[69] Cf. the book of Lamentations, which reflects the struggle of those still back in Palestine.

from us, and we may perhaps sense something of the pain of our spiritual forebears in our own 'groaning' as we wait for it to be revealed (Rom. 8:18–25).[70] Then at last our pain will be over, and we shall be where and what we long to be (Rev. 21:1–5). But there may well be moments along the way, if they have not already come upon us, when the darkness is so intense that we feel forsaken and forgotten – even by God himself.

But such despair, in the end, is irrational and groundless; it simply does not accord with the facts. God, being the God he is, can no more forget his people than a *mother* can *forget the baby at her breast* (15). Like a master architect, he thinks about his plans for them day and night (16). Like a father who is inordinately proud of his daughter, God will not rest until his people are decked out *like a bride* (17–18) and settled like a happy mother with her family about her (19–21). Zion's *children* will return to her, and more besides; she will overflow with them. She herself will not be able to comprehend the full extent of the blessing that will break over her. The images are mixed and do not always cohere logically, but they all affirm God's love for his people and his tireless commitment to their welfare. That is the truth about him and his engagement with them, and if they are too despondent to grasp it now he will carry them until they can (cf. 46:3–4).

b. The choice facing the world (49:22–26)

This, of course, means that the rest of the world has a decision to make. They can cooperate with God by blessing his people (22–23), or they can defy him by continuing to persecute them (24–26). They can share in the blessing God intends to bestow on his people, or they can entirely cut themselves off from it. But they cannot claim any relationship with God that bypasses identification with his people. Saul of Tarsus, centuries later, was to have this truth impressed on him directly by the risen Jesus (Acts 9:3–5). His response was to lay down his arms and become the servant of those he had laboured so determinedly to destroy – and be blessed along with them! The picture of kings and queens serving God's people as *foster fathers* and *nursing mothers* in verse 23 is not one of abject submission but of love and affection; inclusion rather than exclusion.[71]

---

[70] Paul speaks here of the revealing of the children of God rather than of the heavenly city, but the redemption of the body has an obvious link with Phil. 3:21, and hence with the 'heavenly citizenship' idea of that passage. Cf. 2 Cor. 5:1–5.

[71] Even *lick the dust at your feet* is not as harsh as it sounds. It was a conventional posture of submission to a sovereign, and here signifies a complete change of attitude, from oppression to service.

The horror of gruesome defeat is reserved for the *warriors* and the *fierce* of verses 24–26 who are too proud to change. But either way, all will know, in the end, the invincible strength of God's commitment to his people (26b).[72]

c. The divorce that never was (50:1–3)

After this powerful affirmation, the opening verses of chapter 50 look rather anticlimactic. In fact, however, they are more like a quiet appeal at the end of a stirring sermon. They return to the beginning and gently seek to elicit the right response to the issue that was raised there. The sermon began with Zion's sorrowful lament (49:14); it ends by addressing her children (50:1), especially those who would find themselves cruelly separated from her. Has the Lord divorced their mother? No, he has not, for no bill of divorce has been issued (cf. Deut. 24:1–4). Has he sold her to clear a debt? No; the very suggestion that he has creditors is preposterous. The explanation for Zion's destruction is the *sins* and *transgressions* of its people, not any cooling of affection or straitened circumstances on God's part.[73] Since there has been no *divorce* the Lord can take Zion back, and since he has not *sold* her she is still his to claim as by right.[74] Furthermore, as the Creator he has the power to make good everything he has promised her (2b–3).[75] The only hindrance is the one that has always been there, namely, the unresponsiveness of her children to his words and deeds (2a).[76] But the need for change is urgent, for there is the possibility of a new beginning if only God's people will grasp it by faith and move forward into it. That is the challenge with which this sermon ends. Hardly an anticlimax – but a tense and uncertain moment, for the response the Lord seeks is apparently lacking. Or is it? We are about to discover that things are not quite as they seem.

---

[72] There is a play here on *bāśār* (*flesh*), which the NIV misses. The NRSV captures it well: 'eat their own flesh . . . all flesh [humankind] shall know'.

[73] Cf. North (1964), p. 198. And note '*your* sins . . . *your* transgressions' (my emphasis). The children could not blame their mother; they were just as guilty as she was.

[74] I take it that the expressions *sold* and *sent away* are ironic the second time they are used in verse 1.

[75] The Lord's *rebuke* of *the sea* (2) is probably a reference to both the act of creation and the exodus from Egypt. Likewise the darkening of *the heavens* may be a reference to the kind of sandstorms the exiles would have experienced in Babylonia, but also to the plague of darkness in Egypt (Exod. 10:21–23). The general point is the Lord's total control of nature.

[76] The past tenses, *When I came . . . when I called*, imply continuity between the unresponsiveness of the past (which brought about Zion's ruin) and the unresponsiveness of the present (which hinders its recovery). Cf. 2 Kgs 17:13–14.

15. The Servant, the righteous, and the wicked (50:4–11)

Once more the Servant speaks, letting us into some of the most deeply personal areas of his life: his communion with God, the physical and mental suffering which marks his way, and the assurance of final vindication that buoys him up. He speaks more to himself than to others (verses 4–9 have the form of a soliloquy) but there is more than a hint of who is meant to overhear him. It is the *weary* one of verse 4 – the person who, like the Servant himself, is an object of ridicule and abuse, and whose strength to endure is almost exhausted. We are reminded of the 'bruised reed' and the 'smouldering wick' of 42:3. There were many such in Israel, and the words of the Servant here are for them first of all. But, as part of holy Scripture, they are also for us. In this third Servant Song the world at large is left out of the picture, and attention is focused on the Servant himself and his ministry to the people of God.

The Servant has been *given . . . a well-instructed tongue, to know the word that sustains the weary* (4). He is a skilled counsellor because he himself has been taught by the Lord. He is a disciple before he is anything else, and as such his outstanding characteristic is attentiveness to God: *morning by morning* God instructs him, and morning by morning he listens (4b). This, as we recall from chapter 48, is exactly what Israel has failed to do. In stark contrast to Israel, too, he is *not . . . rebellious* (5). His whole intent is to translate the instruction he receives into obedient action, no matter what the cost. As a disciple he does not shrink from the suffering: he does not draw back, or *hide* his *face*, but sets it *like flint* (5–7). There is nothing he will not endure if obedience demands it. But finally – and this is important – his confidence is not in his own power to endure, but in the Lord who helps him, and who will vindicate him in the end (8).[77] No weary one could say that this Servant speaks from a vantage point of lofty and serene detachment. Far from it. No-one has felt the struggle more intensely, or paid a bigger price for obedience. He is the perfect disciple.

Again his identity teases us.[78] But more important at this stage is the question: why the powerful portrait of the Servant at this point? What

---

[77] The language of verse 8 is that of the courtroom. The Servant expects to be the victim of false accusation. Cf. Mark 14:56.

[78] The presentation of the Servant as a disciple has suggested to some that he is a sixth-century disciple of Isaiah (cf. verse 4 with 8:16). But the Servant is a disciple of the Lord rather than of Isaiah. He has many

impact is it intended to have on those still on the knife-edge of belief or unbelief that was reached at the end of the previous section (see comments on 50:1–3)? We do not have far to look, because verses 10–11 at once drive the message home. The Servant is not simply to be admired or wondered at; he is to be obeyed (10).[79] In short, in describing his own discipleship the Servant has shown them what God requires of all his people: not empty profession (as in 48:1–2), but wholehearted, costly obedience. This leads to a quite clear but rather unsettling conclusion introduced by the challenge *Who among you . . . ?* in verse 10. Some fear the Lord as the Servant himself does (10); others do not. Some, though they walk in darkness, *rely* upon the Lord; others choose their own way, lighting *fires* of rebellion that will eventually destroy them (11). The Servant and the challenge that he brings force a separation between the true and the false, the righteous and the wicked, the saved and the lost – among those who profess to be God's people (cf. John 1:10–13)!

While this should exercise our consciences mightily, and cause us to search our hearts, it is at the same time reassuring, and provides some relief from the impasse we were left with in verses 1–3. There will never be a generation of God's people that rises as one to the faith and obedience that he requires of them. Some will and some will not. Some, by their persistence in indifference or rebellion, will show themselves, in the long run, not to be his people at all. But God's ultimate purposes will not be frustrated by their mixed response. There will always be those who genuinely do rely upon their God (10), and they will move on in faith to inherit all the glorious things he has promised. In the end, as we have seen, it will be the Servant, whose testimony we have heard in verses 4–9, who will force the division between the true and the false among God's people. To 'fear the Lord' and 'to obey the word of his Servant' are one and the same thing. We must all decide whether or not we will follow him.

The concept of the people of God is undergoing significant development in these chapters. The people of God are not only Israelites but Gentiles as well, as we saw in 49:8–12. But they are not all of the Gentiles or all of the Israelites, but only those who respond appropriately to God and his

---

characteristics in common with Jeremiah, and with Isaiah himself. Others point to Ps. 129:1–3 and Isa. 1:5–6 as examples of the way Israel can be personified as an abused person. Finally, as North (1964), p. 203, has commented, verses 6–7 contain 'a startling anticipation of the maltreatment of Christ on the morning of the crucifixion' (see Matt. 26:67; 27:26; cf. Luke 9:51). But we will refrain from taking the identification of the Servant further until Isaiah has given us all the relevant data.

79 The speaker in verses 4–9 is not explicitly identified as the Servant, but verse 10 does this retrospectively.

Servant. These are the true citizens of Zion, the city of God, and, as we are about to see, this part of the book, like others before it, is soon to reach its climax with their arrival there.

16. The highway to Zion (51:1–11)

The whole of this passage is coloured by the goal that is reached in verse 11. It is about pilgrimage to Zion – the pilgrims themselves, the doubts that trouble them, the faith that sustains them, and the *joy* that awaits them at their journey's end.

Pilgrimage to Zion was something that every Israelite of Old Testament times knew about. Three times every year, at the three great festivals – Passover, the Feast of Weeks and the Feast of Tabernacles – the pilgrims came, streaming to Zion from every corner of the land (Deut. 16:16–17; Pss 84; 122). Where possible, whole families went together, meeting friends along the way. They laughed, they talked, they sang, and finally they rejoiced together before the Lord in Zion as they recalled God's goodness to them and renewed their commitment to him and to one another. Some of the happiest memories of childhood and family belonged to these occasions. Of course, for those prevented from going any more because of illness or old age, the memories were bitter-sweet. They still cherished them, but their sense of deprivation was terrible (see Pss 42; 43; especially 42:4–5). The exile to Babylon, however, was to produce an experience of deprivation more terrible by far. Many were to grow up with no personal memories of Zion at all, never having seen it, let alone gone there. For them pilgrimage to Zion could only be hoped for, not remembered, and the hope itself must often have seemed like a distant mirage – enticing, but cruelly unreal. Many would simply give up believing that it could happen. A minority, however, would cling to it, not as a kind of mental trick to help them feel better, but as the evidence of an unquenchable confidence in the faithfulness of God and the reliability of his promises. These are the ones the Lord addresses with obvious pleasure in verses 1–7; they are plainly very dear to him.

They are described in verse 1 as those *who pursue righteousness and who seek the Lord*. They have grasped the heart of true religion: holiness of life flowing from a personal relationship with God.[80] Jesus said that the only

---

[80] *Ṣedeq*, translated *righteousness* in the NIV (and the NRSV), is rendered as 'deliverance' in the RSV. It is questionable, however, whether the latter is ever an adequate translation. The most that can be said with confidence is that it can be justified as an interpretive rendering of *ṣedeq* in some contexts. But the NIV is

future that matters (the kingdom of God) belongs to such people (Matt. 5:6). Their expectation of what God will do in the future profoundly shapes how they live in the present. They do not rely on their unaided consciences to tell them how they should live; they *know what is right*, because they have God's *instruction* in their *heart* (7). Their whole character and behaviour are shaped by the word of God. And yet there are things that trouble them. They are so few in number (1b–2), and so despised (7b). How can the future be theirs? The answer, of course, lay in their history. These struggling believers were true children of Abraham; he was *the rock from which* they had been *cut* (1b). They were not just his physical descendants; they also shared in his faith in God. And look what God did with Abraham! He was only *one* when God called him, but he *blessed him and made him many* (2). Cannot God do the same with them? And what of those who mock them? They seem so sophisticated and superior now, but one day they will be no more glorious than cankered garments (8). We have heard this before, of course; in 50:9 the enemies of the Servant were described in exactly the same way. And how appropriate the repetition is here! For the faithful people of God follow in the footsteps of the Servant of the Lord. They will share in his sufferings, but they will also share in his vindication (cf. Rom. 8:17).

These pilgrims, then, are faithful Israelites. They may not have literally set out yet, but they are pilgrims none the less. For they know where their home is and long for the day when they will be there, and it is the promises of God, which they believe, that draw them towards it. Zion will be rebuilt; the *wastelands* around her will blossom again *like the garden of the* LORD (3). It will again become a place of *joy and gladness* and *thanksgiving* (3), and it will stand for ever as undeniable evidence of God's righteous, saving character (8b). And the joy of that place will derive a special richness from the fact that faithful Israelites will find that they are not alone.

Another group of pilgrims is alluded to in verses 4–6. They are a much larger company, coming from *the nations* and the distant *islands*, drawn towards Zion by the promise that light is about to dawn, and the *justice* they long for is soon to become a reality.[81] These are the 'other sheep'

---

certainly right in this instance. The emphasis here is ethical, as indicated by the verb *pursue*. In Isaiah (especially chapters 40–55), 'deliverance' is something one waits for rather than pursues.

[81] It is probable that the nations and isles are addressed directly in verse 4a. The NIV's *my people* and *my nation* suggest an Israelite audience, but the context strongly favours the alternative reading 'peoples' and 'nations', which is attested in a number of Hebrew manuscripts and the Syriac (for details see North [1964], p. 206). In any case the wider world comes quickly into view in what follows. Whether or not faithful Gentiles are addressed directly in verses 4–6, we are certainly reminded of their existence.

Jesus spoke about who would one day hear the shepherd's voice and be gathered into his fold (John 10:16). They have joined the pilgrimage because they are convinced that only the Lord, the God of Israel, can mend the world's ills. And they are right! 'Take one last look at the world you know,' he says to them, 'because it will soon pass away. A new age of *righteousness* – a new world – is about to dawn' (6).

In the end there is only one people of God, *those the Lord has rescued* (or 'ransomed'; cf. Rev. 5:9–10),[82] and when all God's purposes for them have reached their goal they will all be together in one place – Zion, the city of God. They will *enter* it *with singing*, and *joy* will be their *crown* for ever (11).[83]

As so often, Isaiah's vision reaches far beyond the particulars of history to its end; beyond the return from Babylon to the consummation it foreshadowed. And he could hardly wait for the dawning of that final day. There were many obstacles in its way, but he was sure that the strong arm of the Lord had lost none of its ancient power (9).[84] The one who had mastered the waters of the great deep at creation, and parted the sea at the exodus, was surely able to bring his people to their final resting place.[85] Isaiah did not doubt either his ability or his will. But there was what we might call a 'holy impatience' about this great man of faith. 'Do it now,' he cries in effect, 'do it now' (9–10). The Bible itself ends with a very similar cry (Rev. 22:20–21). It should be our cry too.

---

[82] See the footnotes on 'ransom' and 'redemption' at 1:27 and 35:9–10.

[83] This verse is identical to 35:10.

[84] The figure of the Lord's arm as the instrument of deliverance and judgment is frequent in Deuteronomy, usually when recalling the exodus (e.g. Deut. 4:34). The picture is of a heavily gauntleted forearm brandishing a sword, the arm of a warrior (Exod. 15:3).

[85] *The great deep* (10) is almost certainly a reference to the creation account of Gen. 1 (especially verse 2). For *Rahab* (= Egypt) and the other elements of Ancient Near Eastern creation myths in this passage, see the comments on 27:1 and 30:7, with notes. 'The Hebrews took fragments from the creation myths [of other nations], like broken pieces of stained glass, and used them to embellish the story of the Exodus.' North (1964), p. 212. Cf. Ps. 74:12–17.

Isaiah 51:12 – 55:13

6. Grace triumphant

In a sense this part of the book is a rerun of the previous one. It, too, begins with comfort and ends with singing (51:12; 55:11–12). It restates the same general themes, and directs our attention once more to the Servant of the Lord as the key figure in God's plans for his people and for the world (52:13 – 53:12). But what is explored far more intensely here than in the previous section is the forgiveness of sins, and how (on what basis) it is made available to those who so little deserve it. These few chapters reveal the riches of God's grace more brilliantly than any other part of the book. They bring us to the very heart of Isaiah's gospel.

1. Awake, Zion! (51:12 – 52:12)

I, even I, am he who comforts you (12) echoes 40:1 – 'Comfort, comfort my people, says your God.' And there are many more such echoes to follow: *human beings . . . are but grass* (12b; cf. 40:6); *Zion . . . 'my people'* (16; cf. 40:1–2); *those who bring good news . . . 'Your God reigns!'* (52:7; cf. 40:9). It is as though, after the climax that was reached in 51:11, the recording has been restarted, and we hear the opening strains of the previous movement once more. This part of the book sets out from the same point as the previous one, and again the message of comfort moves against the backdrop of the terrible events predicted in 39:5–7.

But at the same time there is continuity and development from the end of the previous unit. Isaiah's cry 'Awake, awake, arm of the LORD' (51:9) is answered here by the challenge *Awake, awake! . . . Jerusalem . . . Awake, awake, Zion* (51:17; 52:1). In other words, the ball is struck very firmly back into the human end of the court. It is not the Lord who needs to awake, but his people! It is not inactivity on his part which is blocking the fulfilment of what he has promised to them, but their own spiritual torpor. Paradoxically, although it was Isaiah's cry in 51:9 which called forth this challenge, the challenge itself is not directed to him. In fact, it is Isaiah himself who delivers it. His own eagerness for God to act is admirable; it is the lack of such eagerness in others that is the problem.

a. God and his people (51:12–16)

This opening part of the passage is basically an affirmation that the covenant between the Lord and Israel is still intact: *I am the* LORD *your God* and *You are my people* (15–16). This is the language God had used when he had first claimed Israel as his own at the exodus (Exod. 20:2; Lev. 26:12). It is the language of relationship and commitment – not their commitment to him, but his commitment to them. And that had always been the solid ground of their security and comfort. God had claimed them for a special relationship with himself, and he was still committed to that relationship. Therefore they had nothing to fear (12–14), and nor do we. As Paul put it, 'If God is for us, who can be against us?' (Rom. 8:31). As a couple's security is in their commitment to each other, or children's in their parents' love, so is our security in God's commitment to us. It is a commitment that is as strong and pure as God himself, and it will never fail.

b. Not condemned (51:17–23)

Security, however, does not justify passivity. Quite the reverse. It calls for decisive action. The first call to action, as we have seen, is to *awake* and *rise up* (51:17). Fear paralyses us; being secure in God and his love for us sets us free. But fear is not the only thing that paralyses. So does a sense of being condemned, of being under judgment. Jerusalem certainly experienced this in the eighth to sixth centuries BC, and for her it was not just a feeling but an actuality. God gave her *the cup of his wrath* to drink, and she staggered and fell under its potent impact. It was a bitter draught, and it unmade her (17b–20). She was down because God had struck her down. But here she is told that that wrath has been removed. God has taken the cup from her and given it to her enemies (21–23).[1] The objective

---

[1] On the cup of wrath, see Ps. 75:8. Most Old Testament references to the cup are from around the beginning of the exile (Jer. 25:15–28; Lam. 4:21; Ezek. 23:31–33). The thought is always present that those to whom God gives the cup are powerless to refuse it. North (1964), p. 216.

facts are that she is not condemned any more; she is forgiven. The problem is that she is still labouring under a sense of condemnation, and it is like a drug which stupefies her. 'Awake,' says Isaiah. 'Rise up. You are not condemned, and you must not go on behaving as though you are!'

Again in this passage, *Jerusalem* stands for the people of Jerusalem who are experiencing the fulfilment of what Isaiah said would happen to them. They have been carried off into exile and are still there. Nothing has changed in their outward circumstances. There is 'terror' on every side, and 'the oppressor' is still bent on their destruction (13b). What they are being asked to respond to is not their circumstances (which will change later), but the word of God that has come to them. They are no longer condemned, because God has said so, and they are to rest their confidence on that alone. Again we are in touch with a great principle. It is the word of God, the gospel of his grace, that sets us free. And what relief it brings to those condemned by care and circumstance (cf. Rom. 5:1–5; 8:1–4)!

c. Loved and valued (52:1–10)

The second call to awake, in verses 1–6, is intended to counter a third deadly cause of spiritual paralysis – a sense of utter worthlessness. Zion had been *defiled* (1), enslaved (2), *sold* (3), *oppressed* (4) and mocked (5). No wonder she felt worthless. The word *nothing* in verses 3 and 5 captures it exactly: she has been *sold for nothing* and *taken away for nothing*. Egypt had treated her as nothing, Assyria had done the same, and so eventually did Babylon (4–5). Sadly, as we all know, those who are treated as nothing eventually come to feel that they *are* nothing, which is exactly how Zion feels here, and it is hard to awaken people to love and life and confidence again when they have sunk so low. Of course Zion's perception is distorted. There is more to the 'nothing' of verses 3 and 5 than she realizes or is willing to see.[2] The fact that she was 'sold for nothing' means in reality that there has been no valid sale at all and that therefore she is still rightfully the Lord's property (see on 50:1). And the fact that she has been taken away for nothing (gratuitously, without due acknowledgment of the Lord as the rightful owner) means that those responsible will have to pay for the wrong they have done.[3] But this does not alter the way Zion feels. It is only the certainty of being loved and valued that can do that.

---

[2] Verses 3–5 play on the various meanings of the Hebrew term *ḥinnām* ('nothing', 'for nothing').

[3] Cf. the two perspectives on the crucifixion of Jesus in Acts 2:23: it happened according to God's determined purpose, yet it was performed by wicked men who are held accountable for their actions.

What 52:1–6 does is challenge Zion to see herself, not as her enemies see her, or even as she sees herself, but as the Lord sees her. In his eyes she is as beautiful as a bride (1a) and as regal as a queen (2a). She is beyond price (3); he calls her citizens *my people* (4–6), and declares that his own *name* is at stake in how they are treated (5–6). No-one whom the Lord values so highly can be worthless, no matter what indignities they have suffered. And the exciting news that breaks out here again and demands to be shouted from the rooftops is that the Lord is about to give fresh expression to his love for Zion by totally reversing her circumstances – and all the world will see him do it (7–10).[4] The *Awake* of this passage is a call to expectation and preparedness. 'Wake up,' says the Lord. 'You are valued, you are precious, and I am coming for you. I want to find you clothed in strength and joy when I arrive' (cf. 1, 9; 43:4).

d. Ready to leave (52:11–12)

The climax is reached in the staccato *Depart, depart* of verse 11, which echoes the *Awake, awake* of the two previous units and brings us to their logical outcome. The people of God are to keep alert because their salvation is near. They are to live as those who are expecting the Lord at any moment, as travellers who are packed and ready for the last leg of their journey home. That is how it had been on the night the Israelites left Egypt: they ate the Passover with their cloaks tucked into their belts, their sandals on their feet and their staffs in their hands (Exod. 12:11). They were not delivered yet, but they were sure they would be – soon. The same air of keen expectancy permeates the present passage. A new exodus is about to take place.

There are many echoes of the original exodus in this passage, but it is the contrasts rather than the similarities that are most significant. When the Israelites left Egypt they took with them whatever they could get from the Egyptians – silver and gold jewellery and clothing (Exod. 12:35–36). This time they will leave behind them everything tainted with paganism. All they will *carry* will be *the articles of the LORD's house* (11), the holy vessels that Nebuchadnezzar removed from the temple when the exile began (Dan. 1:1–2; Ezra 1:7–11). Nor will they *leave in haste*, as their ancestors did when they fled from Egypt. They will go out with dignity and decorum, like priests in procession (12a). But the real glory of this exodus,

---

4 See comments on 40:9–10. The thought of the present passage is fundamentally the same.

as of the first, will be the presence of God with them. He will go before and behind, guiding and protecting them every step of the way (12b).[5]

For those who lived on the eve of the return, these words of Isaiah must have been electrifying, lifting their spirits and concentrating their minds. Of course, they would not be able to set out until Cyrus actually gave the word, but in the meantime the command to depart told them what their mindset was to be. 'Leaving' was to be the reality that controlled all that they said and did. It is the way the people of God are meant to live in every age, including our own. But how little we hear today of the fact that the Lord is coming to take us home, and may do so at any moment (Rev. 22:12–17)! What a difference it would make if this was our waking thought every morning and our retiring meditation every night (1 John 3:1–3). Our expectancy has become dulled, and we are the poorer for it. We, too, need to awake (Rom. 13:11; Eph. 5:14).

We are not quite through with this passage, however. The words *from there* in verse 11 are tantalizingly vague, and almost certainly by design.[6] The most obvious allusion, to be sure, is to the departure from Babylon anticipated in 48:20 and that is the lead we have followed up so far. But there is another, richer meaning of these words, for since the beginning of chapter 49 the primary focus has been not on Cyrus and physical return, but on the Servant and the spiritual recovery that he would bring about (49:1–6; 50:1–10). In this context the commands to *go out from there* have to be seen as a summons to the people of God to respond to the work of the Servant and rise to their high and holy calling as priests of the living God. There is more to be left behind than Babylon; there is the whole ambience of worldliness and estrangement from God that it represents.[7] The physical 'leaving' of 48:20 is here overlaid and transcended by a notion of setting out and pilgrimage which is essentially moral and spiritual.[8] How appropriate, then, that the apostle Paul should allude to this very passage in summoning us to have done with darkness and uncleanness and step out resolutely into the light and holiness of our

---

[5] In the first exodus the ark went before the people (Num. 10:33–36), as did the Lord himself in a pillar of cloud and fire (Exod. 13:21). For *rear guard*, see Num. 10:25; Josh. 6:9, 13.

[6] In addition to what follows, they have implications for the provenance of chapters 40–55. Motyer (p. 421) points out that *'from there* is really a great difficulty for all who propose a Babylonian location for the prophet: how could he say *from there* if he meant "from here"?' Cf. Young, 3, pp. 332–333.

[7] Cf. Motyer, p. 471.

[8] 'The "depart" here is a call to the believing remnant to actualize their faith-position by separation and the homecoming to Yahweh first mentioned in 49:5' (Motyer, in a personal communication).

priestly vocation as the people of God (2 Cor. 6:14–18). He caught the deeper significance of the words. It is by responding to their summons now that we prepare for our final departure on the last day.

2. Man of sorrows (52:13 – 53:12)

Now the Servant steps into full view again. We cannot mistake him, for *See, my servant* in 52:13 echoes the words that first heralded his presence in 42:1. But this time he is going to command our attention for much longer. This fourth Song is the most elaborate and poignant of them all. It is the jewel in the crown of Isaiah's theology, the focal point of his vision. And yet it comes upon us suddenly, almost intrusively. It is as though, just as we were in danger of forgetting his central importance, the Servant steps forward again and insists that we look at him and acknowledge that nothing that we have just been contemplating is possible without him. He is the key to it all. At the same time, however, he is self-effacing. For in this Song he never utters a word. He is as silent as *a lamb* (53:7). His presence is powerful, but it is others who bear witness to him, not he himself. And the first witness is none other than the Lord God: *See, my servant.*

We have already observed that the summons to 'come out' and 'be pure' in 52:11 must be read ultimately with the work of the Servant in mind. Now that is confirmed by further links between this Servant Song and its context. After the references to the 'arm of the Lord' in 51:9 and 52:10 comes the question of 53:1: *To whom has the arm of the Lord been revealed?* The implied answer is that, for those who have eyes to see it, the arm of the Lord (his saving power) is nowhere more clearly revealed than in the work of the Servant. If we ourselves fail to see this, we are like those who give testimony to their own initial blindness in 53:2–3. But the connections run deeper still. We have just seen the people of God as priests carrying holy vessels (52:11). But the previous chapters have repeatedly drawn attention to their endemic sinfulness. How can this tension between sinfulness and holiness be resolved? That question has never been answered. Forgiveness has been announced, but the basis on which it rests has not been clarified. Now at last it is: *my righteous servant will justify many . . . he will bear their iniquities* (53:11). At the very outset of the Song the Servant is pictured as a priest, 'sprinkling' the unclean (52:15),[9] and

---

[9] 'Startle' (NRSV) is a conjectural emendation based on the LXX.

in the heart of the Song he is spoken of as a guilt *offering* (53:10). The Servant is both priest and sacrifice, and it is through his priestly work that the people of God are themselves made fit for priestly service. There are treasures beyond price here, but we must not rush; every part of the Song is rich and worth savouring. There are five stanzas.

a. God's wisdom revealed (52:13–15)

This first stanza is in a sense a summary of the entire Song. *My servant will act wisely*, God says. The significance of that cryptic statement will become clear as the Song draws to a close (53:11), and we will comment further on it then. For the moment, we simply note that the opening stanza begins at the end, so to speak, with the Servant's exaltation (13). It then reverts to his deep suffering (14) and concludes with reflection on the stunned reaction that the sudden reversal in his fortunes will bring (15). Sprinkling, with blood, water or oil, had to do with cleansing, with making a person or thing fit to be in the presence of God.[10] Elsewhere in the Old Testament it always has reference to Israel, but there is no such restriction here. The cleansing the Servant brings is for *many nations* (15a).[11] The one whom people regarded as unclean (they were *appalled at him*, 14) will turn out to be the one who cleanses others. It is a paradox so astounding that it will dry up every accusation and cause every mouth to be stopped (15). The wisdom of God displayed in the Servant will utterly confound human wisdom.[12]

b. Despised and rejected (53:1–3)

The next two stanzas (53:1–3 and 4–6) provide a second, complementary perspective on the Servant. The link is provided by the question in 53:1, *Who has believed our message?* The speakers in 53:1–6 are witnesses. We no longer see the Servant through the eyes of outsiders, but through the eyes of insiders, Israelites who have come to understand the meaning of the Servant's sufferings, and announce it to the world. It is through their witness that those who formerly had not heard come to 'see' and 'understand' (52:15).

---

[10] See Lev. 4:6; 14:7 (blood), 8:11 (oil), Exod. 29:21 (blood and oil), and Exod. 29:4; 30:17–21 (water). Cf., in the New Testament, 1 Pet. 1:2; Heb. 9:13–14; 10:22; 12:24.

[11] Cf. Mark 10:45: 'a ransom for many'.

[12] This is probably the reason why *kings* are mentioned specifically in verse 15, for in the ancient world they were the patrons, and in many cases the most distinguished exponents, of wisdom. Solomon, in Israel, is a prime example.

This is not a new theme, of course. Repeatedly the people of God have been told that they are the Lord's witnesses (43:10, 12; 44:8). But there has been a blockage. Those chosen to be witnesses are blind and deaf. They themselves do not see and understand; much less do they make others do so (42:18–22). Isaiah is confident, however, that it will not always be so. Already there are some who do fear the Lord (50:10). And when at last they grasp the full glory of what the Servant has done, witness will be the natural, inevitable outcome. But notice that it now assumes a more specific form. It is no longer simply witness to the fact that the Lord alone is God (43:12), but witness to his saving power revealed in the suffering, death and exaltation of the Servant. Once the Servant's work is done, witness will focus specifically on what God has achieved through him.

The witnesses begin by reflecting on their own past attitude to the Servant (1–3). At first he had shown promise. He had grown up before the Lord *like a tender shoot*, like a dead plant suddenly springing to life in a wasteland (2a).[13] But that promise did not seem to be fulfilled. The more he grew the less impressive he became. He appeared ordinary, even un-attractive (2b).[14] And when, in the course of his work, he met strong opposition, derision and suffering, he became even less desirable to know (3). Even those who did not actively persecute him found it more prudent to turn away than to take his part. To their shame, the witnesses confess that this is exactly what they themselves had done (3). Perhaps they had not expected the Servant's sufferings to become so severe that he would lose his life. But this is what happened. The words 'pierced' and 'crushed' in verse 5 indicate a violent death.[15] And the witnesses had taken the view (did they really believe it or was it to quieten their consciences?) that the Servant must have deserved it. His human tormentors had merely been instruments that were providentially used; it was 'God' who had struck him down (4b).

c. Healed by his wounds (53:4–6)

How right, and yet at the same time how terribly wrong, they had been! In this third stanza, the witnesses testify to the completely new

---

[13] *Before him* refers to *the LORD* in the previous verse.

[14] *Beauty* (NIV) is *tō'ar*, 'form'. In contrast to the young David, literally 'a man of form' (1 Sam. 16:18), the Servant had 'no form' (no physical attractiveness). Cf. also 52:14 – *his form* (*tō'ar*) was *marred*. Even his very ordinary human features were distorted by physical abuse.

[15] 'Pierced' (*mĕḥōlāl*) is quite specific in this regard (51:9; and cf. Job 26:13; Zech. 12:10). 'Crushed' (*mĕdukkā'*) has similar connotations, which are accentuated here by the poetic parallelism (cf. Pss 89:10; 143:3).

understanding of the Servant's death that they have now arrived at. Yes, it was God, ultimately, who crushed him, but it was not because he deserved it. The original Hebrew is very emphatic in verse 4: 'Surely, it was our infirmities he took up, our sorrows he bore.' And it is clear from the context that it is not sickness or sorrow in general that is being referred to. They are the same sufferings and sorrows that have just been referred to in the previous verse.[16] They are the sufferings which were deliberately inflicted on the Servant and which culminated in his death. The witnesses realize that they themselves deserved those sufferings and that death, but that the Servant took their place. Substitution was not a new thought to the Israelites; it was enshrined in the law of Moses. Ever since that law had been given to Israel, lambs and other animals had been sacrificed in the place of sinners. But now the witnesses see that this same principle is at work in the suffering and death of the Servant. Their peace with God, the healing of their broken relationship with him, was secured by the Servant's death (5). He was *pierced for* their *transgressions* and *crushed for* their *iniquities*. The comfort they have received, the good news of their pardon, has been provided at tremendous cost.

d. The sinless, silent sufferer (53:7–9)

In this fourth stanza a lone witness speaks, most likely Isaiah himself. At his call back in chapter 6, confronted with the awesome holiness of God, he had confessed that he himself was unclean and that he dwelt among unclean people (5). Immediately he was assured of his own cleansing (by the symbolism of a live coal taken from the altar). But what of his fellow Israelites, given their deep-dyed sinfulness exposed in chapters 1–5? How could they ever be pardoned without God's holiness being compromised? Now Isaiah sees the answer: *for the transgression of my people he* [the Servant] *was punished* (8b).[17] They were 'like sheep' that had 'gone astray' (6), but the Servant, *like a lamb*, had been slaughtered in their place (7). In general this stanza repeats the thought of the previous one, but highlights the special significance it had for Isaiah. It does more than this, however. It carries us beyond the Servant's death to his burial, and ends on a rather ambivalent note. The Servant *was assigned a grave with the wicked, and*

---

[16] Older versions of the NIV partly obscured this important connection by translating the same word (*ḥŏlî*) as 'suffering' in verse 3 but 'infirmities' in verse 4. The closeness of the link is emphasized by the chiastic pattern: sorrows, suffering, suffering, sorrows (NIV 2011: *suffering, pain, pain, suffering*).

[17] Cf. Isaiah's use of 'my people' in 22:4; 26:20; 32:13; etc.

with the rich (9). He was an innocent man who had been done to death like a criminal, and his burial was a mixture of honour and dishonour. If his career ended at that point it would be hard to tell what even God's final verdict on him had been. Was his work finished to God's satisfaction or not?

e. Crowned with glory and honour (53:10–12)

This final stanza gives us the answer. First we hear from Isaiah (10–11a), then from the Lord (11b–12), and both affirm the same central truth. The Servant's death will not be the end of his career. God will place his seal of approval on his work by raising and exalting him, *and the will of the* LORD [all God's plans] *will prosper in his hand.* Like *an offering for sin* (or 'guilt offering'), the Servant's death will provide perfect satisfaction for sin (10).[18] But in startling contrast to what happened in a normal guilt offering, the victim, in this case, will not cease to exist. He will die, yes. But afterwards *he will see the light of life, be satisfied* (see the fruit of his sacrifice)[19] and *justify many* (bring them into a right relationship with God) (11). That is, the Servant will accomplish his God-given mission not only by his death, but also by his life beyond death. He will be a new kind of guilt offering that will utterly surpass anything that has gone before.

The reference to the Servant's *knowledge* in verse 11 picks up the theme of wisdom from the very beginning of the Song. The Servant will act wisely (52:13), and *by his knowledge* he will, literally 'cause many to become righteous'. The best commentary on this rather puzzling statement is Daniel 12:3, where we read that 'Those who are wise will shine like the brightness of the heavens, and those who lead many to righteousness, like the stars for ever and ever.' The 'wise' are those who 'know their God' (Dan. 11:32). This is not mere academic knowledge, but personal, intimate knowledge (see 1:3; and cf. Hos. 4:1, 6). And those who know God in this way have a profound influence on others. They become channels by which others find the knowledge of God also; they lead many to righteousness. Righteousness, both here and in Isaiah 53, is more than acquittal; it is a new way of life based on a right relationship with God. The Servant will

---

[18] According to the law of Moses, a guilt offering (*'āšām*) effected atonement (restored relationship with God). It involved the sacrificial slaughter of an animal, and restitution (the payment of compensation with interest). See Lev. 5:14 – 6:7; 7:1–10. It was the most comprehensive type of offering for personal sin, overlapping with other kinds of offering but going beyond them. It is this comprehensiveness which is the point here.

[19] Or perhaps *be satisfied* in the sense of being vindicated at last (see 50:8).

be a supremely wise person in this sense. He will act wisely; he will know God intimately; and he will cause many to become righteous. The wisdom of God will be displayed in him in an unprecedented fashion.

But there is still one more image of the Servant for us to relish before the Song is complete. It is in verse 12. The Servant will return from his mission like a warrior laden with spoil. His weakness will turn to strength, his dishonour into honour, his defeat into victory. The one who was despised and rejected will take the highest place, the place of a conqueror.

And with that the Song is almost over, but not quite. There is one final reflection on who it is that all this is for: *he bore the sin of many, and made intercession for the transgressors* (12b). We began with pagans (52:13–15) and Israelites (53:1–6), witnesses and hearers, insiders and outsiders. But in the end we have only one group – *transgressors, many* of them.[20] And the good news is that it was their sins that the Servant bore, and it was for them he interceded. The witnesses themselves speak in very personal terms in verse 6: 'We all . . . have gone astray, each . . . to our own way . . . the LORD has laid on him the iniquity of us all.' It is as though, while they speak together, each makes his or her own confession: 'I have transgressed; the sacrifice was for me.' And by their own confessions they show the way to others. The message of this fourth Servant Song is for transgressors everywhere. All they have to do is to admit that that is what they are.

Many, many facets of the Servant's character are revealed in this Song. He is sage, priest, sacrifice, servant, sufferer, conqueror and intercessor. He is the channel of God's grace to sinners. In him the holiness and mercy of God are perfectly reconciled. He is the key to all God's plans for his people and for the world. And Isaiah's portrait of him is almost complete. Only one Song remains, in 61:1–3. Then, when all the relevant data are in, we will see the whole in the light of the New Testament. But for the moment we must attend to the more immediate task of following part 6 of Isaiah's vision as it gathers pace again and moves towards its climax in chapter 55.

3. Peace like a river (54:1 – 55:13)

Peace (šālôm) is perhaps the richest word in the Old Testament. It was the word the priests used to bless the people in the name of the Lord, and

---

[20] The *many . . . transgressors* of 53:12 echoes the 'many nations' of 52:15.

the word the people themselves used to greet and bless one another (Num. 6:24–26; 1 Sam. 25:6),[21] as Jews still do today. 'Shalom' stands for complete wholeness, the sum total of covenant blessing, the full enjoyment of all that God has promised. But in practice such peace is an elusive thing, because it depends on being in a right relationship with God. Where the relationship is wrong, peace is lost. 'There is no peace . . . for the wicked' (48:22).

Earlier chapters have spoken of peace as something earnestly longed for. The future Messiah will be the 'Prince of Peace' (9:6). He will bring peace that will last for ever (9:7). At the end of history, the Lord himself will establish peace (26:12). In the meantime, inner peace is reserved for those who trust in him (26:3). One day Zion would experience peace; that is the good news of 52:7. But before peace in this full and final sense could be realized the relationship between God and his people had to be put right. The problem of their sin had to be dealt with to God's total satisfaction. And that, as we saw in chapter 53, is what the Servant achieves. The witnesses in 53:5 are aware that their relationship with God has been fully restored, not by anything they have done, but by what the Servant has done for them: 'the punishment that brought us peace was on him, and by his wounds we are healed'. So as we come to chapters 54 and 55 the blockage has been removed. The floodgates of divine blessing have been flung open, and peace begins to flow like a river. Israel is assured that the peace which has so long eluded her because of her failure to obey (48:18) will now be hers because of what the Servant will accomplish. Notice the references to peace in these chapters. The new relationship between God and his people will be a *covenant of peace* that will never be shaken (54:10). Under it, Zion's children will have *great* peace (54:13), and those presently captive will *be led forth in peace* (55:12), confident that the new age of God's unlimited blessing is about to dawn. *Peace*, then, is the key that links these two chapters together, and connects both of them to the Servant Song of chapter 53. And the promised realization of this peace in all its fullness is the reason for the joyful singing with which the whole section begins (54:1) and ends (55:12–13).

a. Every promise fulfilled (54:1–17)

Isaiah, then, conceived of the ideal future for which he and all God's faithful people longed in terms of a covenant of peace that would be the

---

[21] 'Good health' (NIV) is literally 'peace' (*šālôm*).

culmination of all that was promised in the covenants that had marked Israel's history from the very beginning. In chapters 54 and 55 first one and then another of these covenants comes under review. The situation we have to envisage is that which has been progressively elaborated since the end of chapter 39: the people of God in exile (39:5–7), but no longer condemned (40:1–2), with full restoration to God and his covenant blessings guaranteed by the work of the Servant of the Lord (52:13 – 53:12). Just as in chapter 53 the atoning death of the Servant is viewed from the divine perspective as already accomplished, so here in chapters 54 and 55 it is assumed as the basis of a new covenant of peace which will be the fulfilment of all previous covenants.

First, there was the covenant with Abraham (54:1–3). The *barren woman* (1), the *tent* (2) and the mention of *descendants* (3) all recall Abraham's circumstances and the promises that were made to him. Zion's barrenness during the exile would prove no more an obstacle to the fulfilment of God's promises than was Sarah's. As Abraham received the promises as a tent-dweller in a foreign land, so his descendants are to appropriate them afresh when they dwell precariously in exile. God stands by his promises! Zion's children will repossess and settle in the *desolate cities* of Judah.[22] They *will spread out to the right and to the left* in the land promised to their father Abraham long ago (cf. 51:1–3).

With the reference to the Lord as Israel's *Maker*, *husband* and *Redeemer* in verses 4–8 the focus shifts to the Sinai covenant. In her youth Israel had suffered the shame of slavery in Egypt; in her maturity she was to suffer the disgrace of *widowhood* in Babylon. But as the Lord then took her to be his bride, entering into a covenant with her at Mount Sinai, so he would take her again and renew his relationship with her. He would not cease to be her husband and Redeemer. The Sinai covenant would stand.

The covenant with *Noah* is the next to come into view, in verses 9–17. This is surprising at first, because it takes us backwards in time to a point prior to the previous two covenants. But logically it widens our vision and moves the thought of the chapter a significant step forwards. For the covenant with Noah was a covenant with the entire human race (Gen. 9:8–17). After the flood Noah's family spread out and brought new life and blessing to the whole earth (Gen. 9:17). This adds a whole new dimension to the

---

[22] NIV's '*their* desolate cities' in verse 3 should be '*the* desolate cities'. The reference is to Judah's own cities, which had been occupied by foreigners following the devastation of the area by the Babylonians.

idea of Zion's children spreading out to right and left. The exile is likened to the flood, and Zion's children to the family of Noah. They will be protected by God as Noah was, in order that they might become a blessing to the whole world. God's commitment to them is as firm and unshakeable as his commitment to the world he has created (9). He will not destroy them because he is committed to preserving and blessing his world, and they are the means he has chosen to do it.

What a grand vista opens up before us in verses 11–17 – a whole renewed universe! And at its centre is the *city* of God, the point where heaven and earth meet and God is present with his people for ever (11–17). This city is the final resting place of *the servants of the Lord*, the reward and *vindication* for all that they have suffered because of their faithfulness to God (17). Subtly, but quite unmistakably, Isaiah links them to the greatest Servant of all. As he was a disciple, taught by the Lord (50:4), so are they (13). They have suffered affliction (11) as he did (53:4). And as he will surely be vindicated (50:8), so will they be (17). The *servants of the Lord* follow in the footsteps of the perfect Servant. They share his sufferings, and will also share his glory. They are 'his offspring', the fruit of his sacrifice (53:10), and the city of God will be their home for ever.

b. The banquet spread (55:1–2)

The invitation *Come, all you who are thirsty* must be seen against this background. It is a call to all and sundry to come and share in 'the heritage of the servants of the Lord' that has just been described. The gates of the city of God stand open. A banquet is spread (cf. 25:6–8). All that remains is for the invited guests to come. No *money* is needed; the rich *fare* is free. And when the metaphor gives way to explicit statement in verses 6 and 7, we are told precisely what that delightful and satisfying food is. It is mercy and pardon, and it is freely available because it has already been paid for in full (53:4–6, 12).

c. The everlasting covenant (55:3–5)

All this is explained in verses 3b–5 in terms of *an everlasting covenant* which will mean the fulfilment of all that was once *promised to David*. And, like the earlier covenants, this final covenant will have a sign to confirm it. The covenant with Noah had the rainbow (Gen. 9:13–16). The covenant with Abraham had circumcision (Gen. 17:9–14), and the Sinai covenant had sprinkled blood (Exod. 24:8). Appropriately, the final *everlasting covenant* will have 'an everlasting sign', which will be nothing less than a permanently renewed universe (13). Here is the climax of the whole movement of these two chapters with their review of the various covenants. The final covenant between God and his people will not cancel out the earlier covenants but fulfil them, perfectly and completely. The final outcome of the work of the Servant will be the full realization of all that God has promised from the beginning. All the promises of God will find their 'Yes' and 'Amen' in him (2 Cor 1:20).

But even though the vista opens so very wide as we move to this breathtaking climax, the painful prospect of exile does not disappear from view. The generation which was to experience it is addressed in the *you* (singular) of verse 5 as the surviving remnant of Israel,[23] the nation through whom God has chosen to work. Verses 4 and 5 are closely bound together; as God made David *a witness* and *ruler* of *peoples*, so he will now make his people Israel. David conquered surrounding nations and brought them under his rule, and therefore the rule of the Lord. Now Israel, restored to the land, will do the same. They will conquer other people not physically, as David did, but spiritually. Because of what God does in its midst, Israel will be like a magnet attracting people of *all* nations into the kingdom of God.

d. Sin, pardon, and glory (55:6–13)

All this must have been very hard to grasp for people whose world seemed to be fracturing and contracting rather than expanding. To them it must have appeared too vast to comprehend, too ambitious, like a fantastic dream. But if so, that was because their human minds, like ours, were limited and sinful. God's *thoughts* were as high above theirs as *the heavens* were above *the earth* (8–9). And God is insistent; it is no dream, no mere fancy he has set before them. His plans will shoot and blossom as surely as parched ground when *rain* pours upon it (10). His *word*, which once spoke the universe into existence, has gone forth again, and has lost none of its ancient power. Nothing can frustrate it, or divert it from its course (11). There will be a new creation, a new world, and the return from exile will be the first step towards it (12–13). No wonder chapter 55 throbs with excitement.

---

[23] Cf. the similar use of the singular pronoun for 'Jacob/Israel' in 40:27.

It also rings with a certain urgency, however. There are decisions to be made. There is a banquet spread, but the guests must come. There is *pardon* available, but *the wicked* must *forsake their* own *ways* and *seek the* LORD *while he may be found* (6–7).[24] No-one need be an outsider, but neither will anyone be forced to enter, and the invitation to do so will not be extended indefinitely. In the end, the vision of Isaiah has a very sharp evangelistic edge to it. We will see this even more clearly in chapters 56–66, to which we turn shortly. But first let us reflect on the ground we have traversed since chapter 40.

The resounding affirmations of the power of God's word in 40:6–8 and 55:10–11 form a kind of bracket around the whole of chapters 40–55. This large unit is divided into two parts (40:1 – 51:11 and 51:12 – 55:13) which are very closely related, with passages about the Servant of the Lord occurring in both. But in the first, the Servant shares the stage, so to speak, with Cyrus the Persian. In the second, Cyrus recedes into the background and the Servant becomes everything. The theme of 'grace abounding', which we identified as the keynote of this second section, revolves around him entirely, with chapter 53 as the key that unlocks the mystery of how a holy God can pardon sinners. In him all God's covenant promises find their fulfilment, and all the gospel blessings which are on offer in chapter 55 are benefits that flow from his death. These two parts of the book, and the second in particular, have brought us to the fulcrum on which the whole of Isaiah's vision turns. Only one part remains to bring us to its final outworking in the new heavens and the new earth of chapters 65 and 66.

---

[24] The reference to *the wicked* in verse 7 is best understood as a final appeal to unbelieving Israelites. See 48:22 and comments.

Isaiah 56 – 66

7. Waiting for a new world

Chapter 56 launches us into the seventh and final part of Isaiah's vision. It relates to the period following the arrival of the first returnees from Babylon. Isaiah saw that time in prophetic vision; we see it now in the cold, clear light of history.[1] It was a time of high expectations and immense difficulties. There was tension between the returnees and those, including foreigners, who had been living in the area during their absence. There were the frustrations inevitably associated with limited self-rule. The Judea to which they returned had been incorporated into the Persian empire, so they were home but still not their own masters. Their numbers and resources were limited, and neighbouring groups viewed them with suspicion or outright hostility. In these circumstances the challenges involved in establishing a secure and viable community were almost overwhelming.

But the most serious problems arose from the fact that this small community lived 'between the times', so to speak. The return from exile had begun but was far from complete (56:8). Many Israelites were still scattered in Babylonia, Egypt and elsewhere. The glorious new age the prophets had spoken about had begun to dawn, but much – very much – still awaited fulfilment. Things were not as they had been, but neither were they as they would be. The community lived in the tension between the 'now' and the 'not yet'. They had the beginnings of what God had promised but not the fullness of it. It was a time in many respects like our own, between the first and second comings of Christ. The kingdom of God has come, but is

---

[1] See especially the books of Ezra, Nehemiah, Haggai and Zechariah.

yet to come. It is an exciting time but also a difficult one, when (as Paul puts it) 'we ourselves, who have the firstfruits of the Spirit, groan inwardly as we wait eagerly for . . . the redemption of our bodies' (Rom. 8:23). Waiting tests our patience and our faith. It is too much for some. The interim is a time when tensions develop and some fall away, and when those who do remain faithful are not always sure what is the right thing to do. All these tensions are reflected in Isaiah 56 – 66. This final part of the book is about life in the interim – waiting for a new world.

But we must go one step further. It is not simply that chapters 56–66 may be seen as having an indirect relevance to us because of a perceived similarity between our situation and the earlier one which is in view here. The fact is that what Isaiah says here relates just as directly to both. Certainly there are elements which appear to have more relevance to particular problems that the return from exile would bring. But in the overall shape of Isaiah's vision this last part falls between the death and exaltation of the Servant of the Lord in chapter 53, and the consummation of history in the new heavens and the new earth in chapters 65 and 66. This is the period in which we now live, referred to in the New Testament as 'the last days' (Acts 2:16–21; Heb. 1:1–3). In short, the text has a double focus, and we will need to bear this constantly in mind if we want to appreciate fully its richness and relevance to us.[2]

1. The marks of a redeemed community (56:1–8)

These eight verses are a very fitting introduction to what follows, serving as a kind of charter for the restored community. Those whom God has freed from condemnation and despair have an obligation to do his will, and these verses set forth very clearly the ideals God has for them. They are to be marked by two things: justice and openness.

a. Justice (56:1–2)

It was injustice that had brought Israel to ruin. God had looked for justice, but found only bloodshed and cries of distress (5:7). Religion had become divorced from social responsibility, ritual from right living, and so God destroyed Jerusalem and drove his people out of it rather than permit such monstrous dishonouring of his name to continue. Now those who will

---

[2] This double focus is not limited to chapters 56–66, but is more conspicuous there.

wake on the other side of this nightmare and have the opportunity to make a fresh start are reminded that God has the same passionate commitment to justice that he always had, and that he expects them to share it. They are to *maintain justice and do what is right* because his (the Lord's own) *righteousness* is about to *be revealed* (1). Their life together is to be a visible sign that the kingdom of God – his reign of perfect justice and righteousness – is just around the corner, breaking in and already making its presence felt.

The thought is very similar to that of Jesus in the Sermon on the Mount. After describing the righteousness that is to mark the lives of his disciples, he tells them that they are the light of the world and a city on a hill (Matt. 5:14). Theirs is the kingdom of heaven. They will inherit it fully in the future, but it should also be visible in how they live now. They are to be a sign of what is coming. It is a communal issue, since justice and righteousness are about personal relationships, how people treat one another. But it is also a personal issue. *Blessed is the one who does this – the person who holds it fast* (2). In the end the responsibility for maintaining justice devolves upon each individual; it is not something that can be left to leaders alone.

The fact that maintaining justice (1) is so closely linked to keeping *the Sabbath* (2) may surprise us, but it would not have surprised any Israelite of the Old Testament period. For the Sabbath had to do with rest; not just for masters, but for servants as well, and even for working animals and resident foreigners (Exod. 20:10). To keep the Sabbath meant, among other things, that you served the God who created the world and cared for everyone and everything in it. It also had to do with perfection or completeness. It recalled the completeness of God's original work of creation (Gen. 2:2–3), and looked forward to the time when his work of recreation would also be complete. The Sabbath rest was a sign of the final rest which all God's people will enjoy in the new heavens and new earth (66:22–23). So there is no petty legalism here. The Sabbath is viewed not as an end in itself, but as a sign that the whole of life was to be lived in submission to God, and that meant sharing his concern for justice.[3]

b. Openness (56:3–8)

There is no direct command here, but the implication of what is said is very clear: the Lord accepts the *foreigner* and the *eunuch* who sincerely

---

[3] True Sabbath observance is to refrain from *evil* (2b), not just from work. Cf. chapter 58 on true fasting.

seek him, and his people must do the same. This was a very difficult and sensitive issue, for there were specific statements in the law of Moses excluding emasculated men and foreigners, especially Moabites and Ammonites.[4] These were powerful reminders to Israel that the holiness God demanded of his people was totally incompatible with physical mutilation (as practised in pagan cults), and that his love for them was no casual thing. He was implacably opposed to those who sought to harm them (cf. Deut. 23:3–6 with Gen. 12:2–3). These laws had never been meant to exclude genuine converts, as the stories about Rahab and Ruth show quite plainly (Josh. 6:24–25; Ruth 1 – 4),[5] but the question of how to apply them in the new situation in which they found themselves was to prove very troublesome for the restored community. The danger of being unduly influenced by their pagan environment still existed, but they were also on the threshold of a new age in which God intended to gather outsiders into his kingdom on a totally unprecedented scale (44:1–5; 45:22; 55:1–7). The import of this passage is that they were not to adopt a legalistic attitude which would stand in the way of this happening. They were to be an open community, warmly embracing all who genuinely *bound* themselves *to the Lord* (3, 6). This was part of the justice they were to exhibit as a community of God's people.

Eunuchs in particular were to be treated with compassion. Isaiah had foreseen that members of the royal family would be made eunuchs in Babylon (39:7).[6] How were such people to be regarded in the situation following the exile – as people permanently tainted with paganism and cursed by God? Certainly not. This passage makes it plain that God does not intend to exclude them from his coming kingdom. Nor should his people, who await its arrival.

The great reality which governs everything in this passage is the end, the goal towards which all God's purposes are moving. Something much more is in view than the rebuilding of the Jerusalem temple and the inclusion of formerly excluded people in the worship associated with it.[7] To the degree that these things happened at all in the sixth century BC

---

[4] Deut. 23:1–6. Cf. Lev. 22:24–25, where the offering of emasculated animals is also forbidden.

[5] The case of Ruth is particularly instructive, since she was a Moabitess.

[6] Possibly for harem service, but also as a way of dampening nationalistic expectations associated with a possible revival of the Davidic monarchy.

[7] *Temple*, *walls*, *memorial*, and so on, are not to be taken literally as referring to the particulars of the post-exilic period. The references to the Lord's *holy mountain* and *all nations* in verse 7 suggest that the passage as a whole has the same end-time perspective as 2:1–4.

they were only signs of something that was 'close at hand' and 'soon to be revealed' (1). It was with the coming of Christ that sign finally gave way to substance, and the gathering of the outcasts began in earnest.[8] The conversion of the Ethiopian eunuch in Acts 8:26–40 is a beautiful example of it. This man was both a foreigner and a eunuch, and interestingly it was the scroll of the prophet Isaiah that he was reading when Philip the evangelist met him. What a harvest was to follow in the vast African continent, a harvest still being reaped today! In Acts we see Isaiah's vision moving into top gear as the last days begin (see Acts 2:17).

2. The shattering of the dream: bad leadership and its effects (56:9 – 57:13)

This passage is a rude return to the realities of the waiting time. For a community under stress, the quality of its leadership is critical. Leaders are to be *watchmen* (56:10), alert to dangers that threaten from outside, and *shepherds* (56:11), nurturing and strengthening the inner life of the community. Where such leadership is lacking, the sort of situation develops which we see here. Instead of being open in the right sense – to people sincerely seeking the Lord – the community becomes open to evil people who want to exploit it (56:9). Good people are attacked, and *no one* comes to their defence (57:1–2). Superstition and false religion flourish and become a cover for all kinds of wickedness (57:3–10).[9] The fear of the Lord is lost, and other, unhealthy fears take over (57:11).[10] And finally, God is left with no option but to judge (57:12–13a).

It is a depressing picture, painted in broad, bold brushstrokes and sombre tones. Some of the details are elusive,[11] but the overall impact is

---

[8] Note how Jesus quoted verse 7 at the cleansing of the temple (Matt. 21:13). The trade in the outer courtyard was denying Gentiles even the limited access they were entitled to. Jesus' indignation shows his passionate concern for the outsiders. And cf. verse 8 with Jesus' words in John 10:16 ('I have other sheep that are not of this sheepfold. I must bring them also'). Something more is envisaged than gathering dispersed Jews to their homeland.

[9] In general, verses 3–10 seem to refer to participation in pagan fertility rites and the immoral practices associated with them.

[10] The Lord's having *long been silent* (11b) probably refers to the fact that, for those in view here, the judgment of 587 BC would be long past. Cf. Judg. 2:10.

[11] For example, *You went to Molek* (57:9a) is literally 'You went to the king' (NIV footnote). Does this refer to the child sacrifice associated with the pagan god Molek (see 57:5, and cf. 1 Kgs 11:7; 2 Kgs 23:10), or illicit political activity, as suggested by *You sent your ambassadors far away* (57:9b)? *Children of a sorceress* (57:3) is probably idiomatic for 'having the character of a sorceress' (cf. Judg. 19:22, literally 'sons of Belial'; John 8:44). Note the parallel with *offspring of adulterers and prostitutes* (57:3b). The reference is to the occult and immoral practices associated with idolatry.

very clear. Sin will not be eradicated from God's people until the very end. In the waiting time the struggle against it goes on unabated at both the personal and corporate levels. And where godly leadership is lacking, old evils come flooding back, even after a remarkable experience of God's grace. It proved to be so in the period following the return from Babylon, and it is still so in the church today.

After the ideals laid out in 56:1–8, this passage comes as a shock, like the shattering of a dream. But that is not the whole story. Not all fall away in the waiting time. Isaiah speaks of those who cherish the dream and would rather die than give it up (57:1–3); they take refuge in the Lord, and will finally inherit all things (57:13b).[12] The contrast between them and the apostates whose attitudes and behaviour we have already noted could hardly be more stark. As the pace quickens, and history hurtles more and more rapidly to its end, the difference between the true and false, between those who really are God's people and those who are not, will become more and more obvious. The waiting time is a time of sifting.

This sifting involves pain, and can be very alarming, but it should not cause us to despair. The failure of leadership which in fact happened in the post-exilic community, and the resulting divisions and apostasy on the part of many,[13] did not frustrate God's plan to send Jesus when the time was right (Gal. 4:4). Nor will similar failings in the church today prevent God's purposes from reaching their final goal when Christ returns (2 Tim. 3:12 – 4:1). The dream will not die, because it is God's dream, and those who remain true will share in the fulfilment of it.

3. Comfort for those who mourn (57:14–21)

'Blessed are those who mourn,' Jesus said, 'for they will be comforted' (Matt. 5:4). There could be no more apt summary of this passage. It follows naturally from the previous one, and is addressed to the same situation. But the focus is different. Now it is the faithful, godly ones who are primarily in view; *the wicked* are mentioned only in a footnote (20–21;

---

[12] God's *holy mountain* here, as in 11:9, stands for the kingdom of God that is coming, the new age when God's glory will fill the earth (cf. 65:25).

[13] Of course, there were some great reformers and leaders, such as Ezra and Nehemiah, but a deteriorating situation is evident at the end of the book of Nehemiah (chapter 13). The book of Malachi condemns the priestly leadership in terms very reminiscent of the present passage in Isaiah, and the decline continues through the intertestamental period to the state of affairs which Jesus confronted, culminating in the destruction of Jerusalem in AD 70.

cf. 48:22). And we are taken deeper, here, into what it means to be godly. It is not only to have a robust, indomitable faith in God's promises, or the heroism of a martyr. It is to be *contrite*, to be penitent; to be people who know in their hearts that they are no better than their fellow human beings, and who weep for their own sin and for that of others as well (15, 10).[14] And it is the *mourners* whom God comforts (18–19). The wicked are never comforted, because they will not weep. They have no humility, and are not sorry for their sins.

There are significant echoes here of earlier passages. The promise of comfort harks back to the 'Comfort, comfort my people' of 40:1; *Build up . . . prepare the road* (14)[15] recalls 40:3–4; the reference to God as *the high and exalted One* (15) echoes 6:1 (cf. also 33:5).[16] The effect is to assure the faithful that God still reigns, that he is with them, and that his purposes are on track. But the *way* spoken of here (14) is something rather different from the one back in chapter 40. It is no longer the way back from the exile in Babylon; those on view here have already trodden that way. It is the way through present trials to their final resting place in the kingdom of God which is still to come (13b). In this sense, God's faithful people are always exiles and pilgrims. They will not be fully at home until God's will is done on earth as it is in heaven. Then their mourning will give way to praise from which every tinge of sadness has at last been removed (19).

4. True fasting (58:1–14)

A moment's reflection is all that is needed to see how appropriately the topic of this chapter follows that of the previous passage. For *fasting* was a kind of ritual mourning. From early times it was associated with bereavement (1 Sam. 31:13; 2 Sam. 1:12), repentance (1 Sam. 7:6; 1 Kgs 21:27) and prayer (2 Sam. 12:16–17; Ps. 35:13). The law of Moses prescribed fasting only in connection with the Day of Atonement (Lev. 16:29–31; 23:27–32; Num. 29:7), but fasts were also proclaimed in times of national emergency (Judg. 20:26; 2 Chr. 20:3). In later times the trauma which

---

[14] Cf. Isaiah himself (6:5). He began his ministry as a penitent. Verses 16–17 do not refer to humankind in general. The whole of verses 14–19 refers to those who are now *contrite*, and mourn for their sins. Verse 17 recalls their former rebelliousness.

[15] The indefinite opening *And it will be said* recalls 40:3, 'A voice . . . calling'. The image is of a herald announcing the saving intervention of God.

[16] This description of God is unique to Isaiah.

resulted from the destruction of Jerusalem and the temple in 587 BC gave rise to regular fast days to mark these terrible events (Zech. 7:1–7).

The fast days were impressive, solemn occasions, when the whole community gathered. This was good in itself, but it was also dangerous, for it created an impression of piety which was often far removed from the real state of affairs. It imposed a uniformity of observance which disguised the difference between those who were genuine mourners and those who were not (58:1–2).[17] At its worst it could degenerate into self-righteousness. Religion that drifts into superstition and self-righteousness becomes a hollow thing, lacking integrity and power. This is the inevitable outcome, though, when leaders fail to speak to God's people about their sins and challenge them with the continuing need for repentance. The command of verse 1 is an urgent one, which is still relevant today.[18]

After the exposure of wrong fasting (1–5) comes a description of the kind of fasting that truly pleases God (6–12). It is fasting accompanied by genuine repentance, especially turning away from exploitation and quarrelling (3b, 4a, 6). It is not simply to go without food on the set fast days, but to adopt a lifestyle in which self-indulgence and greed are totally given up and replaced by generosity towards the poor (7).[19] This is the kind of fasting that pleases God and leads to his blessing being released (9). The great paradox of the life of faith to which we are called is that blessing comes through self-denial, that we receive through giving, and that we gain our lives by laying them down (Luke 6:38; 9:24; John 12:24–25). And the only repentance that counts with God is the sort that can be seen in the way we live, especially in how we treat other people (Luke 3:7–14).

Conditions proved to be very difficult in Palestine after the return from exile (Hag. 1:6; Mal. 3:11). On the fast days the people cried out to God to hear them, and give them the good things he had promised (3).[20] The terms *light*, *healing*, *righteousness* and *glory* all refer to the same reality:

---

[17] *My people* in 58:1 is parallel to *the descendants of Jacob*. It is not just the faithful remnant, as in 57:14, but the whole community. Cf. 2:5–6; 8:17; 14:1; 29:22; 48:1. *Your people* (58:12) probably means their descendants. What the present community begins their descendants will complete.

[18] Cf. Paul's solemn charge to Timothy in 2 Tim. 4:1–5.

[19] *The poor wanderer* of verse 7 is probably a foreigner (cf. Deut. 14:29). *Your own flesh and blood* is literally just 'your own flesh'. This probably means 'your fellow human being' rather than 'a member of your own family or race'. Cf. 56:3, 6 (the inclusion of foreigners) and 40:5–6; 49:26; 66:16, 23–24 (where the word for 'flesh', sometimes translated 'people' or 'mankind', means human beings in general).

[20] The expression *just decisions* in verse 2 means the vindication to which they felt they were entitled as God's people (cf. 40:27).

the full realization of covenant blessing for which they were longing (8).[21] But Isaiah here warns all who desire these good things, and even back up their petitions with fasting, that they cannot expect to be heard until they change the way they are living.[22]

After this the closing exhortation to *keep . . . the Sabbath* (13–14) seems like an anticlimax,[23] until we remember the connection between the Sabbath and justice that was made back in 56:1–2. The exploitation of workers denounced in verse 3 may well have involved denying them the rest that the Sabbath provided, and the *idle words* of verse 13 were perhaps the glib rationalizations that justified such behaviour (cf. 59:3–4). In any case, the call for true Sabbath observance, like the call for true fasting, is a call for a changed heart and life, not just the more meticulous observance of a ritual. There is no shortcut to joy and victory (14); they come through repentance, and a willingness to live God's way.[24]

5. A desperate situation (59:1–21)

Repentance does not come easily to any of us, and it is hardest of all for people who have become accustomed to using religion as a cover for their sin. When their prayers go unanswered, they find it easier to blame God than to take a long, hard look at themselves. But Isaiah will not allow such evasion. 'It is not God who is the problem,' he says, 'but you.' *Your iniquities have separated you from your God; your sins have hidden his face from you* (1–2). And then, with devasting directness, he pulls aside their mask and holds up a mirror so that they can see themselves as they really are (3–8).

It is not a pretty sight: violence, *lies*, perversion of *justice*, hearts set on *evil*, 'desolation and destruction' (nrsv), no *peace* (cf. 48:22; 57:21). Can these be the people of God? And yet which of us who has had the courage

---

[21] There are many allusions in verses 8–12 to promises made in previous chapters, e.g. the Lord as *rear guard* (8; cf. 52:12), divine guidance (11; cf. 30:21; 57:18), the land as a *well-watered garden* (11; cf. 51:3).

[22] *Here am I* in verse 9 recalls what Isaiah himself said in 6:8. It indicates a willingness to respond as requested.

[23] The nineteenth-century commentator Duhm and others insist that these verses must be a later addition, possibly from the time of Nehemiah, when the Sabbath was stressed (Neh. 13:15–22). But it is more closely related to its context here in Isa. 58 than they realize. In any case, it is unlikely that abuse of the Sabbath was limited to one particular period.

[24] *Ride . . . on the heights* is an image of victory, recalling the days of the conquest (Deut. 32:13). To *feast on the inheritance of . . . Jacob* is to enjoy full possession of the land promised to him (Gen. 28:13–15). Translated into new-covenant terms it is to inherit the whole (renewed) earth (Matt. 5:5).

to look into the depths of our own hearts has not found such things lurking there? The mirror which the prophet holds up shows us ourselves as well, and as we read on it is as though we have entered a dark tunnel. Here is the rock on which all God's good and loving purposes must surely founder – the inveterate and desperate wickedness of the human heart (Jer. 17:9). It breaks out again and again like some deep-rooted infection and ruins everything. Religion cannot cover it, we cannot face it, and it makes even God hide *his face* and turn away (2). What can we do but weep?

Weeping, in fact, is exactly what we get here. Verses 9–15a are what is generally called a communal lament, of which there are many examples in the Psalms (e.g. Pss 12; 44; 58; 60; 74; 80; 83; 85; 90). It is the kind of prayer that is prayed by desperate people and comes out in long, wracking sobs. The good thing about weeping is that it means we have given up pretending that things are all right, or that we have the resources to deal with them. It means we have come to an end of self-justification and self-trust. We have faced the fact that deliverance, if it is to come at all, must come from outside ourselves.

The speakers in verses 9–15a are the 'mourners' we have already met back in 57:18. There is no trace of self-righteousness or evasiveness in them at all. Like Ezra or Daniel, they confess not only their own sins, but also the sins of those who are too blind or too proud to do so themselves (cf. Ezra 9:6–15; Dan. 9:4–19). The burden of their lament as a whole, however, is the absence of *justice* (*mišpāṭ*, 9, 11, 14). We have had cause to reflect on this important word many times in the book. It means fairness and truth, the 'right' state of affairs that should exist among God's people as they live in obedience to his word and display his character in the way they treat one another (1:17). But it also refers to the 'right' state of affairs that will exist when God has fully established his kingdom on earth. In this sense it is the final salvation or deliverance that only God can bring and which his people eagerly long for (32:15–17; see on 42:1–4). Here it is used in both these senses. Justice is far away in the sense that the deliverance God promised has not yet come to pass (9, 11). Pagan powers still hold sway in the world and God's people have to be subject to them.[25] But justice is also lacking among God's people themselves, so much so that it is hard – even dangerous – for anyone to protest (14–15). At this point in

---

[25] Ezra 9:6–9 shows just how keenly this was in fact felt and resented in the post-exilic period.

the chapter all hope appears to be lost. It is hard to imagine a situation more desperate in the life of God's people than the one described here. But of course there is still one element of hope, and that is the lament itself. As long as there are people who weep, apostasy is not total. The faithful few hold the door ajar, so to speak, for God to enter the situation again and drive the darkness back.

The turnaround comes at last in verses 15b–16: *The Lord looked . . . He saw*. It is not as though he has suddenly become aware of something which up to that point had escaped him. It is quite clear from verse 2 that this is far from the case. He has been well aware of the situation, but unwilling to be used by a community which has no intention of changing its ways. He has withdrawn so that they may taste the full, bitter consequences of their sin. But verse 15 indicates a deliberate change on his part. He decides, in his mercy, to turn his face to the community again, and he does so in response to the lament of verses 9–14. He will intervene for the sake of those who mourn. To them his ears are open. For their sakes he looks, sees and takes action.

Justice in verse 15b carries all the freight it has gathered up to that point. But from here onwards it is justice in the sense of salvation, deliverance from enemies, that comes strongly to the fore. There is no justice within the community, and for that reason it has no legitimate claim on God's help. But God decided to save it anyway. It is characteristic of him to give his people not what they deserve, but what they need, and we certainly see that principle in operation here. He sees that there is *no one to intervene* (the situation is beyond human help), and so he decides to intervene himself; *his own arm* brings *salvation*, and *his own righteousness* sustains him (16b). He is the all-sufficient one; no situation is too dark or desperate for him to deal with.

In verse 17 the Lord girds himself for battle, like a warrior, and the garments he puts on make his purpose very clear. He puts on *righteousness*, *salvation*, *vengeance* and *zeal*. The first two have to do with the deliverance of his people; the last two with the punishment of their *enemies*. In particular, God's *righteousness* refers to his faithfulness to his covenant promises as displayed in his saving acts (see, e.g., 11:4–5; 45:13), and his *zeal* to his intense concern for his people and his determination that their enemies should be destroyed (see 42:13). Taken as a whole, this powerful picture of God girding on his armour expresses the truth that he will not stand by while his people are destroyed; he is totally committed to saving them.[26] And the intervention depicted here is so drastic and so over-whelming that any thought that he is indifferent or powerless is utterly driven from human minds. People everywhere *fear* his *name* and stand in awe of him (19).

As so often in this closing part of the book, Isaiah's vision reaches near-apocalyptic proportions. It is too bold, too absolute, to be exhausted by any historical moment short of the final one, which will bring history itself to an end. There had been many desperate situations in Israel's history when God had girded on his armour to fight for her. She would never have got out of Egypt if he had not done so, or taken possession of Canaan, or survived the period of the judges in the twelfth century, or Sennacherib's invasion in the eighth. His rescue of the exiles from Babylon continued the same tradition (see 40:10). But in the long, weary years following the return, many felt that all this had come to an end. The Jewish community in Palestine was weak and vulnerable. The major players on the world scene were the pagan powers of Persia and Greece, and God seemed remote. It was all too easy to lose any sense of meaning or accountability, to pay lip service to religion but adopt a cynical, 'looking after number one' approach to the practical business of daily living. That is the kind of situation this vision addresses, and it does so with the resounding affirmation that as long as the world endures, deliverance will never be merely a thing of the past; the greatest intervention of God is still to come![27]

Verse 20 reads like a summary of it all: *The Redeemer will come to Zion, to those in Jacob who repent of their sins.* It is fundamentally a promise (*The Redeemer will come*) but also a challenge (*to those . . . who repent*). The mourners of verses 9–15 are repentant already, but what of the rest? The fact that God *will* come makes the need for a change of heart imperative for everyone. The Old Testament as a whole ends on this same note of expectation and challenge (Mal. 4). In due time, of course, the Redeemer came in the person of Jesus the Messiah. He came to the Zion of his day and found some there who received him (John 1:12). Many did not, however, even though Jesus reiterated the demand for repentance in the strongest possible terms (Mark 1:15). But the final coming – the ultimate reference point for Isaiah's vision – still lies before us, and since

---

[26] Paul clearly alludes to this passage in Eph. 6:10–18, although his emphasis is different. In our own con-tinuing struggle against Satan we must rely utterly on God, not on our own resources. Cf. 1 Thess. 5:8.

[27] The past tenses of verses 15b–17 must be understood in the light of the future tenses which follow (esp. verse 20). Isaiah has seen God's coming in vision; the reality to which it points is still future.

we stand much closer to it than earlier generations the demand for repentance is doubly urgent now. When God girds his armour for the last time it will be a glorious day, the day of final salvation for those who have repented of their sins, the culmination of all they have waited for and hoped for, but it will also bring to an end the opportunity for repentance. He will judge the nations who have defied him and persecuted his people (Rev. 11:15–18), but he will also root out and destroy those who are evil among his people themselves (Matt. 7:21–23; cf. Mal. 4:1–3; Matt. 13:24–43). The final intervention of God is good news for God's people; that is where the main emphasis of Isaiah's vision falls. But it must never be viewed with complacency. It calls for readiness and, where necessary, repentance.

Verse 21 draws the chapter to a close with one final word of encouragement. It is addressed particularly to the faithful ones who have just been referred to in the previous verse. God's *covenant* with them stands firm. His *Spirit* rests upon them, and his *words* have been placed in their *mouth* (cf. Mal. 3:16). And these two precious gifts will remain with them and *their descendants . . . for ever.* In other words, apostasy will never destroy the church. In every age God will have those who speak his word and are sustained by his Spirit. It should surely be our fervent desire to be numbered among them.

6. Zion's future glory (60:1–22)

Zion has re-entered by the back door, so to speak, in 59:20.[28] Now in this chapter it expands to fill the whole horizon of the text again, and the atmosphere changes completely. The gloom and darkness of chapter 59 give way to brilliant *light*. Only the merest traces of the *darkness* remain, as something distant and definitely offstage (2, 12). If the previous chapter was like a long, dark tunnel, this is the light at the end of it.

Isaiah must have seen the sunrise over Jerusalem many times, appearing first over the Mount of Olives to the east, and then falling on the city below, driving away the darkness and flooding the whole scene – walls and gates, domes, towers and homes – with its glory. It is a sight tourists still marvel at today. In this chapter, however, that familiar scene, breathtaking in its own right, becomes an image of something infinitely greater. In a vision Isaiah sees the Lord himself rising over Zion like the

---

[28] The last explicit reference to Zion was in 52:8.

sun, and filling the whole city with his *glory*, so that it becomes a magnet drawing all *nations* towards it (1–3; cf. 2:2–4).

Although it is focused on Zion, the vision of this magnificent chapter is worldwide in its scope. It begins with *thick darkness* covering the whole earth, as at the beginning of creation itself (Gen. 1:1–2). But here it is spiritual darkness, the darkness of moral evil and spiritual blindness. It is the 'shroud' of 25:7 that enfolds all peoples and covers all the nations. But then, as in Genesis, the scene is transformed as *light* pierces the darkness, and a new world begins to emerge. If the world called into existence in Genesis 1 was 'very good' (Gen. 1:31), this one is better by far. It has no need of *sun* or *moon*, for *the* Lord himself is its *everlasting light* (19–20; cf. Rev. 21:23). The city at its centre represents everything that was promised in the original creation, now brought to triumphant and glorious fulfilment.[29] And the heartbeat of the city is worship; how could it be anything else (7, 14b)? In this chapter Zion is not the physical city that was rebuilt after the exile. It is the kingdom of God come down to earth; the new creation. Of course the return from exile contained the seed, but it is the full-grown plant, the final outworking, which Isaiah has directly in view here.[30] If we are to understand his words aright we must see them for what they are – a vision of the end comparable to Ezekiel's vision of the city of God (Ezek. 40 – 48), or to John's vision of the new Jerusalem (Rev. 21 – 22).

But now let us note some of the more particular aspects of this vision. The first thing it affirms is that the kingdom of God will conquer all other kingdoms. *Nations* and *kings* will come to Zion, not to conquer it, but to acknowledge that the God who has chosen to reveal himself there is the only God, and to submit to him (3, 14). Those who refuse to do so *will perish* (12). It is a great irony of history that the Rome which crucified Jesus in the first century AD capitulated to him in the fourth, when the emperor Constantine declared himself a Christian. It may have been a mixed blessing, as the nexus between politics and religion tended to corrupt the church in the centuries which followed. It was striking proof, however, that what Isaiah and other prophets had said was no ideal dream (cf. Dan. 2:31–45; 7:13–14). The power of human kingdoms will fail, and the kings

---

[29] The original pair (Adam and Eve) are replaced by a host of redeemed people, and the wealth that pours into the city is striking testimony to the fact that the earth has been 'subdued' in the way God intended it to be (Gen. 1:28).

[30] No *sun* or *moon* (19) clearly implies something beyond history as we know it.

of the earth will amass their *wealth* only to lay it down one day at the feet of the King of kings (5).[31]

The final triumph of the kingdom of God will be absolute and will involve judgment (12). But the second truth that comes through very clearly is that many, from all corners of the globe, will enter it willingly. The *islands* will *look to* the Lord (9), people from *Midian, Ephah* and *Sheba will come*[32] . . . *proclaiming the praise of the* LORD (6), and *foreigners will rebuild* Zion's *walls* (10). Zion's *gates will . . . stand open . . . day* and *night* to welcome all who wish to enter with good intent (11). In other words, citizenship in the kingdom of God will not be limited to Jews only, but will be open to people of all nations. Believing Gentiles will honour those of the faithful who were Zion's children before them and be grateful to share in their heritage. Matthew tells us that soon after Jesus was born, Magi came from the east to Jerusalem, bearing gifts and seeking the one who had been born 'king of the Jews'. They had come to worship him (Matt. 2:1–2). Since then, of course, many have followed in their steps. The light that dawned in Jerusalem has spread to all nations, and many have come to the brightness of its rising.[33]

We could go on unpacking this vision for a very long time; it is so rich. We must content ourselves, however, with one more truth, which emerges strongly in verses 15–22 as it draws to a close. Isaiah bombards us in this final part of the chapter with expressions such as *everlasting, never . . . again, no longer* and *no more*. He is telling us that the confusing flux of history will issue at last in a state of permanent *peace*, 'righteousness' (NRSV; NIV *well-being*) and *praise* (17–18). Human regimes are never entirely benevolent, and sometimes turn upon those they are supposed to protect. The people of God in particular frequently get bruised by the cross-currents of history. Life as we experience it has many loops, dips and detours, when events seem to be turning back upon themselves rather than advancing towards a goal. But here Isaiah assures us yet again that there is indeed a goal, a point of arrival, and that when it is reached there will be no danger of relapse into the frustrations and *sorrow* of the past (20). God's rule, fully realized, will be as perfect and permanent as God himself (19).

---

[31] Note the striking image of conquest in verse 11b, *kings led in triumphal procession*.

[32] *Sheba* was a district in Arabia, possibly modern Yemen. Note the allusion to the visit of the Queen of Sheba (1 Kgs 10). According to Gen. 25:2–4 *Ephah* was the son of *Midian* and the nephew of Jokshan the father of *Sheba*.

[33] See Matt. 4:15–16 (quoting Isa. 9:1–7). The promised light dawned with the coming of Jesus the Messiah.

With that we might expect the passage to end. But no; with exquisite lightness of touch Isaiah brings us back in the very last line to that attitude of poised expectancy which should mark our present living. The end is not yet; it will come *in its time*. But when it does come it will come *swiftly* (22), so we must be ready for it.[34]

7. The year of the Lord's favour (61:1–11)

Two starkly contrasting realities open up before us here: *the year of the LORD's favour and the day of vengeance* (2), and both arise from the truth on which the previous chapter ended. Things will not go on as they are for ever. One day God will bring them to a sudden end. The intervening period, however long or short, is a time of opportunity. But it is not to be taken lightly, for terrible judgment awaits those who carelessly let it pass. Full treatment of the day of vengeance, however, is held over until 63:1–6; chapter 61 concentrates on the time of favour, and above all on the person who ushers it in.

It begins with him in verses 1–6. No-one introduces him; he speaks for himself, demanding our attention quite unselfconsciously and without arrogance, but with tremendous authority: *The Spirit of the Sovereign LORD is on me . . . the LORD has anointed me . . . He has sent me . . .* (1). He is someone of quite extraordinary importance. We have met him before, of course. *The Spirit . . . is on me* recalls 42:1 ('I will put my Spirit on him'), but also 11:2 ('The Spirit of the LORD will rest on him').[35] He is both the Servant of chapters 40–55 and the Messiah of chapters 1–35, for – this is what we must notice – these are one and the same person. Here is the great theological breakthrough of Isaiah's vision and the heart of his gospel. The Messiah must suffer and rise again. Only thus can the year of the Lord's favour be ushered in. No wonder, then, that Jesus took up the scroll of the prophet Isaiah in the synagogue at Nazareth and read this very passage at the beginning of his ministry (Luke 4:17–19). He had been designated the Messiah before his birth (Luke 1:32–33), and in his baptism and temptation he had chosen the path of servanthood and suffering.[36] He knew that

---

[34] Cf. Jesus' teaching in the Gospels about the sudden arrival of the end and the need for watchfulness (e.g. Matt. 25:1–13).

[35] Cf. also 48:16, with reference to the Servant: 'The Sovereign LORD has sent me, endowed with his Spirit.'

[36] Cf. Kidner, p. 667.

Isaiah's vision of a suffering Messiah was to be fulfilled in him; indeed, it had already begun to be fulfilled that day.

We begin this chapter, then, with a speech by the Servant-Messiah (1–6). This is followed by a confirmatory speech by the Lord himself (7–9), and finally by a song of praise by someone who is full of wonder and gratitude for what God has done for him personally (10–11). The references to *the Sovereign* Lord in verses 1 and 11 frame the whole chapter; the salvation which the whole chapter celebrates is his gift (cf. Jon. 2:9).

a. Good news for the poor (61:1–6)

The Servant-Messiah speaks as an anointed preacher, and the burden of his preaching is *the year of the* Lord's *favour* (2). This is almost certainly an allusion to the Year of Jubilee as described in the law of Moses (Lev. 25:8–55). Every fiftieth year was to be proclaimed a year of release in which debts were cancelled, slaves were freed, and people who had been forced to sell their family property because of poverty received it back again. It was called the 'Year of Jubilee', literally 'Year of the Ram's Horn',[37] because of the horn trumpet which was blown to announce its arrival. The expression *proclaim freedom* (1) employs exactly the same Hebrew words as the command in Leviticus 25:10 to 'proclaim liberty' in the Year of Jubilee. The preaching of the Servant-Messiah is like the blast of the ram's horn which ushered in the Year of Jubilee; it proclaims the arrival of a time of grace, a time of release.

Members of the restored community, like many before them, may well have wondered at these words, since the full identity of the preacher was yet to be revealed. Nevertheless, they would have found much here to encourage them in their particular situation. In a sense, the year of the Lord's favour had begun for them with their release from captivity and return to their own land. They had already received comfort and healing for their broken hearts and lives in the good news of their pardon, and they could already see the promise of verse 4 beginning to be fulfilled; a start, however small and feeble, had been made in rebuilding the ancient ruins. So this message would have had a special significance for them.[38] But the

---

[37] Hebrew *yōbēl*, 'ram', occurs in the expression *qeren hayyōbēl*, 'the horn of the ram' (used as a musical instrument, Josh. 6:5; cf. BDB, p. 385). In Lev. 25:28, 'in the [Year of] Jubilee' is simply *bayyōbēl*, 'in the *yōbēl*'.

[38] As in 57:14–19, the audience most directly in view is *those who grieve in Zion* (3), genuinely repentant Jews of the post-exilic period. Their counterparts in the time of Jesus were people such as Simeon and Anna (Luke 2:25, 38).

fulfilment that came with Jesus has given it a far richer meaning for us today. The 'year of the LORD's favour' which he inaugurated is still in force, and will continue to be so right through until his coming again (Luke 4:19; Heb. 2:3; 2 Cor. 6:2).[39] Throughout this whole period the *good news* which is preached is the Christian gospel. Jesus himself was the first to proclaim it after being anointed by the Spirit at his baptism (Luke 3:21–23; 4:1, 14, 18, 31–32, 43; cf. Acts 10:38). Many are the preachers who have followed him. The poor to whom the message is preached are not just *those who grieve in* Zion (3),[40] but the poor in spirit everywhere (Matt. 5:3). The *comfort* they receive is not just release from exile, but release from condemnation through the forgiveness Jesus has won for them (Luke 24:45–47). Through God's grace they become mighty *oaks* displaying the Lord's *splendour* (3), *priests of the LORD* engaged in his service (6a), and the eventual inheritors of all things (6b; cf. Matt. 5:5).[41] The rebuilding of Jerusalem's ruins after the exile was a significant work, made possible by the presence and operation of the Spirit (Hag. 2:5; Zech. 4:6). But the building of the church through the Spirit-empowered preaching of the gospel is a work that surpasses it by far.[42] By reading from this passage in the synagogue at Nazareth Jesus assumed the mantle of the anointed preacher of Isaiah's vision and announced that the final great era of grace had dawned.

b. Grace and justice (61:7–9)

The key word here is *Instead*: a *double portion* of blessing *instead of . . . shame, everlasting joy* instead of *disgrace*, and the inheritance of *land* – a place to live in and call home – instead of exile (7; cf. 3). This is grace at work, and the grace of God is a most powerful agent of change. But grace here is not simply arbitrary largesse, bounty distributed at whim. It is the expression of a relationship in which there is discipline, yes, but also healing and renewal. The double portion of blessing in this passage answers to the double portion of 'hard service' in 40:2, and it is the

---

[39]   Notice, in Luke 4:19–20, that Jesus stopped reading and rolled up the scroll in the middle of a sentence. The 'day of vengeance' awaits his return as judge.

[40]   See n. 38 above.

[41]   According to 1 Pet. 1:22 – 2:10, God's ultimate purpose in choosing Israel to be 'a kingdom of priests' (Exod. 19:6) is fulfilled in the ministry of praise and witness exercised by those who have been born again through believing the gospel.

[42]   According to Acts 15:16–18, the prophecy of Amos (9:11–12) concerning the rebuilding of 'David's fallen tent' (Jerusalem) finds its ultimate fulfilment in the worldwide preaching of the gospel.

ministry of the Servant which is the bridge between the two. Grace rests on atonement as its foundation. It is free, but not cheap. That is why Isaiah can move so naturally from grace in verse 7 to *justice* in verse 8; there is ultimately no conflict between them. His grace in binding up 'the broken-hearted' and setting 'captives' free is just as much an expression of his justice as his punishing their oppressors. For the truth is that he hates *robbery and wrongdoing* (8), and all that he does reflects that in one way or another. His grace is principled or, to put it another way, he is faithful in all his ways. The final demonstration of this will be a new, *everlasting covenant* which he will make with his *people*, in which every promise he ever made will be fulfilled and the whole world will wonder at his grace so powerfully displayed in them (8b–9; cf. Eph. 3:7–11). Isaiah never ceased to be amazed at the sheer grandeur of the grace of God, and nor should we.

c. A song of thanksgiving (61:10–11)

Praise and thanksgiving are the natural response to grace, especially grace that has been personally received and experienced. But often it takes a particularly inspired or gifted individual to give them voice for others. John Newton's famous hymn 'Amazing Grace' and Wesley's 'And Can It Be' are classic examples. Both are intensely personal, but give such powerful expression to what we have all experienced in one way or another that they are our songs too. The same applies here. A single voice rings out: *I delight greatly in the LORD, my soul rejoices in my God* (10a),[43] but the blessing for which he gives thanks is not a new one; it is the common blessings of verse 3 reduced to their essence: he has been *clothed* with *salvation* and *arrayed . . . in a robe of his righteousness* (10b). He has been given a righteousness that is not his own, and he is assured that the same Lord who has set him right will one day set the whole world right: *the Sovereign LORD will make righteousness and praise spring up before all nations* (11). On the most natural reading of the text the speaker is none other than Isaiah himself. His own guilt has been taken away and his sin pardoned (6:7). He himself has already tasted the blessings of the age to come, and as the herald of that age it is entirely appropriate that he should be the one to lead the rest of us in praising God for his glorious grace. It is the theme song of the redeemed in every age.

---

[43] Cf. the song of Hannah (1 Sam. 2:1–10) and the song of Mary (Luke 1:46–55).

8. Bold intercession (62:1–12)

This chapter picks up from where the previous one ended. If righteousness and praise are to spring up before all nations, the question is how and where? The answer has already been given in previous chapters (especially 2:2–4 and 60:1–3), but now it is taken up again with fresh vigour. It is from *Zion* that 'righteousness' (AV; NIV *vindication*) will shine *out like the dawn*, and *salvation like a blazing torch,* and all *nations* will see it (1–2).[44] Zion was profoundly important to Isaiah, not just because he was a patriot, but because he was acutely aware of its strategic significance in God's purposes. He could *not keep silent* about it (1a). The future of Zion in God's plans was the theme of his preaching, and when preaching became impossible[45] it became the theme of his prayers (6–7). In chapter 61 he thanked God for clothing him himself in salvation; now he affirms again that God will do the same for Zion. Isaiah's own words (1–5) merge into those of the Lord (6–12). The prophet and his Lord are completely at one; their hearts are fired by the same vision. In a similar way the historical Zion (Jerusalem) opens out into the city of God of the last days, the kingdom of God come to earth. There is continuity; the new will emerge from the old. But there is also discontinuity. The new will be so different from the old that it will require, and be given, *a new name* (2b–5, 12; cf. Gen. 17:5; 32:28; Rev. 2:17; 3:12).

At times the description of Zion in this chapter is very concrete – its name, its *land,* its *walls.* In other places it is more abstract: glory, salvation, righteousness. But in a sense the last verse of the chapter is the key to it all. The real glory of Zion will be its inhabitants: *the Holy People, the Redeemed of the LORD* (12), gathered in from *the nations* as well as from Israel (10). The chapter as a whole is much more about God's delight in his people than about bricks and mortar. City, land, walls, people, glory, are all aspects of one dazzling reality: God with his people and they with him for ever. Descriptions of Zion in a passage like this are, at their deepest level, descriptions of the people of God in their final, glorified state.

Verses 1–5 rise to the climax of 5b: *your God* will *rejoice over you.* It is an impressive reminder of how significant God's people are to him. His

---

[44] Note how the key terms *salvation* and 'righteousness' are picked up from 61:10, but in reverse order.

[45] See the comments at the start of the chapter on 40:1 – 51:11 on the latter part of Isaiah's life and ministry.

interest in them is not casual, but focused, determined and full of love. They are destined for *glory* (2), to be held aloft as a trophy in the Lord's *hand* (3),[46] and to be *married* to him as his bride for ever (4–5).[47]

The reference in verse 5 to God rejoicing prepares the way for the switch to God as speaker in verse 6. He has a word of encouragement for all those who, like Isaiah, *give* themselves *no rest* but call on the Lord unceasingly to bring his plans for Zion to fruition. They are like *watchmen* whom God has set on Jerusalem's *walls*. He is the one who has raised them up as intercessors, and therefore they are licensed to be bold. They are to give the Lord himself no rest until his promise is fulfilled. The Lord is not offended by such bold intercession; it is precisely the kind of praying that he desires and commands (cf. Luke 18:1–8).

But there is a fine line, as we all know, between boldness and presumption. Boldness of the kind we are talking about here is justified only where prayer is based directly on the revealed will of God. That is why the encouragement to be bold in verses 6 and 7 is followed immediately by a divine oath and a divine proclamation, in which the Lord's purposes are reaffirmed in the strongest possible terms.

The oath (8–9) concerns God's determination to bring his people finally to a position where they will no longer be preyed upon and exploited by their enemies.[48] Instead, they will have a rich reward for their toil, eating and drinking in God's presence and praising him for his goodness. Because there is no-one greater than himself to swear by, the Lord swears by *his* own *right hand and . . . mighty arm* (cf. 45:23; Heb. 6:13; and on 51:9–10). His own invincible power is the guarantee that his oath will be fulfilled.

The *proclamation* (10–12) is in effect an announcement that the time has come for the final great pilgrimage to Zion to begin.[49] The promise of a Saviour is about to be fulfilled (11), so those still in captivity in Babylon

---

[46] Cf. Delitzsch, p. 435: 'Zion is not the ancient crown which the Eternal wears upon His head, but the crown wrought out in time, which He holds in his hand.'

[47] The marriage metaphor is extended in verses 4–5 to include *land* and 'sons' (see NRSV mg.) as well. The idea is of consummation and an indissoluble union between God, people and place. Cf. Kidner, p. 668: 'The godly are as much wedded to as produced by their mother-city.'

[48] As Israel was during the Babylonian exile.

[49] Some see here a reference to the God-inspired proclamation of Cyrus concerning the restoration of Jerusalem (Ezra 1:1–4). There may well be such an allusion, but the focus of the passage as a whole is on something more ultimate than this. Through his inspired prophets and apostles, the Lord has made his purposes concerning Zion known to the whole world. Note how verse 11 echoes 40:10; the redemption experienced in the time of Cyrus anticipates the final deliverance.

(see 56:8b) are to set out quickly[50] as a vanguard to the multitudes who will follow, both Jews and Gentiles (10). The future city of God will be a far cry indeed from the desolate, ruined Jerusalem of the sixth century BC. It will be full of holy, redeemed people, the joy of the whole earth (12).

Rightly understood, there is tremendous encouragement in this passage for us in our own praying, for so much of what Isaiah confidently expected is now happening. We live in the last great era of history. The promised Saviour has come to Zion, a banner has been raised for the nations by the worldwide proclamation of the gospel, and the final great pilgrimage has begun.[51] If Isaiah had good reason to pray boldly for the fulfilment of God's promises concerning Zion, how much more do we! 'Father, may your kingdom come, may your will be done.'

9. The day of vengeance (63:1–6)

This terrible scene bursts upon us almost with the suddenness of the day of judgment itself (Matt. 24:42–44). And yet, paradoxically, it is exactly what we should be expecting at this point, for it is simply the obverse side of the reality that the previous chapter directed us towards – the final coming of God's kingdom. Nor have the previous chapters failed to warn us that this would have a dark side to it. The present passage repeats, with greater intensity, the substance of 59:15b–20: it is Isaiah's description of 'the day of vengeance of our God' whose arrival was anticipated in 61:2 (cf. 34:8; 35:4).

In common usage, *vengeance* is a word which has connotations of deliberately harboured malice and personal vindictiveness. It is the opposite of love (Lev. 19:18; Matt. 5:43–44). And yet the Bible insists that there is a proper time and place for vengeance, for without it a host of evils would never be righted and there would be no moral government in the universe. It is the final calling to account of those who have oppressed others and apparently got away with it. Vengeance is punishment, but punishment with a particularly sharp edge. Its special character arises from the fact that it is the victim him- or herself, or someone closely identified with the

---

[50] The *gates* of verse 10 are best understood as the gates of Babylon through which returning exiles pass as they set out on their journey home. Cf. 52:11.

[51] See on 60:1–12, especially the comments there on the significance of the journey of the Magi in Matt. 2.

victim, who administers the punishment.[52] There is not necessarily any malice or vindictiveness involved; these are aberrations caused by human sin. But the wrongdoer is confronted in a very personal way with the wrong he or she has done and is made to pay for it. In vengeance the tables are finally turned.

Here in Isaiah a lone avenger comes *from Edom*. His *garments* are splendid (is he a king?), but they are also dreadful, covered in *crimson* stains. Isaiah wonders who he is, and what terrible work he has been doing. The questions are natural ones and are answered almost before they have left Isaiah's lips. The avenger is God himself, and the stains on his garments are *blood*. He has *trodden* the *nations* in the *winepress* of his *wrath*. But there is another, even more pressing question which is implicit in the other two. Not just 'Who?' and 'What?' but 'Why?' And this question brings us to the very heart of the passage, for the answer is given in terms of God's special relationship with his people. The key is in verse 4. *The day of vengeance* is *the year* of his 'redeemed' (his people),[53] and he has long had this day in his 'heart' (NRSV; in his plans and purposes) precisely because of his deep commitment to them. Saul of Tarsus was later to learn that the Lord and his people are one; he could not persecute the one without clashing with the other (Acts 9:5). This passage teaches that people everywhere are destined, one day, to learn the same lesson. The judgment in view is final and universal (6), but the reference to Edom in particular gives the passage a special emphasis (1; see on 34:5–17).[54] It is the nations as persecutors of his people which will be the special objects of God's fury on the final day (cf. Rev. 18:20; 19:1–2). They will meet God as the powerful avenger of his people.

God's people are the special objects of the world's hatred (Matt. 5:10–12; John 15:18–25), and it may often seem to us that those who reject the Lord mock us with complete impunity and that there is no redress available to us. But it is not so. This passage assures us that nothing we suffer goes unnoticed, and that every wrong done to us will be repaid in full. It answers our cry for just redress, but takes the responsibility for achieving it out of our hands and places it where it properly belongs. The Lord himself is our avenger (cf. Deut. 32:35; Heb. 10:30).

---

[52] According to the *Concise Oxford Dictionary*, vengeance is 'punishment inflicted or retribution exacted, for wrong to oneself or to a person etc. whose cause one supports'.

[53] The same sense of *gĕʾûlîm* as in 62:12 (which immediately precedes the present passage). See also 35:9; 51:10.

[54] *Bozrah* was a city of Edom.

10. 'Oh, that you would rend the heavens' (63:7 – 64:12)

There have been plenty of incentives for intercession since the beginning of chapter 62, not least the promise of decisive intervention by God in the vision we have just been considering. But so far, intercession has been talked about rather than actually done. Now, however, we move from declarations of intent and exhortation to prayer itself. And what a prayer! There are many fine intercessory prayers in Scripture: Abraham's intercession for Sodom (Gen. 18:16–33), Moses' intercession for Israel after the incident of the golden calf (Exod. 32:31–32), the great prayers of Ezra and Daniel (Ezra 9; Dan. 9), and greatest of all, of course, our Lord's high-priestly prayer (John 17) in which he interceded for us all. The present prayer is less well known, but has the same stamp of greatness on it.

The voice we hear in 63:7 (*I will tell of the kindnesses of the LORD*) is the same as we heard in 61:10 ('I delight greatly in the LORD') and 62:1 ('For Zion's sake I will not keep silent'). The intercessor is Isaiah himself (see on 61:10–11 and 62:1–5). He stands in the prophetic tradition of intercessory prayer which goes right back to Moses. And like Jesus he prays with prophetic vision, not just for himself and his own generation, but for future generations as well. There is much to discourage him in the history of his people. They have always been marked by rebellion, hardness of heart, wandering, and spiritual torpor (63:10, 17; 64:7). Their hold on the land God gave them has always been tenuous; their spiritual weakness has made them easy prey for their enemies (63:18; 64:10–11).[55] And Isaiah sees little prospect of them changing in the future; their sinfulness is too ingrained. Hence the cry at the very centre of the prayer, *Oh, that you would rend the heavens and come down . . . !* (64:1). Intercession glorifies God because it is an expression of utter dependence upon him. It recognizes that we need to be delivered as much from ourselves as from our enemies, and that deliverance of this radical kind can be found only in God. It is his gift, not our achievement (cf. Jon. 2:9b).

But now, having grasped the heart of the prayer, let us note some of its particulars. It begins, as all prayer should, with an acknowledgment of the sheer goodness of God (63:7–9). Isaiah recalls *the days of old*, the acts of

---

[55] The verb *possessed* (63:18) suggests that it is the land as the Lord's sanctuary which is in view here, as in Exod. 15:17. Cf. Deut. 3:18; Ezra 9:7–8.

God that called Israel into existence, and sees that they were marked by grace from beginning to end. Notice the piling up of expressions: *the kindnesses of the LORD, the deeds for which he is to be praised . . . the many good things he has done . . . his compassion . . . his love and mercy.* God's gracious and powerful deliverance of the Israelites from Egyptian bondage established a father–child relationship between him and them, and through the whole wilderness experience he cherished them as his children. He felt their distress, saved them from the perils of the way,[56] lifted them up and carried them when they were weak, and rightly expected that they would return his love by being true to him. But sadly, it was not so. They *rebelled* against him, *and grieved his Holy Spirit* (10a).[57] So in order to preserve his holiness, the father had to become an *enemy* and judge those he loved (10b). The days of old were days of immense grace on the Lord's part, and immense ingratitude on the part of his people. They were days of unrequited love.

The second part of the prayer (63:11–14) is about how 'recalling the days of old' has been central to the relationship between God and his people from generation to generation. The memory of former things has brought assurance of God's power and faithfulness, but also of their own deeply ingrained sinfulness, and has raised painful uncertainties in their minds. Where is the God who *brought* their ancestors *through the sea, set his Holy Spirit among them*, guided them and gave them *rest*? Where is he now? Has his patience at long last been exhausted? Has he withdrawn his protecting presence? Do they now face the world as children without a father? These are the questions which generations of Israelites have asked, especially in times of crisis. But they are also Isaiah's own questions. They trouble him too as he prays.

True prayer, however, must rise above such thoughts. It is not enough to look back or look within. The intercessor must look up, for all true intercession is founded on the conviction that, however we feel, God is sovereign, and deliverance can be found in him alone. That truth had been

---

[56] The *angel of his presence* (63:9) is a heavenly messenger or angel, as other passages make clear (e.g. Exod. 32:34; 33:2; Num. 20:16). He is closely associated with the pillar of cloud (Exod. 14:19–20). But since it is the Lord who speaks to Moses from this cloud (Exod. 33:9), the 'angel of his presence' is in the last analysis indistinguishable from the Lord himself. The 'angel' is his manifested presence.

[57] This probably refers to their rebellion against the leadership of Moses, the leader God had given them and on whom his Spirit rested (Num. 11:17). *Holy* indicates the deity of the Spirit (1:4; 5:19, 24; 10:17, 20; 12:6; etc.), and *grieved* the fact that he is personal (cf. Eph. 4:30). The passage is trinitarian: the Lord (7), the angel of his presence (9) and (literally) 'the Spirit of his holiness' (10). The Spirit is also mentioned in verses 11 and 14.

embedded deeply in Isaiah's soul by the vision of God that had inaugurated his ministry. Now it injects fresh confidence into his praying. He lifts his eyes to the God whose *throne* is *lofty . . . holy and glorious* (63:15; cf. 6:1–5), and calls on him to intervene (64:1).[58] It is not that there are no more questions. There are still a *Where?*, a *Why?* and a *How?* (63:15, 17; 64:5). Where are you, God? Why are things so different from the way they used to be? Why are our hearts so hard?[59] How can we be saved? How much longer will you be angry with us? They are hard questions, all of them, expressing real pain and perplexity. But they are not hostile or arrogant, and they are no longer directed inwards. They are directed upwards to God, who is addressed again and again as *Father* (63:16; 64:8). They are children's questions, expressing penitence, dependence and trust. They are the questions of prodigals come home, daring to hope that their father – simply because that is who he is – will not turn them from his door.

Isaiah has become so identified with those for whom he prays that, as far as his language is concerned, there is no difference between him and them. Their Father is his Father, their sins are his sins, and so are their doubts, perplexities and hard questions. By his praying he brings them to the Father when they are too weak or proud to come themselves. He acts as a true intercessor. It is likely that later generations of Israelites used this very prayer to lament the destruction of the temple and seek God's forgiveness.[60] If so, it did double duty; it lived on after Isaiah himself had died, and became the prayer of the very ones for whom he had interceded. It gave them voice in one of the darkest moments of their history.

11. God answers the cry of his servants (65:1–25)

In chapter 64 it is as though the cry for help has to reach out across infinite space. 'Oh, that you would rend the heavens and come down.' God seems very far away, on the other side of a vast chasm. And the chapter ends with a plaintive question: 'LORD, will you hold yourself back? Will you keep

---

[58] Note the intensification as we move from 63:15 (*Look down from heaven and see*) to 64:1 (*rend the heavens and come down*).

[59] There may be an allusion in 63:17 to the judicial hardening of 6:10, which was to remain in force until the exile, when God's judgment had finally fallen on Jerusalem.

[60] Cf. H. G. M. Williamson, 'Isaiah 63:7 – 64:11: Exilic Lament or Post-Exilic Protest?', *Zeitschrift für die alttestamentliche Wissenschaft* 102 (1990), pp. 48–58.

silent . . . ?' The silence of God is a terrible thing. It mocks our prayers and makes our universe a frightening, forsaken place.

But the truth is that God is not far away, and never has been. All through Israel's history, even when they were too far gone in apostasy, or just sheer hopelessness, to seek him, he had always been seeking them. If he had held himself back, it was only to spare them the full venting of the wrath they so richly deserved. But he had never ceased to reveal himself to them. Generation after generation he had sent his prophets to speak to them in his name, saying, *Here am I, here am I* (1). But they had obstinately chosen their own *ways* rather than his and had sunk deeper and deeper into pagan superstition and uncleanness (2–4), foolishly regarding them as superior to the wholesome, simple trust in the Lord which should have marked them as his children (5). This is the reason their history had been such a long, dark tunnel; not because God was far away, but because they would not listen to him. If there was a chasm between him and them it was of their own making, not his (cf. 59:1–2). But the solemn message of the opening section of chapter 65 is that to call on him to rend the heavens and come down is to invite his judgment as well as his salvation; to bring on the final separation between the saved and the lost among his own people as well as in the world at large. The prayer for God's kingdom to come and his will to be done is a prayer for the end of the world. It is a prayer we should never pray lightly.

There were, however, those who did dare to pray – and went on praying – for the coming of God's kingdom: not just Isaiah himself, but many who have followed in his steps. They are the focus of attention in the second part of the chapter (8–25). They are God's *servants* (9), *people who seek* him (10), his *chosen ones* (22) and *a people blessed by the* LORD (23). They are the faithful remnant, the prayer warriors who have stayed at their post through the long, dark watches of salvation history, never abandoning their trust in God or their confidence that his promises would be fulfilled. And the good news of this chapter is that the new world for which they have waited so long will surely come; God will bring it to pass for their sake (8) and gather them into it (9).

The contours of that new world open up here in ever-widening circles: from the *mountains*, plains and valleys of a renewed Palestine (9–10)[61] to

---

61 'Two extremities of the land are mentioned, Sharon and Achor, the west and the east. *Sharon* was the fertile plain extending from Carmel to Jaffa (cf. 33:9; 35:2). The *Valley of Achor* was named after the episode of Achan (Josh. 7:24ff.; cf. Hos. 2:15).' Young, 3, p. 508.

the *new heavens and a new earth* (17) with a new *Jerusalem* at its centre (18) – a cosmic paradise, one vast sanctuary from which everything harmful has been banished for ever (25). There is something much more here than the mere realization of a utopian dream, a glorified Israel that would be the wonder and envy of the world again, as in the days of Solomon. It is a whole new order of things in which all political structures are transcended. It will be so new that the past will be forgotten entirely (17). The promised land will no longer be Canaan or Israel but the whole earth. As we saw in chapter 62, the new Jerusalem will be so different from the old that it will require a new name. The servants of God will be all who have found mercy and free pardon through the work of the perfect Servant – all God's faithful people in every age. The chapter ends with an unmistakable allusion to the final undoing of the work of the serpent who brought sin and death into the world in the first place (25).[62] The new world will be history perfected and paradise regained, and it will be full of the modest and simple delights that God always intended us to have: joy (18), fullness of life (20), security (21–23a), rewarding work (22b), fellowship with God (23b–24) and peace (25).

Isaiah's vision is breathtaking in its scope: *new heavens and a new earth*. But for all that, he is not a universalist. He does not believe that all will be saved. From verse 8 onwards the contrast between those who are God's servants and those who are not is drawn ever more starkly. There are those who *seek* him and those who do not (10–11), and their destinies are as different as light and darkness (13–15). There are the saved and the lost in this chapter, there is heaven and there is hell.[63] And again we note that the demarcation line is not ethnic or political, but personal and confessional. As far back as 45:22 the call went out: 'Turn to me and be saved, all you ends of the earth; for I am God, and there is no other.' In 55:1, following the death and resurrection of the Servant of the Lord, the invitation was renewed: 'Come, all you who are thirsty, come to the waters.' The door to the kingdom has been thrown open to all and sundry, but the sad fact is that many steadfastly refuse to go in. This chapter speaks of the final and irrevocable separation that will be made on the last day between them and God's servants. But long before then, the choice that

---

[62] There is another hint of curse removed in the positive mention of the *Valley of Achor* in verse 10. See preceding note.

[63] I use the term 'hell' metaphorically of final, irrevocable judgment. We do not have the full New Testament doctrine of hell here, but we do have precursors of it. Cf. 66:24.

people have made becomes clear from the way they live. God calls, but they do *not answer*, he speaks, but they do *not listen* (12). They *forsake* their Maker, choose *Fortune* and *Destiny* (11),[64] and reap *anguish* and *brokenness* (14). Hell, in the end, is God simply giving us what we have chosen. Isaiah is quite clear about this. To be servants of God or not is a personal decision that none of us can avoid, and the consequences are eternal. There will be a new world, but God will not force us into it. The choice is ours.

12. The arrival of the end (66:1–24)

For Isaiah the end would begin to arrive with the return from Babylon. That event was so significant for him because it was ripe with promise, like a woman large with child. The end would emerge from it like a *birth*. And when it came, it would come suddenly, like a premature baby bursting unexpectedly from the womb and announcing its arrival with loud cries. All that the faithful had longed for would be realized in one climactic moment (7–11). But for all the certainty and suddenness of its arrival, the end would not come easily. The pregnancy would be a difficult one.

a. Ecclesiasticism (66:1–6)

Reference to the temple (*the house you will build for me*) anticipates a major aspect of life in the period immediately following the return. The rebuilding of the temple was a project which occupied the community, on and off, for twenty years.[65] When it faltered because of opposition and discouragement, it was the prophets Haggai and Zechariah who stirred up enthusiasm for the work again and enabled it to be brought to a successful conclusion (Ezra 4:23 – 5:2). Yet here it is spoken of with extreme reserve, as though enthusiasm about it were unjustified, or even misguided. What are we to make of this?

It can hardly be the case that Isaiah was opposed in principle to the rebuilding of the temple. It was in the temple that he heard God's call (6:1). As early as 2:2 he spoke of the last days, when 'the mountain of the Lord's

---

[64] Spreading *a table* and filling *bowls of mixed wine* were practices commonly associated with idolatrous worship. The Hebrew words translated *Fortune* and *Destiny* probably stand for pagan gods in general rather than specific deities. The NIV nicely captures a play on *Destiny* and *destine* (same root in Hebrew) in verses 11 and 12.

[65] Approximately 536–516 (Ezra 3:1–13; 6:15).

temple will be established as the highest of the mountains', a theme he returns to in this very chapter (20). Cyrus has been named as the Lord's shepherd, charged with the task of setting the rebuilding process in motion (44:28), and the temple has featured prominently in the promise passages of chapters 56 and 60 (56:5, 7; 60:4–7). He was no more anti-temple than Haggai or Zechariah. He saw the future rebuilding of the temple as a sign of the approaching end, a sacrament of the coming kingdom. But at the same time he was painfully aware of the capacity of human beings to misuse it; to focus on the temple itself instead of the God of the temple, to corrupt it with perfunctory and impure worship. Isaiah understood very well that physical restoration was not enough. Unless there was spiritual renewal the future would simply repeat the sins of the past. He was not against the temple, but against ecclesiasticism, that ugly distortion of true religion which inevitably reasserts itself where there is no recognition of the greatness of God or heartfelt contrition before him (1–2). Where this is lacking, worship, in whatever building, becomes no better than pagan superstition, angering God and calling forth his right-eous judgment (3–4).

But ecclesiasticism bears even more bitter fruit than this. It breeds partisanship and power struggles, theological hatred and religious perse-cution. It turns brother against brother (5). The second part of verse 5 contains a taunt similar to those that Isaiah himself had had to endure (5:19). What finally divides the true from the false in the church is faith-fulness or unfaithfulness to the word of God. Clinging to the promises of God will always seem fanatical and foolish to those who have abandoned them. Jesus warned his disciples that they themselves would experience the same kind of rejection (Matt. 10:22; John 15:18; 17:14; cf. 1 Thess. 2:14).[66] Religion that loses its anchorage in the word of God either becomes pathetically ineffective (Matt. 5:13; 2 Tim. 3:5) or turns into a monster. Persecution is always ugly, religious persecution especially so, and eccle-siasticism is its native soil.

Developments which were to take place soon after the return from exile are glimpsed at several points in this passage, especially the rebuilding of the temple and the beginnings of sectarian tensions within the commu-nity. But in verse 6 these begin to be left behind and the focus settles firmly

---

[66] In the Talmud the expression translated *exclude you* in verse 5 is a technical term for excommunication (cf. Matt. 18:17; John 16:2).

on the final acts of God that will bring salvation history to its triumphant conclusion. In this sense verse 6 is a bridge into what follows, or the hinge on which the whole chapter turns. History begins to give way to eternity.

Like Malachi, Isaiah saw that Jerusalem and its temple would be the scene of God's final judgment on apostate Israel (cf. Mal. 3:1–5). It would begin when the Lord came personally to his temple and made war on his own people who had become his enemies by rejecting his word (6). Judgment would begin at the house of God (cf. Ezek. 9:6; 1 Pet. 4:17). Jesus' preaching, for the most part, was an urgent, eleventh-hour appeal to Israel to repent, and his cleansing of the temple a dramatic sign that the threatened judgment was beginning to take place.[67] Sadly, however, even this did not elicit repentance, but bitter hatred and opposition. Israel's response to God's final warning was to kill the one who brought it, and the destruction of Jerusalem and the temple followed as a matter of course (Matt. 24:1–2).[68]

But this brings us to the mystery which lies at the very heart of this chapter. What seems an end is also a beginning. The death throes of Israel as it existed under the old covenant turn out to be the birth pangs of the new age. Mourning is suddenly turned into joy.

b. Zion's newborn children (66:7–11)

As Zion had once done, so she would do again, but in a far greater way. In Isaiah's day Zion under judgment had given birth to a faithful remnant (see on 7:14). The joyful news he now proclaims is that in the hour of her final judgment she will give *birth* again. Everything in this passage stresses the suddenness and miraculous nature of the event. This birth is, so to speak, already accomplished *before she goes into labour* (7). And it is not the normal one or two who are born, but a whole new people of God (8).[69] It is so sudden and startling that it can only be a work God himself (9).

There is profound prophetic insight here, for in the fullness of time the new age came to birth just as Isaiah predicted. Out of the Israel of the old covenant, judged and rejected by God, emerged the church of Jesus

---

[67] Note how this is preceded by the cursing of the fruitless fig tree in Mark 11:12–19.

[68] In AD 70, following a Jewish revolt, the Roman general Titus forced his way into Jerusalem and destroyed its fortifications and the temple. After a further revolt in AD 132 the city was rebuilt, on a much smaller scale, as a pagan city dedicated to Jupiter. *NBD*, p. 569.

[69] I take *country* ('*eres*) and *nation* here to refer to population – an entire, distinct people group. Cf. the similar use of 'land' ('*eres*) in Judg. 18:30.

Christ.[70] It was already 'born', as it were, before Jerusalem's destruction; that was simply the severing of the umbilical cord. Zion had given birth to a movement that could not be contained within ethnic, territorial or political boundaries. It would spread to the ends of the earth, but always owe a debt to the mother who gave it birth. Zion's children would always remember that they had been suckled at her breasts, and be thankful (10–11).[71]

c. 'I will comfort you' (66:12–17)

Isaiah is almost ready now to bring his grand vision to a close by drawing out its full missionary implications. But first he has some comforting words for the faithful within Israel. For them the prospect of Jerusalem's coming destruction by God was exceedingly painful. They could not view it with the equanimity of which others might be capable. Did the sentence passed on Israel mean that Jerusalem had no further place in God's purposes? And what of their own place in the new order of things?[72]

His first word for them picks up and confirms all that has been said about the future city of God in preceding chapters (especially chapter 62). The new Jerusalem will be everything that the old failed to be – a city of *peace*, rich to overflowing with the blessing of God (12a). And those who grieved over the passing of the old *will be comforted* in the new (12b–13).[73] The faithful need not fear that they will be discarded with apostate Israel; the new Jerusalem will be the home of all God's faithful people, the old as well as the new.

His second word answers the disquiet they feel at the severity of the sentence passed on Israel. Is it not unreasonably harsh? The answer is that it is no more so than the *judgment* he will visit on all his enemies everywhere, Jew and Gentile alike (14–17). The judgment that begins with

---

[70] The scene is already set by the allusion back to Isa. 7:14 in Matt. 1:23.

[71] There is a sense, of course, in which the church continues to draw nourishment from its Jewish heritage. The Old Testament is three-quarters of the Christian Bible! Cf. Paul's image of the root and the branches in Rom. 11:11–24.

[72] I take verses 12ff. to be addressed particularly to the 'mourners' of verse 10b who, in view of the preceding chapters, are repentant Israelites (57:18; 61:2–3). The connecting *For* of verse 12 suggests a close connection with verses 9–10, where they are already included, by implication, in the larger category of Zion's children. Now the spotlight falls especially on them.

[73] Note how in verse 13 the image of the comforting *mother* is extended to God himself. This is one of the few places where the Old Testament breaks through its normal reserve and attributes feminine qualities to God (cf. 49:15). The promise of comfort here lifts the promise of 40:1 onto a higher plane. 40:1 and 66:13 form a frame around the whole of 40–66. There are further echoes of chapter 40 in verses 18–24, especially the idea of all 'nations' seeing God's glory.

the house of God has its significance not simply in itself but in what it points to. It is a sign of the final, universal judgment to come.[74] It puts the whole world on notice.[75]

But this introduces a note of urgency which launches us into the final movement of the vision. If the world has been put on notice, what of those who remain ignorant? How is the revelation to be published? How are the nations to be apprised of the judgment to come and the means of escape from it?

d. To the ends of the earth (66:18–24)

This last, tremendous paragraph contains God's entire programme for the evangelization of the world. It is summarized in verse 18. In a word, God's fundamental response to the evil actions and imaginations of his creatures is one of grace. His gathering, rescuing activity, once restricted to the dispersed of Israel, is to be extended to all people. He will *come and gather* people of *all nations and languages* so that they may *see* his *glory* (18).[76] The goal of mission is the glory of God, that God might be known and honoured for who he really is. How this goal is to be achieved is spelled out in what follows.[77]

God *will set a sign* in the midst of the nations (19). In context this can surely be nothing other than the wondrous birth of verses 7–8.[78] It is the whole miraculous complex of events which occurred when Israel was judged and the church was born,[79] and the 'survivors' are the faithful remnant of verses 12–16.[80] The final proof that God has not rejected them is that they have been chosen to spearhead his mission to the nations.[81] The place names in the last part of verse 19 are drawn from Isaiah's own world, but as the farthest outposts they stand symbolically for the whole

---

[74] Note the *all people* of verse 16. Some details of verse 17 are obscure, but the general sense is clear. The wide-ranging judgment of verse 16 narrows here to those who practise idolatrous rites (cf. 65:3–7). The judgment is on the heathen and on those (including apostate Jews) who have become like them.

[75] This is why Jesus can pass so easily in Matt. 24 from the destruction of the temple to his return to judge the world.

[76] As Isaiah himself had once seen it (6:1–5).

[77] Cf. Kidner, p. 670: 'V. 18 [states] his purpose for the world, and vv. 19–21 his means of carrying it out.'

[78] Cf. 7:14, where the connection between 'sign' and 'miraculous birth' is explicit. There the sign was for Ahaz; here it is for the nations.

[79] Note the reference in Acts 2:22 to the signs associated with Jesus' ministry. Cf. Young, 3, p. 532.

[80] Peter, himself a survivor, pleads with his fellow Israelites on the day of Pentecost to save themselves from 'this corrupt generation' (Acts 2:40). Cf. Young, 3, p. 532.

[81] This choice is confirmed by Jesus in the Great Commission (Matt. 28:18–20), and in his further words to his disciples after his resurrection (Acts 1:8).

earth.[82] Mission is to know no ethnic, geographical or national boundaries. It is to extend everywhere (again, cf. Matt. 28:18–20; Acts 1:8).

The mention of *grain offerings* in verse 20 introduces the figure of a great harvest,[83] and with it what must have been one of the most startling and controversial aspects of Isaiah's missionary vision. Again the terms are drawn from the familiar world of Isaiah's immediate audience (*offering, Jerusalem, temple, priests and Levites*), but the vision itself turns that world upside down. It is *the nations* that are harvested, and converts from all nations who are presented to the Lord as holy offerings. Converted Jew and converted Gentile become one covenant *people* (20),[84] united in a new kind of priestly ministry in which both alike, in due course, share in the privileges and responsibilities of leadership (21).[85] What a stunningly accurate portrayal this is of things to come! No prophet understood more deeply the missionary nature of God's heart, or the shape of the mission he would put into effect when the time was right.

Only one reflection remains, and it has to do with the origin and outcome of God's mission, its beginning and its end. Verse 22 contains one final word of assurance to faithful Israelites, the true children of Abraham of the Old Testament period. The promise of an enduring *name* and many *descendants* will not fail; they will have their perfect fulfilment in *the new heavens and the new earth*, where the redeemed of the entire human race will offer unending worship to their creator (cf. Gen. 12:2; 15:5); but the final verse contains a chilling reminder that those same promises to Abraham implied judgment. They confronted men and women with the unavoidable responsibility to respond: to bless or curse, and be blessed or cursed themselves (Gen. 12:3). The last verse does not detract in any way from the victory of the previous verse, but rather testifies to the completeness of it. God will not stoop to conversion by force. He will give us what we choose, and be glorified as much by his righteous judgment as by his saving grace.[86]

---

[82] *Tarshish* was probably Tartessus in Spain. *Tubal* is located in the far north in Ezek. 39:1–5. 'This is the first sure and certain mention of mission as we today employ the term' (Westermann, p. 425).

[83] Already anticipated in the 'gathering' of verse 18.

[84] In view of the particulars given in verse 19, *your people, from all the nations* cannot be restricted to Jews.

[85] *Priests and Levites* is clearly figurative in this context. It is not the perpetuation of the old priestly orders which is in view, but their passing. See Rom. 15:15–16. At first it was Jews such as Peter and Paul who exercised leadership, but Gentiles soon did as well (e.g. Titus, Gal. 2:3). Note Paul's insistence that Titus did not need to be circumcised to be acceptable.

[86] The image of verse 24 may be that of a smouldering battlefield, or of the Valley of Hinnom (Jerusalem's rubbish dump) to the south of the city (Jer. 7:31–33). As it stands, it seems to depict annihilation rather than

At its most fundamental level, this closing paragraph brings us back to the basic truth that God is creator, and therefore ruler, of his world. The book of Isaiah, like the Bible itself, moves from the heavens and the earth (1:2) to the new heavens and new earth (66:22; cf. Gen. 1:1; Rev. 21:1). God's mission is simply the outworking of the intentions he had at the beginning, expressed in the blessing he pronounced on the first pair and confirmed in the promises he made to Abraham. And Isaiah leaves us in no doubt that the key to it all is God's perfect Servant, our Lord Jesus Christ. How eloquently and simply the apostle John put it! Isaiah, he says, 'saw Jesus' glory and spoke about him' (John 12:41). In the second half of the book the new creation unfolds from his saving work like a bud bursting into bloom, and the last verse challenges us never to take it lightly, but to ponder (as we shall for all eternity) the greatness of our redemption and the terrible fate from which we have been saved.[87] What can we do but worship?

---

eternal torment. The bodies are dead; the undying worm and ever-burning fire exclude any possibility of recovery. Destruction is total and permanent. In the New Testament, however, the same imagery is taken more in the direction of eternal torment (Mark 9:47–48; and, more clearly, Luke 16:23–24; Rev. 14:9–11).

[87] This is the force of *they will go out and look*. It is not gloating, but sober reflection that is in view. Cf. Young, 3, p. 537.

Listen to God's Word speaking to the world today

The complete NIV text, with over 2,300 notes from the Bible Speaks Today series, in beautiful fine leather- and clothbound editions. Ideal for devotional reading, studying and teaching the Bible.

Leatherbound edition with slipcase
£50.00 • 978 1 78974 139 1

Clothbound edition
£34.99 • 978 1 78359 613 3

ivpbooks.com /IVPbooks @IVPbookcentre @IVPbooks

The Bible Speaks Today: Old Testament series

The Message of Genesis 1 – 11
The dawn of creation
David Atkinson

The Message of Genesis 12 – 50
From Abraham to Joseph
Joyce G. Baldwin

The Message of Exodus
The days of our pilgrimage
Alec Motyer

The Message of Leviticus
Free to be holy
Derek Tidball

The Message of Numbers
Journey to the Promised Land
Raymond Brown

The Message of Deuteronomy
Not by bread alone
Raymond Brown

The Message of Joshua
Promise and people
David G. Firth

The Message of Judges
Grace abounding
Michael Wilcock

The Message of Ruth
The wings of refuge
David Atkinson

The Message of 1 and 2 Samuel
Personalities, potential, politics and power
Mary J. Evans

The Message of 1 and 2 Kings
God is present
John W. Olley

The Message of 1 and 2 Chronicles
One church, one faith, one Lord
Michael Wilcock

The Message of Ezra and Haggai
Building for God
Robert Fyall

The Message of Nehemiah
God's servant in a time of change
Raymond Brown

The Message of Esther
God present but unseen
David G. Firth

The Message of Job
Suffering and grace
David Atkinson

The Bible Speaks Today: New Testament series

The Message of Matthew
The kingdom of heaven
Michael Green

The Message of Mark
The mystery of faith
Donald English

The Message of Luke
The Saviour of the world
Michael Wilcock

The Message of John
Here is your King!
Bruce Milne

The Message of the Sermon on the Mount (Matthew 5 – 7)
Christian counter-culture
John Stott

The Message of Acts
To the ends of the earth
John Stott

The Message of Romans
God's good news for the world
John Stott

The Message of 1 Corinthians
Life in the local church
David Prior

The Message of 2 Corinthians
Power in weakness
Paul Barnett

The Message of Galatians
Only one way
John Stott

The Message of Ephesians
God's new society
John Stott

The Message of Philippians
Jesus our joy
Alec Motyer

The Message of Colossians and Philemon
Fullness and freedom
Dick Lucas

The Message of 1 and 2 Thessalonians
Preparing for the coming King
John Stott

The Bible Speaks Today:
Bible Themes series

The Message of the Living God
His glory, his people, his world
Peter Lewis

The Message of the Resurrection
Christ is risen!
Paul Beasley-Murray

The Message of the Cross
Wisdom unsearchable, love indestructible
Derek Tidball

The Message of Salvation
By God's grace, for God's glory
Philip Graham Ryken

The Message of Creation
Encountering the Lord of the universe
David Wilkinson

The Message of Heaven and Hell
Grace and destiny
Bruce Milne

The Message of Mission
The glory of Christ in all time and space
Howard Peskett and Vinoth Ramachandra

The Message of Prayer
Approaching the throne of grace
Tim Chester

The Message of the Trinity
Life in God
Brian Edgar

The Message of Evil and Suffering
Light into darkness
Peter Hicks

The Message of the Holy Spirit
The Spirit of encounter
Keith Warrington

The Message of Holiness
Restoring God's masterpiece
Derek Tidball

The Message of Sonship
At home in God's household
Trevor Burke

The Message of the Word of God
The glory of God made known
Tim Meadowcroft

The Message of Women
Creation, grace and gender
Derek and Dianne Tidball

The Message of the Church
Assemble the people before me
Chris Green

The Message of the Person of Christ
The Word made flesh
Robert Letham

The Message of Worship
Celebrating the glory of God in the whole of life
John Risbridger

The Message of Spiritual Warfare
The Lord is a warrior; the Lord is his name
Keith Ferdinando

The Message of Discipleship
Authentic followers of Jesus in today's world
Peter Morden

The Message of Love
The only thing that counts
Patrick Mitchel

The Message of Wisdom
Learning and living the way of the Lord
Daniel J. Estes

The Message of the Second Coming
Ending all things well
Steve Motyer